"The writing is strong, heartfelt, but not syrupy, at points hard-hitting and at others tender. The way you tell your story is realistic and elegant."

-Janet Hill, former Executive VP of Doubleday Broadway
and founder of the Harlem Moon imprint

IN BLACK IN WHITE

L. T. WOODY

iUniverse, Inc.
New York   Bloomington

IN BLACK IN WHITE

Copyright © by L. T. Woody

iUniverse books may be ordered through booksellers or by contacting:
iUniverse
1663 Liberty Drive
Bloomington, IN 47403
www.iuniverse.com
1-800-Authors (1-800-288-4677)

ISBN: 978-1-4401-3050-2 (pbk)
ISBN: 978-1-4401-3051-9 (ebk)

Printed in the United States of America
iUniverse rev. date: 3/17/09

It was always in my mind to come back up here. I stumbled upon this spot, quite by accident, during my first exploratory walk into the woods. It is so weird for someone like me to be living where, for an adventure; you can casually set off into dense and unfamiliar woods and feel relatively safe. The two black snakes I saw, sunbathing on opposite sides of the entrance to that little grey stone footbridge, were about the only things that caused me any alarm the first time I came here. What are the odds of something like that happening? There they were, like two glistening black, sinister looking sentries, guarding the path to what lay beyond. I couldn't believe it. I nearly turned back, but then I long-jumped over them. The snakes barely seemed to notice me.

I came back because I wanted to see what it looked like when there was snow on the ground. It was sunny and mild when I was first here. The surrounding woods were so much more alive. Most of the trees were in full autumn blush, birds and insects were buzzing about, and occasionally, I would hear indistinct rustling sounds in the brush.

Then there was that woman who rode by on a dark horse. She didn't seem surprised to see me; at least, not that I could discern. She smiled and waved.

This time, with all the snow and little sunlight, everything here amongst the bare trees looks a shadowy black and white, and it is reassuringly quiet, somehow. All I can hear is the whispery whine of an unforgiving New Hampshire winter's wind, and the sound of my own labored breathing. This cold is brutal. It almost hurts to breathe. My hands are warm, at least. I knew these ski gloves that I ripped-off from somebody would come in handy one day.

If I don't find what I'm looking for soon, I can't remain out here too much longer. I'm not even sure if I'm heading in the right direction. Everything looks so different now. I'll never find it. I should have asked someone, but I wanted to do this alone.

I'm thinking there has to be a path or something that goes uphill - sharply. That must be how I got up there the first time, but I can't remember exactly. It was so unexpected. At first, I didn't know what it was I was seeing, probably because I had approached it from near the top, rather than seeing it from a position below it. It was made of wood, and it looked rickety to me. The wood was dry, grey and weather-beaten, but there was no doubt about it, it was a ski jump. Other than on television, I had never seen one before, but this one didn't look too sturdy, in my opinion.

Looking at it, I found it hard to imagine how anyone could be brave enough to ski down that ramp, going all out, and then launch into that wide-open space, the way ski jumpers do. To me, it seemed not much different from jumping out of a plane without a parachute. The ground below is a good ways down. I don't know, maybe it is far less frightening when there is a ton of snow on the ground.

I climbed out to near the edge at the top, to look down into the valley below. What a view. It was magnificent. I could see for a great distance out over the tops of the dense trees, which were a glorious array of autumnal colors, framing the landing zone below. I tried to visualize how it might look if the ground were snow covered, but I couldn't. Right then I resolved to come back, after a snowfall, to get the full effect.

What's that - are those the noontime chapel bells? I'm a little surprised that I can hear them from so far away, but it is quiet out here, and I'm freezing and getting hungry. Maybe this wasn't such a great idea. It's dangerous being in the woods in this cold. The fact that it is snowing is no help, and it's really starting to come down. The snow looks beautiful, but it will make it more difficult for me to follow my footprints back. It'd be a lovely sight if I were not so cold. Meanwhile, I can't help thinking of that poem by Robert Frost, the one Mr. Logan had me memorize, about the 'lovely, dark and deep woods.' Is it possible that I have walked for miles? I certainly hope not.

The sound of the chapel bells seemed to be coming from that direction, but that can't be the way back. That's not how I got here - I don't think. I'll wait to hear those bells again, that'll set me straight. They'll sound again in about ten minutes. I'll wait, and in the meantime enjoy the view of these woods filling with snow. I know I mustn't panic because I know I'm not lost, per se. However, where am I, really?

*****

CHAPTER 1 – IMMEDIATE FAMILY

Our household consisted of my father Reverend Johnnie Watkins, a Pentecostal preacher; my serene mother Mary Jane (maiden name Mary Jane Woody), my older sister Velma, whom we called Plum and the twins Anthony and Angela. It has now become clear to me that while in many ways we shared a familial bond between us, we were a rather loosely knit clan, my mother being the strong thin tie that bound us all together.

My older sister Plum was born of a union between my mother and some mystery person of whom I have never heard anyone in the family ever speak. The twins were the youngest and they were Reverend Johnnie Watkins's offspring.

It was not until I was an adult that I learned my biological father was a man named John Penson. One of my aunts gave me a few scattered details about him, and helped me to go to his home and meet his wife some years after my Mom died in 1979, and only a year after my father John Penson died.

"Aunt Vinnie, I would like to know about my father." I asked her.

She looked at me somewhat shocked, and then blurted out, "Baby, I want you to know it wasn't his fault. Reverend Watkins wouldn't ever let him see you."

At my father's home, I saw photos of half-brothers and sisters of whom I had no knowledge. They seemed to have been living a very comfortable life. I was a little jealous. That should have been my life.

My Mom never talked to me about my father - except one time!

I was standing at a window in her bedroom when she walks up to me with this bemused expression on her face. She looked very young, almost girlish, as she leans into me, and half-whispers.

"Guess who I saw today?

I sensed that what she was about to say was somehow momentous for us both. Yet, I wasn't sure how I should react to her, so I stood there and kept looking at her sort of puzzled. I suspect I was trying to act grownup, since everyone thought of me as wise beyond my years. I wasn't.

Then, she leans into me again and very distinctly mouths the words, "YOUR FATHER!"

After first allowing her big pronouncement to float there in the air between us, she backs away and studies my face. I had never seen her like this. She seemed so enormously pleased to have been able to say this to me.

I'm standing there and my mind is racing. What is she getting at?

My first thought was, 'Is she saying that she saw Reverend Johnnie Watkins sneaking around on her? Maybe she saw him downtown, somewhere he wasn't supposed to be?'

Then - it was like, "Well, what was he... oh - oh – OOOH you mean my real father?" Now I'm half-whispering.

My mother calmly looks me up and down and says, almost regally, "Yes."

Then she quickly adds, "He was downtown."

I had no idea what I should say. In a vague sort of way, I knew that I had a father out there somewhere, yet I cannot remember ever being concerned about it, certainly not enough to ask about it. Now, it appears that my flesh and blood father is not at all far away. It is even possible to run into him on the streets, right here in Baltimore. Wow!

The only thing I could think to say was "Oh really...downtown?" I thought that sounded real grownup-like.

Therefore, I said, "Oh really...downtown?"

We stood there in that moment, saying nothing at all. I tried to come up with something to say. It appeared something from me was required, it felt like she was watching me, maybe even studying me. Unfortunately, I had nothing to offer her - nothing. Then, per a life-long and tacit agreement between my mother and I, that now astounds me, we simply - let it go. It is heartbreaking for me now to see how I let that opportunity to learn something of my father get past me. That, however, is how we did things in our family, and I suspect, many others do the same.

There was a rather strained dynamic at work in our family. My mother had to take extraordinary care not to exhibit any traces of favoritism towards my older sister Plum or me; at least not at the expense of the twins. Johnnie could be an unpredictably volatile, and at times, irrationally petty man. Although, I must point out that, to his credit, he did marry a woman with two kids who were not his own, and remained with her until the day she died. You have to give the man some respect for that.

Plum chose to deal with the disparities in our family by being rebellious and at times spoiled rotten, fairly screaming for her rightful share of attention, and several times even running away from home to make her point.

Me - I became an over-achiever and tried to disconnect myself from the whole messy business, while every single day, quietly searching for a way out of it all. My Mom had married herself into a tight corner as far as I could see. She did not need any trouble from me. I was determined that she would never have any trouble from me, and as I look back, I now know it is that singular decision that unwittingly condemned me to a lifetime of what has been a simmering, barely repressed sense of loneliness. Everything has its price.

I vividly remember April 11, 1963, the actual date we arrived on Edmondson Avenue in the neighborhood of Harlem Park in Baltimore. I was nine years old. We had come from a section of Baltimore called Cherry Hill. Cherry Hill was a great place for a kid. There were railroad tracks where we could watch freight trains come by, and nice hills for sledding and kids, kids, kids. Everyone living out there was dirt poor, but of course, that was not important - then.

The day we were to move away, I was playing with a softball with some of my boys. When our ball rolled into a sewage drain, we decided, like always, to get it back by lifting off the manhole cover above the sewer hole. A large iron manhole cover is extremely heavy, and it was especially heavy for our scrawny little nine-year-old arms.

After we got the ball, and we were replacing the manhole cover, I caught my hand under it as it slid back into place, and it tore one of my fingernails completely off. Shocked, bleeding and crying, I ran home where my mother cleaned it for me like a good Mom, but she was pissed as hell. She was entirely convinced that I had ripped my whole fingernail off deliberately, so that we would not have to move.

Like I'm out there saying, "Hey man, why don't y'all drop that big heavy-ass manhole cover on my finger, and if you do it just right you should tear my fingernail off, and then maybe we won't have to move, see?"

The first time I ever saw my mother cry was that day. She was sitting at the kitchen-table sobbing while being comforted by Ms. Susie who was her best friend from next door. I figured that she was probably crying about the fact that we had to move away.

Ms. Susie was rubbing her shoulders and saying that it was going to be all right but - well - it wasn't. Ms. Susie was a good friend to my Mom. She had three small boys of her own, and apparently, from all accounts, a no accounts husband.

None of the other moms was stupid enough to mess with her because she could crush you with the force of her personality, and some of those other women out there were pretty rough themselves. Sometimes the women there would get into fights with each other, usually because of their kids. The moms would be out there throwing bricks and shit. I witnessed it many times. It was great!

I had a crush on Ms. Susie and I wanted to be everywhere near her. In my mind's eye, I can still see her on those steamy hot Baltimore summer days. Ms. Susie would be holding court with the other moms and their kids. She would be walking around, gloriously young and fantastic, playing with us kids, and just laughing.

"Come on out here Mary Jane. Your children showin' this new thang called the hula-hoop. Where did Johnnie find this?"

When he wasn't preaching, my father worked on the loading dock of Hoschild Kohn, a department store in downtown Baltimore, and he had brought home some hula-hoops. It was a new and cheap toy, but no one else in Cherry Hill had one.

"You got to move your hips honey. Mary Jane I don't know if these children should be out here movin' their behinds like this…ah sookey-now!"

Ms. Susie had that hula-hoop twirling pretty well. It seemed as though Ms. Susie could do anything.

"I don't know Susie. I don't have time right now. I got cookin' to do," Mom replies.

My Mom could be shy. I loved my Mom.

"Girl, you come on out here right this minute and show these kids how to shake it Mary Jane."

Ms. Susie knew how to have a good time and only she could persuade my Mom to leave her housework and come outside to do the hula-hoop. Ms. Susie teased us all in turn and kept us laughing. Her laughter always ended with her trademark, 'Lord Child!'

She and my Mom were very close. If we got out of line, Ms. Susie would beat our asses as though we were her own, and my Mom would do the same to her kids. The two of them were always doing that corny "See ya later alligator - after a while crocodile" bit. When we left, I know my Mom really missed her.

*****

CHAPTER 2 - 1315 EDMONDSON AVENUE

Our three-story row house at 1315 Edmondson Avenue was huge, or so it seemed when compared to the very small two-story row house we had vacated in Cherry Hill. This new house was already pretty rundown, but you could see that it had been a pretty nice place once upon a time. My brother told me that he was pretty disappointed when he first saw it, but I think he was only lacking in imagination.

It had long ornate wood banisters that I liked to slide down, and there was a lot of other nice ornate woodwork all over the house, much of which had paint slathered all over it. There were French doors between the rooms, with most of the glass panes still in them. There was also a front and a back staircase (sweet!), and lots of neat looking doorknobs.

On the first floor were a living room, dining room, a fair-sized kitchen and a room we dubbed the "Summer Kitchen." Sounds nice, doesn't it? The Summer Kitchen! It was really just a bare room near the back porch that served little purpose except to suck outside what little heat our oil furnace could generate during the winters. There was even a space out there for an extra bathroom, but all the plumbing was gone. It was a beat up old house, but there was stuff that a kid could work with.

Two large bedrooms were on the second floor. My parents and my sisters took those. One other very tiny bedroom was also on the second floor, but it went unutilized. There was a bathroom in the back with a giant tub. My brother and I shared a back bedroom on the third floor. There was another bedroom up there, at the front of the house, that my father sometimes rented out.

Next door to our house on the one side was a small restaurant and carryout, although it was hardly ever open and often going out of business soon after it did open. Next to that was the infamous Club Astoria, once a well-known bar and lounge, but by the time we arrived it was just another neighborhood bar. They say Billie Holiday once sang there, but they say that about every bar in Baltimore.

Caplan's Drugstore was up the block at Edmondson Avenue and Carey Street, as well as a couple of corner grocery stores and the hardware store. Directly across the street from our house was a small luncheonette run by an old man named Mr. James. He was quiet and a little cranky, too.

The Traynham barbershop was diagonally across the street, where the star of the show was a barber named Jesse, who was a fair Billy Dee Williams look-a-like at that time. Jesse was such a good barber that it was not a good idea to go to him unless you had at least two hours of time to wait for a haircut. Still, everybody came to Jesse if just to hear him talk. Jesse knew something about everything. That had to be true because Jesse said so himself.

If you happened to forget to comb your knotty hair before you got into his chair he had no mercy on you as he went about busting them knots. Jesse would have your ass crying. If you had dirty hair, it would really set him off.

"Boy, when was the last time you washed your hair? I can't hardly get a comb through your nappy stuff. I would bet big money that your Momma don't know your head looks like this. Damn boy! You got all kinds of flakes and stuff coming from your head. I don't mean no harm boy, but you have to wash your hair sometimes!"

The whole place is laughing at your ass.

"Don't your Momma ever tell you to wash your hair? Ain't no way in the world that my Momma would let me come to the barbershop with my hair looking like this. Especially when you know someone will be looking at your head all-close up. See…come here; look right here, all that is dandruff and stuff."

Jesse will have parted your hair and called people over to see.

"This don't make a bit of sense! That's what I've been saying in here. These young single mothers nowadays don't know what they doing. Things just ain't like they used to be."

Your hair looked good when he was finished though. You smelled good too. At one time or another, there was always one other barbershop in a building two doors down from Jesse's. Eventually they would just give up and close shop.

Close by the Traynham barbershop was the Yat-Gaw-Mein Joint. That is what everyone called it. The actual name of the place was Chop Suey. They had Yat-Gaw-Mein on the menu with chicken, beef or pork and that was a preferred dish in the neighborhood, especially the 'pork yat.'

Lots of us bought the Yat-Gaw-Mein because it was cheap, only .45 cents, an amount even we kids could scrape together from odd jobs, or on payday, when our folks were feeling generous. You really had something a bit substantial in that pint of noodles, pork and onions with catsup ($.05 extra). It could fill the belly of a grown-up and would easily have us kids feeling bloated and satisfied.

Most of their business happened on the weekends when people got paid. In the case of the adults and older teens, that often meant a person who had first stopped to get liquored-up at Club Astoria. They would then go to the Yat-Gaw-Mein Joint, where it was the accepted sport to make fun of the Lee's imperfect English and generally berate them.

I guess folk were trying to feel superior to someone...anyone! They were behaving as though those hard working Asian people were somehow beneath all of us good Black people. I thought folk shouldn't treat other folk like that, but hardly anybody was going to be dumb enough to take up for the Lee family. I mean, on the wrong night that could be one stupid way to get shot!

Back on our side of the street in the other direction were more row houses, and then the Pawnshop. The Pawnshop was off-limits to us kids, but we sure liked looking at all the stuff in the window, you know... guitars, horns, jewelry, guns, tools and all.

Just past the Pawnshop at Calhoun Street was another drugstore called Adam's Drugstore, which was not as nice as Caplan's up at Carey Street. Caplan's was another place where we kids could go to buy candy, and where we would often end up having them chase our loud black asses out of the store. Usually, we just stuck to Adam's Drugstore where they were a little more tolerant.

The neighborhood of Harlem Park was virtually 100% Black; as was the other neighborhood I left behind in Cherry Hill. Consequently, until I finally left Harlem Park, I had never been to school with a white child or even had a teacher who was not Black. Yet, with the exceptions of the Traynham barbershop, Club Astoria and a few other smaller businesses, most of the businesses in our neighborhood were white-owned, primarily by Jewish folk. This was a fact which only registered with me slightly at the time because at nine-years-old - who cared?

After the riots of '68, things changed for everyone. However, this was 1963, when I still had many hard lessons to learn, many people to know.

*****

CHAPTER 3 – MY PEOPLE

I have heard that the creation of the universe (in the context of the Big-Bang theory) was "A mutation from zero to everything." Well, so it was for me with the start of my life in the neighborhood of Harlem Park; and it had everything to do with the people there - the good and the bad - because they became my people. The foundation for the life I was to create.

The center of our universe was Ms. Alma's row house at 1417 Edmondson Avenue, in the next block up from my block. Her home became the staging point for much of what our circle of friends did. Ms. Alma Pope had six children, three boys and three girls, all of them around my age or just slightly older. They all shared the same father, but her ex-husband was not living with them at that juncture in their lives.

Although I did not know it at that time, Ms. Alma's family had arrived on Edmondson Avenue only two days before the day that my family moved in. They had moved to Maryland after living for some time in Virginia. Almost immediately, we found each other. More specifically, Ms. Alma's son Allen Pope and I found each other.

Allen was in Ms. Woodfield's third grade class at P.S. 95, Franklin Square Elementary School. So was I, as well as one other boy who would become a key member of our tribe. Bruce Johnson lived at 518 N. Calhoun Street, which Allen and I had to pass as we walked the four blocks to school.

The trip to school was marginally dangerous. We had to cross Franklin Street (Rt. 40), a notoriously dangerous thoroughfare. Our parents showed us that we were supposed to stand and wait for the light to turn red and stop the traffic. However, where was the fun in that?

No! The trick was to just step on out there and time it so that you had to use stutter-steps and dramatic pauses; ducking and weaving to negotiate the fast moving traffic, much as a guard does in basketball or a running-back in football, stiff-arming cars and shit. That Heisman pose!

At times, those cars would skim by within inches of our frail bodies with the angry drivers screaming at us and cussing our dumb asses. Then, if you made it across the westbound side, you had earned the right to walk one more block and do it all over again on the eastbound side of Route 40 (Mulberry Street). We did this every day of the school year. Cars did hit kids from time-to-time, but it was never any of us. I am now old enough to know better, and yet, at times I will cross a street in the exact same manner.

Actually, an even more pressing concern during that walk south on Calhoun St. was the ever-present fear of Franklin Square boys and the other solo bandits roaming the streets. These guys were only five or six years older than we were, but in some cases, they had citywide reputations as juvenile delinquents.

Johnny Murphy, Doody-pig, Eggy-mule and Flubber would jack

you up for your measly .25 cents lunch money, just as surely as they would snatch some unlucky old lady's pocketbook or stick somebody up with a pistol.

I sort of liked Johnny Murphy, who was shorter than average, stocky, and pretty scary looking. He was a genuine outlaw, but he lived around the way, knew me by my name and made me feel like a true homeboy. He never robbed me. Everybody hated that fucking Doody-Pig who was just a mean son-of-a-bitch. He would take your money and then beat you up for no rational reason. The one called Eggy-mule was supposedly a genuine bonafide killer. You did not even want to dream about him.

It was my bad luck to get stopped by Flubber one day. I happened to be walking to school alone that day, moronically flipping my lunch money in the air, I was so happy to have it. Flubber started in on me the way they all did, by asking me to 'loan him some money?' and we all knew what that meant! They always asked you for the loan as though you were old friends or something.

"Hey little muthafucka, loan me some money?"

Therefore, of course, I say, "I don't have any money."

"Well...what's that in your hand then, nigga?" he says.

"Just my lunch money" and I'm trying hard not to look like I might begin sobbing, at this point.

"Well... let me see it muthafucka," he says, still smiling and everything.

I manage to whimper out, "I can't!"

I did not want to give up that money, because it was a rare thing for me to have money to buy my lunch and if I had to give it to him, I would have to go hungry that day.

Flubber roughly grabs my arm and tries to pry my paltry little quarter from my hand, but I wouldn't release it. Can you believe it?

"Let go of the money you stupid little muthafucka. Don't make me kick your skinny ass!"

So now, he's a little angry, and he began twisting my wrist like a corkscrew in an effort to force me to let go of my money. To his amazement and mine, I went down on my knees and twisted my entire body around on the ground in an attempt to relieve the pressure he was putting on my arm.

"C'mon you dumb-ass muthafucka let it go!"

It looked ridiculous, although for a few seconds my squirming around on the ground actually worked. Even Flubber laughed a little bit.

Flubber took my money anyway, as though there was ever any doubt. At least he was good enough not to beat the shit out of me, which I guess he had every right to do.

Still, it all goes to show you that Flubber was not a killer or anything – not yet. He was still just another sorry punk out there making his reputation by jumping school kids. That day, I went home hungry, but when you think about it, that's not so bad.

Ultimately, Allen, Bruce and I were just three skinny black kids who formed a bond as a way of getting safely to school on a daily basis. It helped us that Allen had two older brothers, Glascoe and Hubert, who were reasonably well known and very athletic, and who were both tough guys themselves. We could somewhat ride on their coat tails as long as we did not behave too much like scared pussies.

While there was always the potential for violence in that neighborhood, it was not impossible to negotiate life in relative peace as long as you did not deliberately go out of your way to fuck with other people. Harlem Park had a hard reputation then; as did Lexington

Terrace, Pennsylvania Avenue, Park Heights, Pimlico and any number of other West Side neighborhoods.

And the East Side of Baltimore! You did not want to think about going over there unless you were begging for trouble. No doubt, they probably thought the same thing about us, but we were scared of those boys - for real!

Everybody was always worried about getting shot, which was a legitimate fear in Baltimore. Even way back then it seemed that Baltimoreans had a fascination with handguns that was way out of proportion to its perception as a relatively small urban center.

There was gun violence enough to keep you afraid, but it was of a variety, at least at that time, that you felt could be avoided unless you were really - really - unlucky. Everyone knew, when gunfire did break out, the thing to do was to 'Stay Down,' no mystery there.

Essentially, if you wanted to get out of there alive, what you did was to stick close to your own neighborhood with your own homeboys, the good ones and the bad. It was smart to know them all. However, who the hell was going to confine themselves to a few square blocks in their own neighborhood. I mean - the guys and gals who were a little bit older than us had shit to do. They had to get to their parties and jobs. You can't just hide on your block like some kind of punk.

You see - it helped to look at your survival this way, it was a lot like when we were crossing Mulberry Street to get to school. You had to get over your fears, step off the curb, and get on out there into the fast moving flow of Baltimore City. Just remember to stay low and use that stutter-step, duck and weave. You do that, and most of the bad shit will probably miss you, if only by inches, sometimes.

*****

CHAPTER 4 – THE PLAYERS

Every boy needs to have those two other boys in his neighborhood who become his two best friends. In my case, that was Bruce Johnson and Allen Pope. Allen Pope had charisma. As a kid, he was a born leader. He was not a big kid, but he carried himself in a way that made you think of him as big and strong. Nobody ever wanted to pick a fight with Allen because he was so quick with a fierce determination.

When I would wrestle with him, as we all loved to do with each other, Allen would never give up. Sometimes I was not sure if the wrestling match had not degenerated into an actual fight. He would engage me with such intensity that most of the time; I would be the first to quit.

We did something else that we called body punching. It was a way of standing toe-to-toe with another guy and using your fist to pound the other guy's body, hitting him above the waist and below the neck as hard as you could punch him. Oh man! Allen could hit hard, and he stoically took whatever punishment you could dish out.

It probably helped that he had older brothers and he would have to body-punch with them sometimes, you know that rite of passage stuff and whatnot. I watched Allen and his brother Glascoe go at it once and Glascoe was fucking him up, and this was his brother!

The boy had heart! I knew that I was not going to be doing any body punching with Glascoe, and none of the rest of our boys was either. I mean, shit! Glascoe was quicker and a lot stronger than Allen was. Glascoe was going to inflict some real pain.

All of us knew that if there were ever any trouble, Allen would always have your back. He was an enormously loyal and honest person who was also a good athlete and incredibly industrious. During the summer months, Allen could always think of something we could do. At that time, it was usually chasing after the neighborhood girls or playing softball. Everyone knows what happens when you have a bunch of kids, with no imagination, standing around doing that dumb,

"What do you want to do?"

"I dunno man, what do you want to do?" etc., etc.

Unbelievably, we actually did that. There was always a need for someone to step up with some authority, and remind all of us dopes that we should do what it is that everyone wants to do anyway, which is to chase girls or play softball. That was Allen's role.

Running after the girls was mostly a nighttime activity, so boy did we play a lot of softball. That is a fact that somewhat goes against the conventional wisdom at the time regarding black boys and inner-city sports. Everyone would think that we would be playing basketball, but we rarely ever did.

For one thing, there was no basketball court nearby, and for another, man... we just really liked playing softball. We would be out there in that blistering hot Baltimore summer heat and humidity, sometimes from 10:00AM until 5:00PM. The scores would be like, 120-98 or 143-120.

Most of the players for our marathon games were our age or slightly younger, a few of them slightly older. Guys like our boy William Newman, who liked to pitch and who also liked to suck on his middle two fingers. Once, while crossing a street, William was hit by a motorcycle, because after he was more than halfway across and the light suddenly changed, he decided to run back rather than continue on to the other side.

"Why run back William? You were almost to the other side!"

William never had an answer for that question. He would only giggle.

That story always cracked us up.

There was one girl, Joanne, who often played with us. She was a thick girl with strong arms, short powerful legs and a gruff, loud speaking voice. Joanne always talked non-stop. That damn Joanne could hit a baseball too. She could embarrass you if you were not a very good, fast pitcher. Other than big 'ol Butch, nobody threw hard enough, except maybe Allen.

When she was not playing ball with us she would sometimes chase us around the neighborhood, which was weird fun, especially since nobody ever knew why she was chasing us. Maybe it was just because we were running. It was like one of those 'chicken or the egg?' things. I don't know.

If she did catch you, she would usually just grab you, kind of hug you very tightly, maybe try to kiss you, and then let you go. That was it. The whole thing did not make a whole lot of sense but it was something to do. She especially liked hugging the one guy Butch who was a couple of years older than the rest of us, but who would play ball with us anyway, Joanne luuved Butch.

I've heard it said that Joanne was a little 'slow' mentally, and people would make fun of her at times. I never saw anything to substantiate her being 'slow.' She was talkative and slightly goofy at times, like everybody else. As far as I can tell, her life in later years all but completely refuted what people were saying. She went on to become an honor student in college, a good athlete, and appeared headed for an exemplary life.

That is, until someone pumped a bullet into her body and left her to die on the side of a road somewhere far from Harlem Park, in Baltimore County. That is what I heard anyway. All of Harlem Park grieved for her. All of Baltimore City grieved for Joanne. People sure did seem to like Joanne after that happened. How fucked up is that?

Anyway, the core group of players for our softball games consisted of Allen, Bruce, Butch and me. All of us developed whatever skills we were to possess as softball players out there on that makeshift baseball field. Quite honestly many of us did become pretty good players. We understood the rules of the game reasonably well and we were all avid fans of the Baltimore Orioles, who were an exciting baseball team around that time.

Butch fueled much of our interest in professional baseball. Since he was older and had a job working in Adam's drugstore he could afford to go to the Oriole games at Memorial Stadium. Butch had us all wanting to go. Sometimes we did.

Although all of us had TV sets at home, what we really liked to do was to listen to the Oriole games on the radio as the old folk did, with the mellifluous voice of Chuck Thompson doing the play-by-play. When somebody like Brooks Robinson would hit a home run, he had this great way of saying, "And ain't the beer cold!"

Allen's grandmother Ms. Katie, who lived on the third floor of their house, always had her radio tuned to the Orioles games. Sometimes we would listen to the game with her. She liked to impress us with her knowledge of the game – which was considerable. I learned what a grapefruit game was from Ms. Katie.

*****

CHAPTER 5 – ROLE MODELS

All of us paid close attention to what the older guys were doing. They were our immediate (day-to-day) role models for what it took to be a man, although none of us thought of it that way then. We were lucky; they were good guys. They weren't perfect, but nobody is.

After those softball games we would often go back to Allen's house for water, most of the time without Butch, who often had to work. Usually Allen, Bruce and me would go in through Allen's back yard and enter a door that opened to the basement of his house.

That basement could be a cool place to be on a hot day. Allen and his two older brothers shared the basement as their living quarters. It was not a 'finished basement.' It was a rustic arrangement with a lot of pipes and vents around, but made considerably more comfortable by the creative handiwork of Hubert and Glascoe, complimented by Allen's artwork. This was the place where they would entertain their women. You had to hook it up as best you could, you understand.

Scrub it down! Put up some soft low lights, curtains, and a couple of posters or whatever. It was not the Belvedere hotel, but it would do.

Everyone knew that if you came up to that cellar door, either from the entrance on the first floor inside the house or the backyard entrance, if that door was locked - don't even knock. Just Leave! Even Ms. Alma, an absolutely righteous woman, generally adopted a 'don't ask - don't tell' policy regarding her boys in the cellar.

We were allowed down there whenever Hubert and Glascoe were 'without woman,' as it were. Most of the time, Hubert was a lot more accommodating about things than Glascoe (who never hesitated to tell us to beat it). Sometimes, Allen would bravely bang on the first floor cellar door.

"Hey Glascoe, I need to get that new football. We're gettin up a real game with some boys."

After a few moments, Glascoe would yell up, "I'm busy."

"You can just throw it up the stairs Glascoe, I'll catch it"

There would be another long pause.

"Go away fool!"

That would bring us all to the door whining and begging, "Aw, C'mon Glascoe. We wanna use the good ball."

Pause.

"Go on fools," we can hear him and the girl laughing at us.

Then, Allen gets an idea.

"Hey Glascoe, why don't you just throw it out the back door to the backyard?"

Allen knew that this would not require much effort from Glascoe. He could do it and quickly get back to what he was doing.

There was a slightly different kind of pause, then "Go away fool."

Allen looked at us and said excitedly, "C'mon y'all!"

All of us would then crowd out of the front door and run around the block to the backyard. The football would be sitting there on the ground, rocking back and forth.

Glascoe!

I was always a little in awe of Hubert. He was a tall-ish and very soft-spoken guy with a warm smile. Hubert, despite the conspicuous absence of his father, bravely shouldered the responsibility that his place as the eldest son in his large family conferred upon him. He always appeared to be working at a job somewhere to help out his Mom, and to make sure that he looked good. He was after all, still a teenager. Everybody, his Mom included, gave Hubert his space because he was trying to do the right thing by his family.

Sometimes he would talk with us in the backyard or even come out to the alley and hit a few fly balls for us. That was a real treat. Hubert was left-handed. Some of the older boys called him "Lefty" and he could hit a ball what seemed to us, a mile high.

There was one time in particular when I found myself especially impressed by Hubert's gentle nature. He and his younger brother Allen were doing target practice with a B.B. Rifle that Allen had purchased. From a kitchen window, one of them fired point-blank at a bird sitting in a tree, killing it. Allen told us how badly they felt about killing that stupid bird and how they decided that day that they would never shoot at birds again because the birds weren't hurting anybody or anything. Allen said that they even gave the bird a burial. I was pretty sure that the burial was Hubert's idea. The whole thing sounded like something Hubert would say and do.

Year's later, when I mentioned this story to Allen; he said that it was actually Hubert who shot that bird.

Anyway - I remember Hubert as nice.

All of us were out there every day trying to shoot a bird - any bird - with our own B.B. guns, which were not terribly accurate. However, we too stopped doing that simply because it did not feel right anymore after what Allen and Hubert had done. Of course, that did not stop us from shooting at mice and rats. It was a badge of honor to kill one of those.

Another time, Hubert was out in the alley with us and we were all throwing bricks at rats scurrying in and out of a garbage heap. After Hubert had managed to wound one of them badly and it was completely defenseless, we all pelted it a few more times for good measure.

Then, Hubert went into his house and returned with a can of spray paint. I had no idea what he planned to do with it, and I could not believe it when he lit a match and then pressed the nozzle on the spray-can. That ignited it into a kind of blowtorch. Hubert burned that screaming rat to a black crisp. Oh yeah, Hubert was a nice guy all right, but let's face it, that was a rat of the kind which might sometime turn up in the basement where he and his brothers slept at night.

A statement was required. It was like...fuck you!

Often, in the relative cool of Ms. Alma's cellar, we would end up just sitting around doing nothing in particular, perhaps enjoying a frozen-cup (frozen flavored-syrup and water) and some cookies we had purchased for a dime from Ms. Mary's house across the way. Ms. Mary was the mother of Ben (the crybaby) and Tony P. She would make extra money by selling frozen-cups. She also sold cookies she baked herself, a tasty combination on a hot afternoon.

All the kids in the neighborhood knew about Ms. Mary's impromptu store. A large part of its appeal for us boys was that her daughter, whom everyone called, Sister, served those treats up. Sister was one healthy girl. She had nice legs and a bodacious ass that we coveted, despite the fact that we did not know (that we really did not know!) exactly what we would do with it. She liked to wear cut-off jeans.

Even at the tender age of nine or ten, we were not very naive about matters regarding sex. As far back as seven-years- old, in my old neighborhood of Cherry Hill, I can remember fooling around with one of my sister's older girl friends while in a closet in our house. When we came out, my sister Plum demanded to know what we were doing.

"I was looking all over for y'all. Were y'all in that closet all this time? Oooooh! I'm gonna tell! I know what y'all were doing."

Her girlfriend counters with a smile and some attitude, "what were we doin' Plum?"

My sister was not about to back down, even though she was younger,

"Let me smell your fingers. I know you. I know you were doing something with him."

Her girlfriend says, "Plum ain't no way I'm lettin' you smell my fingers."

Plum fires back, "See, I'm not asking to smell your fingers... I didn't say that I wanted to smell your fingers - see, but he's gonna' let me smell his fingers. Y'all know you were doing something nasty."

The whole time I 'm trying to sneak a whiff of my fingers to see what she was talking about, but she was looking right at me. When she grabbed my hand, I let her smell my fingers, and Plum looked confused.

"Well...I'm not sure if I can smell anything. She must have just taken a bath or something, but y'all can't be hiding in my Mom's closet like that."

You have to wonder how my sister knew about this sort of stuff anyway. To this day I don't know why she could not smell anything, because I sure 'nuff did have my hands inside that girl's panties. My fingers were between her legs, inside her vagina, finger popping her, something she had shown me how to do. I remember the warm musky smell.

That was a close call.

Any chance we got, we would assail Allen's older brothers with blunt questions about girls, fucking, titties, kissing, and they were glad to talk to us - some of the time. Also, since I was an avid reader of just about anything, I spent untold hours looking for books, pictures, sympathetic older girls, anything or anyone who could help me unravel the mysteries of sex. Then, I would share any information I could gather with my boys Allen and Bruce. That was my role.

Allen could make good use of the information since he was a good-looking kid with nice wavy-hair and everything. Wavy-hair went a long way with the girls in the Black community. Girls found him attractive and he had the confidence and self-possession to capitalize on that. I was a bit awkward, but some girls thought I was kind of cute. Then, there was our boy Bruce...

*****

CHAPTER 6 – BRUCE

Bruce Johnson was our neighborhood's approximation of the poor little rich kid. Sure, his family was not all that much better off than our families, but his life was unquestionably a tad softer than ours was. He lived with his Mom, his Dad and older brother Lawrence, on Calhoun Street. They had been in the neighborhood longer than either Allen or me.

Bruce's Dad was out there working hard every day, which enabled him to take good care of his wife and two boys. He had a very good job as a manager of an Electrical Warehouse and their family lived in an apartment rather than renting a row house as our families did. Having such a great job and only two children meant Bruce's father had a few extra dollars for other amenities, like ample food, summer camp and a car.

One might assume that Bruce would have been successful with the ladies. He had a pleasant round face, which made him look almost stocky when compared with most of us. He was light-skinned. That was another plus with black folk, and he had hazel eyes and nice hair.

Yet, most of the girls gave him a hard time. I mean, he was kind and generally well liked, but the girls were reluctant to spend any time with him on an intimate basis. However, any possibility of understanding Bruce must include some specific mention of the role his mother Ms. Sarah played in his life.

As we all used to say, "Ms. Sarah was a trip!"

Taking care of her youngest boy Bruce appeared to be Ms. Sarah's primary reason for living. Our boy Bruce was spoiled rotten, and unashamedly so. There were times, although rare, when we would go to Bruce's house to hang out. This did not occur often because his Mom had a tendency to nag him; something that he hated and something that was painful for us to witness.

Nonetheless, it was simply stunning for us to see how his mother would cater to him, as though he was completely helpless. Bruce would say, "What else does she have to do?" Ms. Sarah never worked a day outside of her home, and as a result, she was able to be an omnipresent force in the life of her baby boy. From her perch in their second floor kitchen window, she had an outstanding vantage point for observing the moment-to-moment movements of her boy in the back alley playground.

There were a few kids who were plainly jealous of Bruce and openly resentful of the relative opulence in which he lived in Harlem Park. For this reason, they would pick on him, and Bruce had to do a good deal of fighting. It was always over some dumb shit, but Bruce lacked the physical presence or the quick thinking to talk trash and bluff his way out of trouble.

This one kid in particular, Black Jesus, was always up in Bruce's face. He was very, very dark skinned and he did not actually live in the immediate area, but was a regular fixture in the back alley. His real name was Gregory, but in those years, when black folk were still referred to as Colored or Negroes, one of the worst things you could call somebody was black, and since not very many people liked Gregory, he somehow acquired the nickname of Black Jesus. It could be that the Jesus part of his name helped to soften the insult of being called "Black."

I have often felt that some darker-skinned black folk, like Gregory, were ornery simply because the rest of us black folk could treat them so cruelly. They were subject to discrimination from white folk, which they could somewhat understand - but from their own people?

When Ms. Sarah would see Black Jesus bothering Bruce and invariably come outside to intervene, Black Jesus refused to back off one inch. He would sometimes verbally tear into Ms. Sarah with little respect for her age or the fact that she was someone's mom.

Yet, even though nobody liked Black Jesus very much and we all hated the way he would disrespect Bruce's Mom, usually no one would get involved because there was something of a feeling that Bruce's Mom should never have come out there to fight Bruce's battles in the first place.

Besides, Black Jesus wasn't stupid enough to assault Ms. Sarah physically, because then the whole neighborhood would have been honor-bound to kick his ass. Mostly what he did was a lot of mouthing off.

You would see Black Jesus and Bruce out in the alley locked in the usual street fight pose, where the two guys stand face to face with one guy's chest pushed up against the other guy's chest, trying to stare one another down. Bruce is too puffed-up angry to speak. Black Jesus is at his most belligerent.

"I ain't scared of none of y'all niggas around here. That's right Bruce...and I ain't scared of your boy Allen or that tall skinny nigga.
"

"Shut the fuck up Black Jesus," I say.

"I ain't scared of you man," he spits back.

"Let's go Bruce." Ms. Sarah has come up behind us. I'm hoping she didn't hear me cussing.

"And I ain't gonna run just 'cause your Moms is out here. Ain't nobody out here scared of your Moms. Shit! I should bang you in your face right now…right in front of her. She always is tryin' to fight for you. Why you don't let him fight his own battles Ms. Sarah?"

Ms. Sarah barely looks at Black Jesus.

"He is not that important Bruce. You don't have anything to prove to that boy." She quietly pleads with Bruce.

Actually, Black Jesus knows that it would be best if this whole thing de-escalates, before he has to fight the whole neighborhood.

He says, "And she better not put her hands on me 'cause then…. I don't know…but I would have to bring a whole lotta niggas down here."

There was a chorus of, 'Yeah…sure!' at this declaration.

Anyone who knows Black Jesus knows there is no way anyone is going to come around here to fight for his benefit.

The whole time he's talking, he has to keep his face like 1/4 inch away from Bruce's face. Of course, he's spitting all over Bruce, but Bruce can't punk out and leave.

Ms. Sarah could hear everything Black Jesus was saying. She was standing her ground smartly, being careful not to give him a reason to come after her.

"Come on Bruce. You don't have to fight with him. Just get your stuff and come on home. Let's go home Bruce, now!"

Bruce was holding his ground as well. We could see that he had made up his mind to give Black Jesus a good fight today. Black Jesus could probably sense it too. Wisely, they walked away from each other. The thing is – if your mom comes out there too much, it's not good. That's all I'm trying to say.

Stuff like that did not do a lot to help with Bruce's standing in the neighborhood pecking order. Unfortunately, Bruce had no leadership ability and he was not a very good athlete; two attributes which might have improved matters for him.

In fact, he was that kind of kid who, when we were playing tackle football on a dirt-covered patch of that glass strewn back alley playground, would be the only kid wearing football pants, kneepads, shoulder pads and a helmet. Well - maybe one other kid might have a beat-up helmet on. Then, when there was a big pile-up of players on the ground, Bruce would all too often be the only one to come out of it badly injured, even with all those pads and shit on! It became a running joke.

However, he was shrewd enough to hook-up with Allen and me and that gave him legitimacy enough on our little playground. Bruce does deserve some credit for trying. He worked at sports steadily, and over the years, he became a much-improved athlete in many respects. Always he had a good heart. I remember once seeing his eyes glaze over at the sight of a homeless woman.

"Do I detect a tear in your eye, man?" I asked.

Bruce was staring at her, lost in thought, and he answered without taking his eyes off of the old woman.

"I just hate to see an old lady doing bad like that. I look at her and it makes me think, what if she was my Mom?"

His reaction to her was intense even for him. It mystified me, and I thought I knew him well.

Fortunately, Bruce knew how to make the right friends and that is not a bad thing to know in a place like Harlem Park. As best we could, we covered for him and defended him because he needed our help. In many cases, the best way to help him was to let a fight happen, once it developed. We made sure to stay close, to insure that it was a fair fight.

Really, the last thing any of us wanted was trouble. Still, even if you did everything to avoid it, in Harlem Park trouble could find you. Then, there are always those who can't seem to survive without purposefully cultivating danger. One of our boys, Huggie, was a perfect example of that sort.

*****

CHAPTER 7 – OUTLAWS

The boys and I did our best to be good guys. Whenever we could, we tried to find some odd job to make a few pennies, thereby avoiding the temptation of petty thievery in the neighborhood stores. We also went to school everyday and none of us played hooky even though that was something many kids did. Together, the three of us made a conscious decision that we would not use a lot of profanity (maybe some for effect). We simply decided that we did not want to be cussing all the time, like some of the other kids.

Jumping on the back bumper of the old transit buses and hitching a ride for a few blocks, while holding on for dear life, was a big thing then. For some guys, this was their sole means of transportation for riding downtown or just getting around looking for some trouble. A bus would come by, and I'd see crazy-ass Sponge (Carlton Dixon) leaning from the back bumper, waving. I wanted to try it. I hopped on the back of an idling bus once, but jumped off after it had only gone a few feet. I was a coward.

We didn't smoke cigarettes and we had not developed an interest in alcohol or drugs. Lots of kids our age did some of these things to varying degrees. However, in our corner of Harlem Park it was not so terrible to be a moderately decent kid. At least no one ever had to come and pick us up from jail.

We had this friend, Huggie, who was also in our class at school. He often hung out with the three of us. Huggie lived with his mother Ms. Bobbie and his younger brother on Calhoun Street, in the same block as Bruce. He was a so-so student in school, choosing to disguise his academic deficiencies by being a cut-up.

Despite this, we liked Huggie and he was welcome to spend as much time with us as he wanted. He did come around intermittently, but there would be long stretches when we would not see him. It was not very hard to guess what he might be doing.

At some point early on, it became clear to us that Huggie had made the decision to be a tough guy, an outlaw. We would see him running with some pretty rough boys, the kind of guys who were sure to lead you into situations that would get you hurt at the very least, killed in the worst case scenario.

Huggie was hanging out with two boys in particular. The lesser of the two bad guys, was a guy named Tyrone Lewis, who would later earn the nickname of "Wine." Wine lived on Calhoun Street on the same block as Bruce and Huggie. Wine's sister was Joanne, who played softball with and who they found dead.

Wine was a homeboy but he was a rough customer who was already way beyond the control of his mother. He knew all of us kids by our names and he was about two or three years older than we were. Wine hung out with Sammy who was Wine's cousin, supposedly. Sammy was one cruel, sadistic, rotten muthafucka.

For us, having to live in fear of Sammy, and the few dumb thugs who followed him around everywhere like puppies, was bad enough;

but Sammy would never show up with only his flunkies. When you saw Sammy, there were always two or three big-ass German shepherd dogs or Pit Bulls, tugging him along. These dogs were way scary and vicious. Sammy did everything he could to keep them hungry and angry, usually by beating the shit out of them.

On several nightmarish occasions, we would be out playing in the back alley lot when we would see Sammy and his squad turn the corner with those dogs. Everybody with any sense knew to drop everything and find something high on which to start climbing, and it had better be high enough so that the dogs could not easily drag you down from it.

Once, when we were around twelve or so, we were playing softball in the spacious new playground at Harlem Park Junior High, when someone started yelling.

"Run y'all, here comes Sammy. Sammayyyy!"

We looked up to see Sammy and those German shepherds coming through the gates and heading straight towards us. He was still easily about a hundred yards away, but this time Sammy let those dogs run ahead of him sending terrified kids running and screaming before them.

One good thing about the new playground was that the walls surrounding it were high, and topped-off with a very high chain link fence. If you ran at the wall with some speed, you could vault high enough to pull yourself up to the chain link section, safe from the dogs and the thugs running with Sammy.

However, that day Sammy obviously had something particular in mind. That day, he was not there just to harass and terrorize us. He was there to get Huggie, who was right up there cowering on the fence with the rest of us. Not a good sign I'd say.

Right away, that bastard Sammy came over and ordered Huggie to climb down. Poor Huggie had no choice. After all, he did hang out with those morons sometimes. Looking a little sickly, Huggie resignedly jumps down. We all watch them surround him and hustle him off across the playground, heading north on Calhoun Street. Everybody felt bad for Huggie, but the sad truth is, we were all relieved that he only wanted Huggie.

I jumped down and ran to get Huggie's Mom, Ms Bobbie. Those guys were practically dragging Huggie away with them and despite his attempt at a brave face; I could see that Huggie was scared. While I went for Huggie's Mom, Allen and some of the others followed Sammy and his stooges, at a distance, to see where they went.

Soon, with Huggie's Mom, Ms. Bobbie, following behind me, I began slowly jogging north on Calhoun Street in the direction I had last seen everyone headed. Up ahead, we could see Allen and the others peeking up an alley. That is when Ms. Bobbie, knowing that her child was in trouble, went charging by me up that alley and man - she was pissed! What she saw when she got back there must have truly horrified her.

Sammy, and two kids everyone knew as 'The Twins,' were holding a badly bruised and bloodied Huggie suspended in the air above their heads and dangling over a fence surrounding someone's backyard. Inside the yard was an enormous German shepherd that was somewhat legendary in Harlem Park for its size and its viciousness. I would have bet money that Sammy was planning to steal that dog, and Huggie was some kind of bait.

They were threatening to drop Huggie into the yard with that big, mean-ass dog if he didn't agree to fight one of the Twins. However, they had not reckoned on Ms. Bobbie showing up, and without a moment's hesitation Ms. Bobbie stalked right up to them and spat out,

"Put-my-got-damned-son-down!"

For the rest of us watching, it was like, "WHOA!"

Now, all those boys knew that Ms. Bobbie was Huggie's Mom and that she was a tough woman, who incidentally, was gorgeous. They were just so stunned to see her standing there. They froze... and for a few moments, they simply held him up there. Then, not knowing what else to do and being in no mood to confront Ms. Bobbie, who looked dangerous as only a Mom could, they put him down.

She was clearly ready to kick all their asses - and their dogs' too. Still, they roughly dropped Huggie onto the ground at her feet. Then, in an effort to save some face, they very slowly and deliberately strutted away with their wild dogs, who all this time had been barking and straining at their leashes from where they had been tied to a fence.

Ms. Bobbie helped Huggie get up, dusted him off and looked him over real good. He was pretty beat up to be sure, but he would live. Huggie was a pretty tough kid after all, and it was crystal clear that he had to be tough, given the kind of bad life choices he seemed to be making.

All of us began walking the three blocks home, during which Huggie had to explain to his Mom what those boys, who were supposed to be his friends, had done to him. She kept smacking him in the back of the head and giving him hell.

"It's bad enough that he goes around makin' those dogs fight. But, I will be got-damned if he is gonna have my son fighting like a got-damned dog. I can't believe that he's out here trying to make people fight each other. That boy has lost his mind, or did you do something to one of them?"

"Mom, I didn't do nothing to them. I don't know why they always wantin' me to fight him."

Whap! Ms. Bobbie smacked him up beside his head.

"I don't have time for this shit Huggie. I have to get to work. I don't know why you runnin' with them boys. Not a one of them is any good James. I should have slapped that got-damned Sammy in his face. That boy is a sneaky bastard. Stop hangin' out with that boy Huggie! He's just too mean to be messin' with."

Whap! Ms. Bobbie slapped his head again.

Huggie laughed when she popped him beside his head. I liked him for that.

Apparently, what happened was that Sammy had decided in his twisted mind that it would be fun to watch Huggie and one of The Twins fight one another. Now, in a fair fight Huggie stood a chance of coming out of it reasonably well. Huggie was almost as big as either one of them and he could handle himself.

Of course, there was no way it was going to be a fair fight. That other twin was going to be standing close by holding an angry dog on a leash, making sure that his brother came out on top. Huggie was smart enough to figure this out, so of course he said no to the fight.

At that point, they let him know that if he did not fight one of the twins they would throw him into the yard with that big agitated German shepherd. He put up a hell of a fight to keep them from throwing him into that yard, and it was during that struggle that they ended up having to drag him across that back alley. Broken glass littered the concrete surface of the alley, so he had cuts all over his hands and legs.

The sad irony of it all was that, a couple of days later, Huggie would be right back out there hanging with Sammy and that bunch. That was a hard thing for the rest of us to digest.

It was likely at about this time in my life I concluded that I was not ever going to be a real outlaw. The bad guys were too unpredictable and could turn on you in a flash. Any idiot could figure out that there is no way that running with those boys could bring you anything but trouble, but Huggie had made up his mind to be a tough guy, an outlaw.

*****

CHAPTER 8 – SUMMER'S EVE

Very few people we knew had an air-conditioner in their home. However, when a fan is all you can afford, you develop an appreciation for it, and those fans would be humming on any given night on Edmondson Avenue, moving that hot air around and around and around.

Most people spent their summer evenings sitting outdoors on the white marble steps for which Baltimore was so famous. Those muggy evenings are the fuzzy, precious, golden moments many of us would reflect upon nostalgically years later, as we cranked up our air conditioners another notch. For us young boys in Harlem Park it was the time when we had our best opportunity to pursue our rapidly budding interest in girls. They were all out there, hot and sweaty.

After nearly a full day in the searing heat of that back alley playground all of us would eventually make our way home for some kind of dinner. In my house, that meant going into the kitchen and making a meal of whatever was in the pots and pans left on the stove by my Mom or Dad. Except on rare occasions, our family only ate together on Sundays at breakfast and dinner.

Dinner was something to be completed with all due haste in order to get back outside and up the street to the 1400 block of Edmondson Avenue, so as not to miss anything. After gobbling down a typical meal of mackerel cakes and rice, I would make my way through the drunks and other patrons of Club Astoria, who would be sitting on our front steps or standing nearby. Excited and expectant, I would strike off, headed up the street for 1417 Edmondson Avenue.

Immediately after walking across Calhoun Street, I pass by Adam's drugstore. Through the glass door, soaking up that cool conditioned air, I see Butch behind the counter stacking boxes or something like that. Sometimes he would even be a temporary clerk, selling candy to the small kids who would come in. Butch was an important young man in our little world because he had managed to find a steady job. Many of the corner storeowners gave jobs to the teenage boys and girls from the neighborhood. They also employed some of the adults. These jobs were coveted because they kept a little cash in your pocket and that never hurts.

Continuing up the block, I pass the cousins Rhonda and Stephanie sitting on the front steps of their grandmother's house. It would not be quite accurate to describe their family as well-to-do, but they did have a sort of Black lower-middle-class kind of thing working, and people respected them and their property. They owned their own home and kept it up.

Old Mrs. Carr had a son Teddy, who was in his late thirties and who was an unfortunate source of embarrassment to their family. He had a serious drinking problem. Occasionally Teddy would appear at my house, usually followed by his scruffy, dusty black mutt of a dog, Jumping Jack.

While his mutt waited at the curb, Teddy would come inside and stay long enough for a meal and some casual talk with my father. When you live with a preacher, someone is always dropping in. They sometimes had a stiff drink together. As a preacher, my father was not really supposed be doing that. It was one of those loosely held family secrets.

On one such occasion while sitting at the table, Teddy removed his full set of dentures from his mouth in order to eat. Then, he very matter-of-factly dropped them into his glass of drinking water to allow them to soak. He then drank the water, with his teeth still in the glass, we could see them bouncing around in there. Allen and I thought that was damn funny. We roared!

Further on up the street are Sherry and Debbie, who are cousins. They would be sitting on their grandmother's steps. Debbie was the younger sister of Butch who worked at the corner drugstore. Good ol' Debbie always had money because Butch was pretty generous with his cash.

Quite a few of the kids lived with their grandparents on a permanent basis or they stayed with them in the summer because they wanted to be on Edmondson Avenue, where more often than not, something that was fun was bound to happen.

Only a couple of doors more up the street, at 1417 Edmondson Avenue, on any given night, there is a small knot of people sitting on the steps and leaning against the cars parked along the street. Music is wafting into the air from transistor radios, car radios or maybe from a speaker that was sitting in a window inside the house.

Nearly every radio is set to the same station, WWIN on your AM dial, where they are playing the latest thing from Smokey or the Temptations, the Delphonics, Supremes, Intruders, Dionne Warwick, Marvin Gay and on and on. Practically everybody up and down the street will be singing and humming along, bullshitting and passing the time. Oh man, the delicious possibilities. Each person has come seeking some form of affirmation; irresistibly drawn here to play some part in the story, a role in this fleeting moment on the West Side, on a summer evening in Harlem Park.

The early evening hours before dark were primarily devoted to visiting the clusters of people along the street. Some people on the block could not stand one another, but over time and out of necessity, they had managed to find ways to peacefully coexist on the block - most of the time anyway.

Sometimes, all it took to upset this delicate balance was something as innocuous as a new family on the block, perhaps someone like Ms. Alma, who has come to Harlem Park with her three fine daughters. This was a source of bitterness for some of the other girls, and a delight for the boys in the neighborhood.

Mary was the oldest, about eleven years old in 1963. She was short with nicely shaped legs and a tight little butt. Mary was extremely bright and a somewhat serious girl who seemed mature beyond her years. She was hopelessly beyond the reach of us young boys, although we were actually only a couple of years younger than she was. Girls mature faster, as we well know.

Linda and Brenda were ten years old fraternal twins. Linda was taller and thinner with nice legs and lips and an outgoing nature. Brenda was shorter, softer, already bosomy and more matronly

Ms. Alma raised her three girls to conduct themselves as ladies. That, and the presence of three strong healthy boys in the house, was some guarantee that they received the proper respect and consideration. The older boys around, seeing the possibilities, took due notice of the three girls, but publicly confined their ardor to mild flirting. Privately, each boy, in his own sneaky way, devised various means to compete for each girl's respective attentions. Ms. Alma's girls were as popular as her boys were, so the area around their house was a busy place.

It was a good time. These girls were our girls in our neighborhood.

They were good girls who were a lot like us good boys, for the time being at least. There was just no way, for any of us to know what was coming in a few short years; and besides, we were too young to be looking that far down the road. At that time, we were only hoping, as children do, that the summer would never end; but of course, all things must end.

****

CHAPTER 9 – HARLEM PARK ELEMENTARY SCHOOL

Another summer's end meant the beginning of our fourth grade year and an autumn return to Franklin Square Elementary School. My boys and I all landed in the same class once again and those first couple of months passed by uneventfully. Then, something got everyone's attention.

Our teacher, Mrs. Ball, was standing near the door to the classroom when another teacher entered and furtively whispered something in her ear. We watched her listen for a few moments and then there was a sudden sharp intake of breath by Mrs. Ball. Her eyes widened in shock and she clamped both hands over her mouth.

Trembling, she said, "I am going to need all of you to sit quietly with your hands folded on your desk. Something very important has happened and I have to go see about it. Cynthia, I want you to write down the names of anyone who misbehaves." She then hurriedly left the room.

It was November 22, 1963 and she had just been informed that President John F. Kennedy had been shot dead in Dallas, Texas. Now, while we all knew who he was in a vague sort of way, it was nonetheless difficult for us to understand why she and so many other teachers were so terribly upset. They were actually crying. The most important grown-ups in our world were weeping. That was certainly not something you see every day.

For us small kids, what stood out most was that we got out of school and there were no cartoons on television. This was due to the media coverage of the shooting of Lee Harvey Oswald and then the news coverage of the funeral. For us, if there were not going to be any cartoons on television then we may as well be back in school. Then, there was another novel event.

Harlem Park Junior High and Elementary School had finally been completed and those of us who lived north of Franklin Street were instructed to proceed, en masse, to our new school. On one gorgeously sunny mid-morning day in the early winter of 1963, a long line of grade school students headed north on Calhoun Street for the six-block walk to Harlem Park Elementary School. Once there, Bruce moved to a different classroom. Allen and I were fortunate enough to finish out our fourth grade year in the same class.

Our fifth grade year began with all three of us assigned to different classrooms. Many of the kids at our new elementary school were from the north, west and eastern boundaries of Harlem Park and were therefore unfamiliar to those of us who had attended Franklin Square Elementary School. The fifth grade was when I first discovered something of myself that would have far-reaching implications.

At some point during that year, my mother informed my brother and me that we would be missing a few days of school. It turned out that we were going for a short stay in a hospital to be circumcised. Somehow at my birth, this little detail (don't laugh!) had been missed.

On the day of my return to school, as I hurriedly entered the schoolyard I became aware of a slight buzz going through the crowd and I noticed teachers pointing me out. I didn't give it much thought at the time because I was very close to being late that morning and in a hurry to get into the building. Besides, how could all of those people possibly know that I was returning from having my pee-pee cut?

That day, the first announcement over the intercom was about me. The school Principal was congratulating me for having gotten a very high reading score on the citywide standardized test we had all taken a short while before I went into the hospital. At the time, I wasn't sure why it was such a big deal, but apparently, the school's faculty understood. I heard that I was reading at the level of a high school junior or senior, which was notable for a fifth grader in an inner-city public school. They were all impressed.

The whole thing was embarrassing and I recall feeling the skin on my face tighten. Everyone was staring at me. It was the first time at school that I had received some specific confirmation there was something about, even me, which was special.

Later that same week, Allen and Bruce stopped by my house with some pornographic playing cards. I really wanted to look at them, but I was concerned that if I got an erection I would rupture the stitches around my penis (see - I really was a smart guy). It was like…hmm… what a dilemma…to look, or not to look at dirty, nasty pictures.

My carnal instincts won out. It is not every day that you get to see something so dirty. Those cards were smokin' hot and my stitches held. Shit, by that time I was nearly healed anyway. So, the citywide test notwithstanding, nothing much was different for me I guess. I was still just one of the boys, and that is mostly what I wanted to be.

It seemed that in no time at all, we were finished with the fifth grade and had cruised into our sixth grade year. I was in Mrs. Rosalie

Jenkins's class and I thought that she was an outstanding teacher. She was a tough woman, but she was fair and treated us with respect.

That year, the school had a flag football league for the fifth and sixth grades; and to my giddy delight, there was also a softball league. My team lost the softball league championship game that year when I managed to drop a routine fly ball in left field, allowing a grand slam home run to win the game in the final inning. One of my boys named Eggy hit that home run. He was laughing his ass off at me as he rounded the bases. I felt terrible.

As bad as I felt at the time, that may have been my last year of true childhood, the last year that I still had a 'child's heart.' The mean world outside of our insular neighborhood of Harlem Park had breeched the gates, and would soon come crashing down upon us. We had seen some portentous signs, and we were in fear of it - but - it was our turn for middle school boys and girls.

*****

CHAPTER 10 – HARLEM PARK JUNIOR HIGH

The sprawling red brick building that was Harlem Park Junior High School was like an ominous, living, breathing beast to us. From its resting place, directly across the street on Edmondson Avenue, the beast watched us with its fierce eyes (windows), and salivated from its gaping jaws (doors).

Hyperbole, yes, but it was a scary place, and not just for the relatively benign reasons one might expect to be of concern to any child moving into a new school in his early teenage years. At Harlem Park, suddenly, kids from different areas found themselves thrust together, and the results were not always positive.

After only two years, Harlem Park Junior High had acquired a reputation all over the city for a certain level of violence. Its' location meant that it was drawing kids from a wide variety of neighborhoods, some from as far away as the Lexington Terrace projects. Those were some tough boys and girls down there and they were bound to be a little edgy, being so far from home.

There were rumors of pistols and knives being confiscated from lockers and there were fights almost daily. The talk of guns was alarming because we were still in a time, or so we thought, when disputes were generally settled with a fistfight. There had been no one shot inside the school, at least not yet anyway. It was difficult to say what might have been happening in the back streets and alleys surrounding the school, but it is safe to say that it was certainly not all good.

Many times, as we walked home from our day in elementary school, we would see large crowds gathered around a pair of fighting kids near one of several exits from Harlem Park Junior High. These informal gatherings were obviously the fallout from someone declaring earlier in the day, "Your ass better not come outside after school today!"

Even the girls would get into it, and we once witnessed an incredibly vicious fight between two girls. As I watched them, I was surprised to see that simply winning the fight was not going to be quite enough for them. Each girl seemed intent upon nothing less than the total degradation of the other girl.

They would start out by standing a short distance apart with all of their friends arrayed behind them feverishly attempting to provoke something. The girls would be shouting and cursing at one another.

"All you are is a skank bitch, you and your whole family."

"Your mother's a bitch!"

It was like a rule that they had to say that to one another before the fight could be official.

"Don't be calling my Mom a bitch...Bitch!"

"I didn't call your Mom a bitch... but that's only because that nasty bitch ain't here...skank."

"Don't be callin' me no skank… hoe!"

"Your mother's a hoe!"

The crowd responds with, "oooooooooooh"

Now, there is no going back! Somebody has got to get beat down. They have reached a critical point of no return. Then…Bam! They explode at each other, heads bowed and hands thrust forward, grabbing for that other bitch's hair, standard practice whenever girls fought.

At this point, some of the onlookers from each girl's respective camp will rush in and pretend to pull them apart, but only momentarily. Those girls will have at each other again, and things now have to leap to another level because now both wounded ladies are determined to walk away the clear winner.

The next round will be ferocious and it is in this round that you can bet money that they will invariably attempt to strip that other bitch of as much of her clothing as possible, especially her bra.

More than once, we saw some teenage girl with her hair standing wildly on her head, her ears bleeding from an earring being snatched from her ear and long scratches all over her face. Her white bra dangling against her black skin, she would be frantically holding onto her shredded clothing in an attempt to cover her exposed breast. Of course, we lived for these exhibitions.

The faculty over at Harlem Park was doing what it could to keep the fights off the school premises. So, the kids took the action to the back alleys that everyone used as a shortcut to school. Since we lived in the houses directly across the street from Harlem Park, it was often possible to see this type of activity by simply opening a window or stepping out my back door.

As the school year approached, it was becoming increasingly difficult to suppress my own fears of attending Harlem Park Junior High.

Particularly after one cold winter day when I witnessed two Harlem Park students fight from my back porch. It was pretty disgusting.

One of the boys had pinned the other kid to the ground in the snow by sitting on his chest. Then, he used his legs to immobilize the now helpless kid's arms. He began spitting into the prostrate kid's face over and over in as disgusting a manner as he could muster, if you know what I'm saying?

"What you got to say now muthafucka?" hawking and spitting right in the crying kid's face.

You almost felt it would be better to get shot than to have someone spit in your face like that, when you had no possible way to stop it from happening. I must tell you; it was nothing short of stupid that I would soon be going to school with those crazy-ass muthafuckas. This was only Junior High School for god's sake!

Rather than go to Harlem Park, some kids elected to ride the city buses to safer schools in other neighborhoods, which added an hour to what would have been a five-minute morning commute. Not to mention the extra financial burden on their parents that came with such a choice. Most of us saw that as punking out, and punking out wasn't a workable option for me.

There was some minor comfort for me in the knowledge that Allen's siblings, Glascoe, Mary and Linda were already over at Harlem Park. They were getting by fine so I figured, how bad could it be? The way I figured it, most of the other kids around were feeling just like me, so we all had to suck it up and head on over.

One hot August day during the summer before my entrance into Harlem Park Junior High, I was walking up the alley that leads to Allen's backyard, on my way to find out what he and Bruce were doing. Allen's brother Glascoe spotted me from his kitchen window and calls out to me.

"I hear you're coming over there with the big boys now. Are you ready for it?"

"Yeah, I guess I am Coe," I replied.

"What unit are you in?" he asked

"I don't know. I got this card in the mail that says I'm in 7-D," I answer, sounding a little confused.

Then he asked me, "7-D what?"

So now I am confused, "I don't know. The card says 7-D, with a little mark next to it."

Glascoe's face brightens, "Is it a 1...or a 2...or what?

"You know what ... I guess it's a little (1)... I was wondering what that tiny mark was," I reply.

"Damn - fool! You in 7D1, the smart class in unit-D... like my sister Mary was. You, Mary, and Allen are all in the same unit. That's all right boy," he yells at me.

"Yeah... It's gonna be all right," I answer, not really believing it, but feeling somewhat comforted by the news nonetheless.

*****

CHAPTER 11 – HARLEM PARK, SEVENTH GRADE

When I entered Harlem Park in the fall of 1966, it had been in operation nearly three years. Much of the violence associated with the first two years had subsided and was likely attributable to a necessary adjustment for the administration, faculty, students and the community at large. Many of those students of the first two years had moved on to high school. The school was still a hard place, but once I was on the inside, I quickly began to feel that I could handle it.

Harlem Park Junior High School had four sections, called units. A letter of the alphabet designated each unit: i.e. unit-A, unit-B, C and D. Although Allen and I were both in unit-D, we would not see one another very often while in school. Usually, we only saw one another in passing in the hallways or maybe in the cafeteria at lunch. We were all required to sit with our own 7th grade class in the cafeteria.

Bruce did not make the move to Junior High School with us. He had run into some academic troubles a couple of years back and consequently had to repeat a year. That meant we would not be seeing him at all during the day. We assured him that we would pave the way for him.

As it turned out, there was not a single kid in my 7th grade class whom I had known previous to that year. The class was made up of the brightest students from a number of elementary schools. To my chagrin, some of those kids were not only smart but there were some pretty hardened guys among them as well.

Obviously, they were not incorrigible. They had attended school often enough, and had done well enough while in school, to be assigned to this elite class of students. Therefore, what you had was a collection of very bright boys at big bad Harlem Park who were hell-bent on proving that they were not a bunch of punks.

Some of my least pleasant experiences came courtesy of some boys who were from the Lexington Terrace projects. There seemed to be some inexplicable, natural antipathy, between them and those of us from around Harlem Park. Almost from day one, it was obvious to me that I would have to keep an eye out for one particular group of boys from the projects: Andre, Quentin, Ricardo, and Tyrone.

Andre was the meanest, Quentin was sneaky, and the last two, Ricardo and Tyrone, were chronic instigators of trouble. In a way, the last three were often more troublesome because they were instrumental in legitimizing the extreme mischief of Andre, who had the loudest mouth.

They were not particularly original and operated the way most bullies did. One of them would whisper something inflammatory to Ricardo or Tyrone.

"Yo' man, y'all see how that boy is starin' at Andre."

The two of them would scan all the boys in the room.

"Which one?"

"That one - that tall skinny boy."

Ricardo would say something like, "Man, that dude ain't paying Andre no nevermind.

However, Tyrone would go along with anything that Quentin said, "Yo' Andre. That tall guy over there is lookin' at you like he don't like you."

"Which one, show me?" Andre replies.

"That one over there, answering all the questions, we saw him lookin' at you man, for real. You don't believe me, ask Ricardo?"

Quentin suggests, "He lookin' at you like he don't like you man."

Now, Ricardo realizes that he wants in on this. "I don't know about y'all, but I don't think I like the nigga."

The stage is set. It makes no sense, but they have found the trouble they were seeking. The four of them were exceptionally intelligent boys. Go figure!

On the morning of our very first day of school, we have assembled in our homeroom class and our homeroom teacher, Mrs. Delmita P. Reid, is introducing herself to the class.

"Let me first welcome all of you to Harlem Park Junior High School. My name is Mrs. Delmita P. Reid... and I will write that on the board for those of you..."

"What does the P. in your name stand for?" blurts out Ricardo.

"Well, I guess that I could tell you, but I really don't think that is of any importance." Mrs. Reid remarks.

"C'mon, what does it stand for? You can tell us.," insists Tyrone.

You could almost smell the blood in the water.

She replies, "I think we should move on. There is a lot that...."

In an instant, Andre jumps in.

"I think it stands for...Delmata Potata...!"

At which point the entire class exploded into raucous laughter. I mean everybody was laughing. Andre knew that what he said was mean, and unfortunately, the inexperienced and very delicate Mrs. Reid responded by bursting into tears.

Andre had established his reputation in that class for the duration; he made the teacher cry! After that exchange, Mrs. Reid always had a contentious relationship with Andre, which was a damn shame. Mrs. Reid was a sweet and sensitive woman, as well as a conscientious teacher. She never stood a chance with those guys.

A few days later, as we were preparing to exit homeroom for our first period class, Mrs. Reid requested that the boys and girls form separate lines in single file, and the girls promptly complied. The boys, however, piled out of the room as a loud, loose pack of adolescent bodies.

It was my stupid bad luck to end up near the back of the pack, with those Lexington Terrace boys right behind me. That had me a little nervous and I am sure they sensed as much. Just at the moment when the group of boys began moving, I heard some snickering behind me.

With a kind of a sick feeling, I turned to see what was up. Each one of them had his most innocent looking expression plastered across his smart-assed face. However, as I turned away from them to move on, I heard, felt, and partially saw Andre in the act of spitting onto the back of my shirt.

After what had happened to Mrs. Reid, I knew enough to understand that an immediate response was required or I would have to put up with this kind of crap for the rest of the school year. Yet, it was not lost on me that I was all on my own here against all of them. This was it, a pivotal moment for me. For about a split second, I debated my response and then did something I had never done before. Something I did not know that I could do.

Feeling Andre directly behind me, I spun around suddenly and summoning all my strength I slammed my fist into the center of his chest....BOOM, catching him completely by surprise and knocking him back hard against those other three smirking idiots, almost knocking that sneaky assed Quentin down. An audible, "OOOH!" rippled through the entire group of boys. It was pretty goddamned impressive, if I have to say so myself.

Thankfully, and to my everlasting relief, it appeared that Andre was far too stunned to respond. We stood there glowering at one another, neither one of us knowing what to do next. Then, there was Mrs. Reid's voice.

"Andre, go to your next class. Both of you leave my classroom before something gets started in here."

I was glad when Mrs. Reid quickly came over and stood between us. Luckily, that was enough to allow the drama to subside. Slowly, everyone moved on. I realized that what the big boys had always been telling me was true. When confronted with a mob, knock out the head guy and pray. If that doesn't work...run, like it ain't no thang.

That was that. Andre never physically challenged me again, although, his boys would still occasionally harass me in other ways, but much less so than some of the other guys around. For me, an important first test had been passed and I came away from it feeling good, and filled with a sense of relief at the same time. Maybe this thing wouldn't be so bad.

Andre, like so many other bullies, was only one more pathetically insecure, and in his case, spoiled child. He was not an uninteresting person to talk to, really. I was able to see that over the course of the year, when in a few unguarded moments, Andre was not being the usual dick-head.

Sometimes I got the feeling he hated himself for having a well functioning brain. At times, in class, you would see flashes of brilliance from him. Sadly, much more common was to see him engage in activities like extorting money from the timid and weaker kids.

It is important to note that Andre was not a part of any gang. The whole gang thing was a phenomenon that was rather uncommon, in Harlem Park anyway, if not in the entire city. The bad guys around would back-up one another sometimes, but primarily they preferred to operate independently. This is something that potentially made any one of them singularly dangerous.

****

CHAPTER 12 – JOEL FINNEY, THE SMARTEST KID

I quickly learned that most of my fears about Harlem Park Junior High were baseless. I discovered that I was reasonably well equipped to handle whatever Harlem Park could throw at me. There were ways to insulate one's self from much of the bullshit, one of which was to combine academics and athletics judiciously. Being 'smart' could make you somewhat of a target for abuse, but if you had some athletic skills as well, then that could carry you a long way. Fortunately, I had a few things going for me.

I was in the band. That meant that I arrived at school early every day, thus avoiding contact with the unruly crowds of students moving about in the morning. That morning rush, with too many kids too close together, was a prime time (and arena) for the start of fights.

I also discovered that I could run, jump, throw and hit with anyone my age. It was in gym class that a lot of these bad guys took a measure of you. When we had wrestling, I would win often enough.

In the major sports, I could hold my own although I had trouble with basketball, which many of these boys played well. However, I was tall and I learned things quickly, so I managed to fake my way through that. In the sport of football, I did all right because I could catch well and I was fast. My grades were excellent, but like an idiot, I tended to downplay that.

One day near the end of the first semester, I was sitting in the school auditorium waiting for band practice to begin. The band was to play during a school assembly at which some students were to receive academic awards. There was this kid up on the stage. He stood before a microphone and he was clowning around and being generally uncooperative with the faculty coordinating this rehearsal. He had a toothpick in his mouth.

His name was Joel Finney. I had heard of him. He was supposed to be the smartest kid in the entire school, and he had won a scholarship to a fancy private boarding school through a scholarship program called A Better Chance (ABC).

Sitting there that day and watching him on stage was a defining moment for me. He had everyone laughing because he was clever with a good sense of humor, and he was a little bit of a smart-ass. The guy was cracking me up, and I think it was because I was so completely thrilled to see that he appeared so damned ordinary.

I was thinking, there is no way that the kid up on that stage could be the person I was hearing about. If he really was Joel Finney, and he was, then I was going to be all right. His roughneck antics had shown me that it was possible to do well academically, and not necessarily be a stiff. I mean - after seeing him I was encouraged.

You see, much like my boy Huggie, I was fascinated with those boys who were out there on the edge, the outlaws. Unlike Huggie, I could never bring myself to emulate them to any significant degree. Call me a coward, but I think I wanted to stay alive for the long run.

It was all right to pal around with them sometimes, but they always understood, and I never forgot, that my thing was scholastics.

This kid Joel seemed to combine a bit of both extremes into what I thought was a cool package. If I could replicate it, it was the kind of thing I could work with.

To my genuine surprise, at the end of the first grading period that year, I had the highest grade point average of any seventh grader in the entire school. I shared the honor of the highest grade point average in any grade with an eighth grader, who was also in unit-D. Harlem Park Junior High was going to be a breeze and I was going to be a star.

However, good grades were not going to be enough to ensure that I was not going to have a bumpy ride through Harlem Park.

For example, there was an illustrative incident that occurred just at the end of our first Christmas vacation. I had returned to school with nothing new and ostentatious to show or wear, as is the custom. That Christmas had not been a particularly good one in our house.

"Hello Mom…it's me …your son? We just got home and it looks like somebody broke into the house…it looks like they came in through my window on the third floor, from the roof."

Then I whispered into the phone.

"Hey Mom, all the Christmas presents are gone… you know… presents… the ones you hide in the closet in your room…they're all gone. Everybody's crying! They even took my shoeshine kit! We looked around and there's nobody here now… OK. I'll call him."

The guys who robbed us turned out to be two teenaged guys who would sometimes come to visit Brother Herbert, who was renting the front room on the third floor of our house. He caught them by waiting at the house the next day, and they actually came back for another load. Brother Herbert said that they would do that. I don't know how he knew.

"Johnnie, man, you should have seen their faces when they came through that window and saw me standing there with my baseball bat." Brother Herbert chuckled. We never got any of our stuff back. They had already gotten rid of it.

I told my Mom that I did not need any new clothes to wear and that they should spend their money on my brother and sisters. I don't mean to suggest that I was being especially noble in doing so either. This was simply how I had learned to seek approval in my family, specifically from my mother. In many ways, I felt she was all I had. To please her and to take her off the hook with Johnnie Watkins, I tried to behave unselfishly. I often ended up feeling shortchanged as a result, but that is what I get for my well-meaning duplicity!

Therefore, with Christmas behind us, and a new semester beginning, we all filtered back into Harlem Park Junior High School. Tyrone, who was a fucking pain-in-the-ass and who, to me, always seemed to have especially nice clothing to wear and extra money to spend, had noticed in the hallway that I was wearing the same tired clothing that they were accustomed to seeing me wear in the months before Christmas vacation.

He craftily waited for the precise moment as I entered our homeroom, when everyone was typically looking up to see who was walking in. Then, he approached me and dramatically looked me up and down. Pointing me out to everyone, he loudly declared for all to hear,

"Hey y'all...You can always tell smart people...because they don't have new clothes."

Oh boy did that get a huge laugh, which even in my intense humiliation I suppose I could understand on some level. It was funny.

Intellectually, I understood that all of us were poor, relatively speaking. Still, for all my alleged smarts I just could not help feeling ashamed of being poor. It seemed to me at the time that my family struggled more than most and I could not help piteously wondering why it had to be me.

Once, Andre humiliated me in front of the entire class when he joked about the winter coat that my mother had picked up from the Goodwill organization. It was an ungodly ugly, yellow and green striped thing. I would wear it on only the very coldest days, resigned to suffer the cold the rest of the time. When I walked into class on one of those freezing days, Andre announced to everyone in the class,

"Everybody in here better tell y'all Moms to get ready for a blizzard. He done walked up in here in his chinchilla coat."

Man, everybody rolled in the aisles.

*****

CHAPTER 13 – BOZY AND KENARD

In a house directly across the street from mine lived Dolly, who sometimes worked behind the bar at Club Astoria. Her hair was a silvery gray and I thought she was stunning with her round afro hairstyle, rugged face, and still attractive figure for her age. Dolly was about forty years old. She had two daughters; one of them named Marie, who was about ten or eleven years old with the tiniest squeaky voice imaginable and a big Afro, like her Mom.

The other daughter, Peaches, was in her late teens or early twenties, with exotic eyes, a short haircut and a slim athletic figure. Judging by the amount of attitude she conveyed and the company she kept, Peaches was a tough girl. Her boyfriend, Bozy, seemed to be at their house every day.

Bozy's appearance on Edmondson Avenue was one of the earliest and most conspicuous signs of a change occurring in the complexion of the 1300 block of Edmondson Avenue. He did what he did quietly and unobtrusively and I think professionally, at first.

His business was drugs, and as far as I could tell, it was heroin. Most likely, he also dabbled in weed and perhaps a little cocaine but those drugs were available almost anywhere. Bozy was on a higher level than that, judging by the kind of respect he commanded from the older men frequenting Club Astoria. More than likely, that was where he would make contact with some of his customers. Bozy spent a lot of time in the Club.

I practically lived right next door to Club Astoria and I spent a lot of time out on my front steps, talking and listening to the men and women who hung around there. People saw me as a part of the scenery so I saw them with their defenses down, and although I was somewhat naive at times, I was not stupid at any time. I could pick a junkie out of a crowd, even the most covert junkies. The younger junkies didn't seem to care who knew what they were doing.

At that time, I had very little hands-on specific knowledge about drugs. My boys and I had no real interest in that stuff, yet. Much of what I knew, I learned from some of the older boys around who were beginning to hang out around the Club. Through witnessing their drug use and through my conversations with them, I learned a lot about which of the guys were smoking weed and drinking a little wine or shooting smack. I saw that a lot of the guys were using cough syrup to get high; or sniffing (huffing) airplane glue, the cheapest kind of high.

All you had to do was to go up to Harlem Park Square, near that building on the east side of the square and you would see all the brown paper bags with the tops of the bags rolled over in the fashion the glue-sniffers preferred. They did that to cushion the top of the bag where they would have it pressed hard over their nose and mouth.

Also scattered around would be empty bottles of Robitussin cough syrup, which when consumed made you seem drunk, with slurred speech and everything. Back in the day, you could get that in a drugstore without a prescription.

The teenagers would go up to the square at night to party. The trees and the low light of the square made it an ideal place for getting high without drawing any unwanted attention. A whole lot of kids were into that stuff, but my boys and I managed to steer clear of it. We did not have the money to spend on it and we were still more interested in having fun. Stumbling around drunk and high did not look like fun.

Bozy represented a different level of the drug game. While heroin had always been around in a 'back room down in the basement' kind of way, it now seemed a little more in your face, however, only a little more so. You never saw it being dealt on the street. You knew it was going on but you mostly only saw the end result. You would see things like a junkie who was high and nodding out, but not the actual hand-to-hand business of drug dealing. Heroin was coming onto the streets however - bit by bit.

Sometimes, from my perch on my front doorsteps I would watch this guy named Dinky. He and his girlfriend often sat on the steps next to Bozy's house and they would usually be in a deep junkie nod. I would marvel at how they managed to regain their balance, just in that instant when it appeared they would topple over onto the sidewalk.

To me, Bozy was so discreet with his real business that it was pretty much a non-issue in the day-to-day events of the 1300 block of Edmondson Avenue. What most fascinated me about him was his commanding presence on the streets. He was like the neighborhood CEO. He walked the block as if it belonged to him. To say he walked the streets is not accurate. Bozy strutted on the pavement, in an arrogant and almost comical way, as though he were invincible.

He had a long stride, although his legs were actually not very long. You would see him crossing the street on the way to the Club, head thrown back, chest thrust out rooster-like. His strong arms and big hands hanging at his side, with those large hands subtly swinging and sweeping away the air before him; moving in what almost seemed like slow motion and just begging for somebody to get in his way who was looking for an ass whipping.

Predictably, he was a flashy dresser, partial to bright neon-like reds, lime green, neon orange and the like. Given the questionable business he was in, his style of dress might have seemed liable to draw unwelcome attention to him, but since a lot of guys dressed this way, Bozy was really no more conspicuous than anyone else was. Granted, the stuff he wore was a bit more expensive, but still, it allowed him to blend in well enough.

There was one incident in particular that spoke volumes to me regarding Bozy's place in the hierarchy of the streets. It started while I was in the living room of our house, on a Saturday afternoon. I heard shrill screaming coming from the outside and a whole lot of cussing. I immediately ran to the door to see what was up, because like everyone else I hated to miss anything exciting and then have to hear about it second hand.

As I came out the front door, I spotted Bozy. He was standing on the sidewalk directly across the street, slapping the shit out of his girlfriend Peaches; holding her up by her clothing and using the front and back of his big hands to repeatedly snap her head back and forth so that she looked like a rag doll. It was hard to tell what he was yelling at her, but he was royally pissed. After a couple of minutes of this he finally pushed her to the ground, where she started crawling backwards in a kind of crab-like manner across the pavement in an attempt to get away from him, but he stayed on her, occasionally giving her a little kick.

Finally, she was able to get to her feet and frantically tried to make a run for it across the street in the direction of Club Astoria. Bozy was right behind her. When he caught up to her, he snatched her back towards him by her hair, spun her around and started slapping her in the face all over again.

Her mother Dolly was nowhere in sight, although I cannot imagine what she could possibly have done to stop this madness, Bozy was so angry. However, her younger sister Marie was out there, seeing everything and crying hysterically. I felt so sorry for Marie. She looked so small and helpless standing in the crowd of onlookers.

The number of people gathered to watch this ugly spectacle was rather considerable. Many young kids were out there, as always, for anything resembling a fight. In addition, the screams had drawn the attention of the men and women inside Club Astoria, because by this time Bozy had shoved her down on the ground again at the mouth of the little alley that ran alongside the Club. The Club Astoria crowd came rushing outside, practically crashing into Bozy and Peaches.

Again, Bozy started kicking at Peach as she lay there in a pathetic heap, curling up to ward off the blows from his feet. By now however, it was becoming obvious that there was very little conviction in his actions. You could see that Bozy's fury had diminished and he was now only standing there, completely out of breath and glowering down on her, seemingly at a loss as to what to do next.

Not one person had tried to intercede in any way, by word or deed. Everyone elected to stand by silently, looking intently at Bozy, wondering what his next move would be. Bozy seemed to sense this, and turned to confront the entire crowd. He then shouted, "Marie... go over to the house and get my pistol." Marie, in tears and probably grateful to have an excuse to get away, darted across the street to their house.

Undoubtedly, Marie understood like all the rest of us that there was no way that Bozy would actually shoot somebody with so many witnesses present. On that score, there was no cause for alarm from anyone, including his girlfriend Peaches, who is still on the ground. Therefore, nobody made a move to exit.

Then, Bozy directly challenged the entire, deadly silent crowd.

"Anybody out here don't like it?" he demanded.

Silence...

The moments following this pronouncement left me nothing short of - astonished. I remember thinking certainly someone will say something. Surely, one of the adults will tell him that it is cowardly to beat up on a woman so small and defenseless, or maybe someone would make some kind of move to help the girl off the ground. However, not a whisper, and no one dared go help her.

Not only that, no one even seemed willing to leave the scene at all. We all just stood there. It was about then that Marie ran over and handed Bozy a big old-fashioned revolver that he tucked into his belt at the back of his pants.

At that precise moment, a voice suddenly issued forth from the silent crowd. It came from a guy named Kenard, who was then a relatively unassuming person, but who was beginning to move in some tough circles. He was still young, maybe fifteen years old. What Kenard said was succinct, but it set him apart from everyone else there as a force with whom to be reckoned in Harlem Park. What he said was, "It's your woman, man."

That is all that he said. Then he turned away and walked off.

Silence..., but there were heads everywhere nodding in agreement.

The tension now effectively diffused, everyone else began to drift away as Bozy himself gathered up his girlfriend and ushered her back across the street. Having made his point, whatever that might have been, it was now time to make his peace with his woman. Just before they disappeared into the house, I could see him kissing her and trying to tidy her up a bit.

In the aftermath of this, my thoughts kept returning to Kenard. He was the only person bold enough to speak out. Kenard had, I thought, brilliantly established his growing ascendancy in the street pecking order. What he said was the absolute perfect thing to say, because it served several purposes at once.

There was nothing to challenge, provoke or otherwise embarrass Bozy. At the same time, he had unequivocally announced to anyone who might care that Kenard was no punk who was afraid to speak up, even in the face of someone holding a gun! His comment was precisely timed for optimal benefit, just when everyone's attention was riveted on that pistol.

Undoubtedly Kenard, like everyone else out there, felt some compassion for that poor girl Peaches. At the same time, you knew that Kenard and everyone else was thinking that she knew well who she was in bed with. What happened to her was the price she paid for her grievously poor choice of a mate. Kind of like, 'You ride with an outlaw, you die with an outlaw.' It's a cold way to think - but that is how it was. I sometimes wonder what I would have done to help that girl, were I an adult at the time.

As I watched Kenard head up the street towards Carrolton Avenue where his girlfriend lived, it washed over me that I would never again view him in the same way. He had long been an infrequent sight on this block but he always seemed to me to be somewhat quiet and thoughtful, almost sweet in a macho kind of way. It was now evident that he was not your typical teenager. He was a person who took himself... seriously.

*****

CHAPTER 14 – NEW JACKS

Kenard was one of several new guys who had been living in other parts of Harlem Park but were now beginning to show up around Club Astoria in the 1300 block of Edmondson Avenue, and to a lesser extent the 1400 block.

Some of the others coming around included a guy named Alfred who wore thick black glasses and had a knack for making people laugh, and a guy called Cardy who was short and kind of slick. These guys simply drifted in and quickly became a part of the overall scenery.

I recall overhearing some of the girls practically swooning over a new boy who was light-skinned with pretty eyes and he was..., "Oh-my-lord, he's bow-legged?" Being slightly bow-legged is sexy for some reason that I could never exactly fathom.

His name was Tony Stewart and he lived two blocks up the street, on Carrolton Avenue. He and Kenard were close friends. In fact, Kenard later married Tony's sister. While I did not know it at the time,

Tony was to become a sizeable contributing player, for good or ill, in my own development as a young man.

All of these new faces helped to affirm that Harlem Park was in the throes of transition. Whatever this new thing was, it was unmistakably growing. Theirs were new faces and they were fourteen, sixteen, eighteen years old and beginning to think of themselves as men, all of them drawn down to the action around Club Astoria. Most of them smoked cigarettes, drank liquor, got high, sold a little weed, made a few dollars, and were mightily attractive to the girls in the neighborhood, who were themselves ready to stretch out.

There were enough of the old faces around to help affirm that things were still the same, and that was some consolation, but even we were all a little older now. I was 12 years old and I was starting to see and hear things in a way that had somehow eluded me before. Consequently, although not all of the new guys were outlaws, I could now tell that some of them were that and much more.

It brings to mind the case of this guy named Wheeler, whom I would sometimes see walking on Edmondson Avenue, up around Carey Street and Carrolton Avenue. He was quiet and seemed to keep to himself, and I cannot ever recall seeing him standing around chatting or anything like that. He had a reputation for being good at the martial arts, but other than that, there was not a lot of talk about him in any overt way. There were furtively whispered observations about him, however. It was as though no one wanted to be overheard speculating about him, and I noticed that suddenly he was coming around Club Astoria more than he had been.

When Wheeler would pass by me on my block, he would on rare occasions acknowledge me with a nod of his head or a terse, "Hey now." I have to say, that of all the people I had observed while sitting on my front doorsteps, without any doubt, Wheeler was the most frightening, and it was not because of anything I ever saw him do. I never even heard him raise his voice.

He did have a way, however, of looking at you, as though he were seeing you better than you have ever been seen, and at the same time, it appeared that he barely noticed you. If you caught his eye, he seemed to absorb all of who you were instantly and completely with a lightning-quick glance.

It was whispered that he had killed several people and gotten away with it. It was whispered that he was a professional Hit Man. These had only been whispers, but now with a rapidly changing feel to the neighborhood, with people like Bozy on the block, and to a lesser extent Kenard, this low-level buzz about Wheeler suddenly seemed reasonable enough.

More than ten years later, Wheeler and me encountered one another again. He was then an inmate at the Maryland Penitentiary, purportedly for having shot a cop. I was an actor in a play called Streamers that we were performing for the inmates. Ironically, I was playing a character (Carlyle) that possessed the same sort of menace that guys like Wheeler exuded as a matter of course.

In the days before our anticipated performance, our director learned that we could not bring any weapons inside the prison. A blunt tipped metal knife that I used in the play worried some of the prison officials. They reluctantly agreed to allow us to use a knife made of rubber. I put the metal knife in my bag anyway hoping they might reconsider, and they never noticed it.

We were escorted to a stage in what appeared to be their recreation room. While I was standing at the edge of the proscenium stage looking down at the assembly, an inmate came over to the stage. He gave me the impression that he was some sort of trustee, because unlike most of the others it appeared that he could move about the room as he pleased. I could see that he was intently studying my face.

It was Wheeler, and he very suddenly pointed his finger at me.

"You from down the way aren't you ... down Harlem Park?"

"Yeah... from Edmondson Avenue...I thought I recognized you... and I know your brother, Bruce," I replied.

Oh, man! There is no way to express how I was feeling during this exchange. Before that day, I had never had any occasion to say much more than a single word to Wheeler, little more than 'Hey'. I was barely a teen when he was sent to prison, and I was at a loss to explain how it was that he remembered my obscure face. As I said, he had a way of looking at you.

He tapped his hand on the stage indicating that he wanted me to sit, and he nimbly lifted himself up to the stage in order to sit down next to me.

"Y'all coming back here tomorrow...aren't you?"

"Yeah...we'll do one more show." I told him.

"Look here..." his voice lowering; "when y'all come back here tomorrow...why don't you bring me a couple of them good ones (marijuana)?"

I remember I took a long look around the room at all those incarcerated men.

"All right... I guess I can do that." I replied.

Who knows what I was thinking when I agreed to that, but quite honestly I could not help being somewhat flattered that someone as notorious as Wheeler actually knew who I was. I was always on the extreme fringes of most of the illegitimate stuff that was being done on Edmondson Avenue, but by the time he went to prison, I was probably a little closer to the action than was good for me.

Wheeler was the kind of person who would have noticed this, since it was now obvious that he had made some kind of note of me and knew I could do what he asked. Besides, all we were talking about was a couple of joints, no big deal. Following our brief exchange, he returned to the floor area.

On the following day, I secreted three fat joints in the shirt pocket of the military costume I had to wear for the play. Once on the stage, I decided to hold the joints in the palm of my hand, making a fist. I had no idea how I was supposed to get them to Wheeler, but I figured he would work that out and I would be ready for whatever. Emboldened by the events of the previous day and by what I was about to do, I was feeling - invincible.

Upon seeing me enter the recreation room, Wheeler had come over to the stage and again sat down on the edge of it. When he felt the time was right, he tapped the space next to him, indicating I was to sit. He then casually placed his hand on the stage between us.

"Lay 'em on me." he directed.

I placed my fist down on the stage, releasing the contraband. He smoothly covered my fist with his own substantial hand, at which point I removed my hand and we both moved away from each other. It was like something you might see in a movie and I have to admit, as stupid as my actions were, I liked the rush it gave me.

****

CHAPTER 15 – GUIDANCE COUNSELOR

In the first week at Harlem Park Junior High School, the guidance counselor for Unit-D visited us in our homeroom class. Her name was Adele Fing. She had come to our class to give us an overview of how things worked at the school and to explain to us what was expected of each student.

One of the things she explained to us was the way in which academic standing at Harlem Park was determined. She explained that there were three significant levels of achievement, the Success Role for students with a C average, the Honor Role for students with a B average and the Distinction Role for students with an A average.

As she was explaining all of this, I was seated very near her and I was listening intently, because this was all so very different from elementary school. Back there, if you got good grades, it meant maybe a little more attention directed towards you from your teacher and a pat on the back from Mom and Dad; but nothing like what I was hearing now. Here, they gave you awards and stuff if you performed well. I thought that was kind of nice.

When Mrs. Fing mentioned the Distinction role, I remember interrupting her to say that I thought that I would make that role.

"What kind of awards do you get if you make the Distinction Role?" I asked her.

"Well, let's see if you make it first," she said laughing.

"I think I'm going to try to make that high one, Mrs. Fing."

"That's good, aim high. I hope you do," she answered.

It was an arrogant thing for me to say and I was as surprised as anyone to hear myself say it, particularly in a room full of people who I did not know very well. Mrs. Fing looked at me and gave me a smile. I liked her immediately.

As I said, that first semester ended with me making the Distinction Role as I had jokingly predicted, and they announced to the entire school over the public address system. So, somewhat like that smart assed kid in my class, Andre, I had secured my reputation at Harlem Park for the duration. Other than the occasional bump in the road, the remainder of that first year consisted of more of the same for me; making the Distinction Role each of the four grading periods.

Although it was not as good as being a top athlete or being a tough guy, I was afforded a sort of grudging respect by the entire student body. Everyone knew who I was at least. I had discovered through my observations of that smart kid Joel Finney that it was possible to achieve a balance between academics and being a total pussy, and I was able to manage that reasonably well. Life was good.

I was aware that I was doing well at Harlem Park. At the annual end-of-the-year awards assembly, I learned just how well. Achievement awards, gift certificates and pins were given out to those students with the highest averages in the various academic subjects.

To my genuine surprise, I received top honors in six of my eight subjects. I also got an award for having the highest grade-point average for a seventh grader for the year, and tied with another student for the highest average of any student in the entire school. Not a bad start - and another summer had come.

We were on the threshold of the summer of 1967 and the boys and me had survived and thrived. We were all thirteen years old. Like me, Allen had also gotten through his first year at Harlem Park unscathed. He had developed a stronger interest in art, and more specifically, drawing. Our boy Bruce was heading over to the Junior High in the coming school year and that was good news. It appeared that everything was on track for all of us, so we could now turn our attention to what we were going to do to have some fun for the summer, now that we were all horny young teenagers.

*****

CHAPTER 16 – SEX ED

So much had changed since we were nine years old, when the bulk of our summer was spent playing softball and running up and down the block after the girls. While we still loved softball, we now had to find a way to fit it in around the time we spent pursuing girls. We now thought of that pursuit in terms that are more indelicate: chasing pussy. We were hoping for more than a kiss or a light touch of their ass. We were looking for a chance to stick it in.

Our previous experiences had been of the, humping the neighborhood sweetie variety. The type of circumstance where a few guys get together with one or two girls who, owing to fostering a crush on one of the boys, is willing to screw that boy and possibly a couple of his friends; usually down in someone's basement or maybe even outside in a back playground.

I know some people might think that only the lowest sort of girl would stoop to such a thing, but I don't know if I would go along with that idea. These girls were often our close friends. To describe these girls as "bad girls" would be unfair, because they were simply trying to explore their burgeoning sexuality in much the same way as us boys, making them no better or worse than us. I thought that then and I think that now. We all gained a basic hands-on knowledge of where the female equipment was and how everything fit together. I would have to guess that the same idea was true for the girls.

Once, while my Mom and Dad were at work, Huggie and I had sneaked this girl named Vanessa up to my room. Vanessa had been sending me these very sexy letters in school, and then started hanging out with us in our neighborhood. For some reason she had decided that she wanted to give me some pussy. I know that sounds blunt, but that is about how she put it to me in those letters.

I think that she was only interested in me, but on that day, the timing was right and each one of us could see that Huggie wasn't about to go home, so he lucked out. I told Vanessa to wait in my room while I went to talk to Huggie.

"She said you can stay Huggie, but you are gonna have to be the lookout while I go first."

"Naw…let me go first man. She might change her mind after you finished." Huggie had a good point.

"I don't think she's gonna go for that man. She came down here because of me. If we ask her to let you go first, she might get mad and leave."

Huggie persisted, and said, "Why don't you go ask her man. Go ask her."

I opened the door, went into my room, and then closed the door so that Huggie couldn't hear us.

"Look Vanessa, we need Huggie to look out for us, and he said he won't do that unless he gets to go first."

"I don't care. He can go first. I just want to find out if you hot like

I think you are. That's why I was writing you those letters. It's not like it's my first time," she said right away.

I remember feeling a rush of blood to the head when she said that.

"OK. Just wait a second. Don't move…just wait a second. OK?" I went back out to Huggie in the hall.

"Yo' Huggie, she won't let you go first man. She said that she will give you some, but only if I go first. I tried hard to talk her into it, but she wasn't going for it. You know how girls are?"

Huggie said, "Damn. All right man, but she better not be lyin."

I assured him, "Trust me man. I got you."

Vanessa kept her word. She was young, she was wild, and she knew what she was doing in bed too.

That is how it would be, and even back then, we all knew enough to use condoms. No one wanted to get anyone knocked-up.

There were a lot of attractive young ladies around the neighborhood and we were now acutely aware that they were no longer little girls. We were very sure that we were no longer little boys, but quickly a flaw in our logic became glaringly apparent to us and we did not like it, not one bit.

Our wonderful girls, with whom we had spent so much time and who we knew so well, were showing signs they had outgrown us. The evidence was right there before us and it was unequivocal.

Harlem Park was now a much bigger place. It had always been a rather large area, but many of us were just beginning to expand our vision of it to include the streets and neighborhoods beyond the two or three-square blocks in the immediate vicinity of Edmondson Avenue and Calhoun Streets. By this, I mean those places like the neighborhoods up around Gilmore Street, Lafayette Avenue, Fulton Avenue and Carrolton Avenue, to name a few.

Before now, we had only dealt with the guys and gals living in those other areas when we were on the playground, and when we were all involved in team sports through the Harlem Park Recreation Center. By virtue of our enrollment at Harlem Park Junior High School, we had all increased the extent of our circle of friends.

Many of these new friends were finding their way down to Edmondson Avenue rather than the other way around. Edmondson Avenue was still a viable small business corridor at that time. There was also the growing availability of drugs that attracted some of them. A person could easily find a variety of reasons to take a walk down our way.

They were streaming in and they were new, exciting and unfamiliar faces to the girls on Edmondson Avenue. It quickly became obvious to my boys and me that we were fast becoming - tiresome. These new guys were slightly older with a bit more style and wit. They had traveled around the city more and seen more and they were much more aggressive in their pursuit of the girls.

They were not all outlaws either. Some of them had legitimate jobs, making what was some decent money for a young guy. They looked smooth holding their cigarettes, which they smoked openly. Many of them had no trouble acquiring beer or a bottle of wine and they always had a little weed on them.

They could stay out as late as they liked and had money to take a girl up to the Harlem Park Movie Theater on Gilmore Street. A lot of them were outstanding athletes and used their prowess at sports to beguile the girls, who would come to see them over at the basketball courts or in the softball league or just playing a pick-up game of touch football.

Once they started coming around, and adding to their allure was the mere fact that they were not at all afraid to come around, my boys and me were finished. The three of us would sit on his front steps commiserating about how everything seemed to change so suddenly.

When the brothers Mutty and Richard and that pretty boy Bruce Robinson and 'left handed' Jerry and on and on, came onto the block, all of a sudden we were viewed as young boys. It seemed our primary purpose had now become to amuse the girls in the interim periods when the big boys were not around.

The change in many of the girls was palpable. We noticed that some of them were sneaking a smoke when they thought no one was looking and sometimes you might see one of the girls nursing a beer in a brown paper bag. At night, they might get together, head up to Harlem Park Square, and hang out while the boys got high. If all that were not enough to guarantee that me and my boys would look like young punks, according to Mutty and some of the others, a few of the girls were giving up that pussy. Damnit those were our girls!

Even as we sat around lamenting the lost of our women, my two buddies and I knew deep down that this was the natural order of things. Even we knew that our testosterone driven reach, far exceeded our abilities to deliver. We knew it, the girls knew it and the older boys knew it. They just loved to mess with us by pointing out our diminished position to us. They would say to the girls,

"Baby, them young boys don't know how to make no love to a woman; time for you to stop messin around with them young-boy muthafuckas. Come with me and I'll make them toes curl baby."

Older guys like Tony Stewart or Alfred and even Allen's brother Glascoe would also get a kick out of punching us in the chest around that time, because they knew that the nipples on our chest were painfully sensitive as part of the whole process of puberty. Man, it would hurt like hell when they did that.

In my case, I had made the mistake of asking Tony Stewart if he knew why my nipples were so sore. That gave him a good laugh. I had thought to ask my mother this question because we were open with one another, but in this case, I just could not do it.

For some reason, I thought that she would somehow know that I was having sex if I revealed this mysterious detail to her. Don't ask me why! So for a short while, I did not mention it to anyone, not even my two best pals. You tell me how you tell your two best friends that you think you might be growing titties.

There's just no way!

Despite our disappointment at having been shunted aside in favor of these older guys, there was no significant amount of animosity in our young hearts for most of them. In fact, it was quite the contrary. Those guys could be a lot of fun when they were just hanging around and goofing off with us.

A semi-regular thing between Tony Stewart and Alfred and me and my boys, was a game in which the point was to catch one of them when he was alone, surround him, then try to pile on top of him and pin his ass down on the ground. Then, we would try to punch him unmercifully and make sure that we got away before he had a chance to retaliate.

Allen would usually have no trouble escaping because he could run fast. The same was true for me most of the time. Bruce could sometimes run into a little problem when he tried to run because he just wasn't all that fast. In addition, he had an unfortunate habit of falling down at the most inopportune moments.

To help Bruce out, we would try to hold Tony or Alfred down until Bruce had managed to put some distance between himself and our victim. This was especially true when it came to that damn Tony, who was so goddamned quick.

Tony caught up to me once just after we had finished pummeling on him. I knew I was in for it, because he could punch a whole lot harder than we could and he was honor bound to prove that. He got me down on the ground and very methodically began to pound on me in the muscle at the back of my thigh; something he knew was unbelievably painful. I really tried to take my punishment like a man, until a painful cramp hit me just where he was pounding on my leg.

"Wait a minute Tony...hold up...hold up for a minute, man...I got a cramp in my thigh."

"O.K. man ...where's the cramp...in your thigh...back here?" he asked, concerned.

"Yeah, Tony...let me get up so I can walk it off...alright man...?" I said with a grimace.

"Sorry I can't do it man...If we were fighting I wouldn't let you up," he said, and he resumed driving his fist into the rigidly knotted cramp in the muscle of my leg.

This was one of many lessons I picked up from Tony, about how it's a hard world out here, and some of the times when it gets you down; it's not going to let up. So you had better not be a pussy! You had better learn to keep fighting no matter what!

Allen and Bruce tried to help me out, but Tony did a pretty good job of fending them off with one arm while he held me down with the other. Then, after he had administered a few more well placed licks, he eventually let me go. As I limped off, I did my best not to cry.

I swear. Good times, so many good times.

*****

CHAPTER 17 – WHITE EDUCATION

We too had begun to widen the boundaries of our own playing field. One of the very first things we learned is that there were fresh new girls out there, and they were glad to see us. Now, the boys out there were not so welcoming. Therefore, we quickly realized the extent to which we had to be extremely careful and watch each other's backs. We also had to get some cash in our pockets.

This was not a new concept for us. We had often found ways to make a few coins, by shoveling snow or running errands and that sort of thing, but a lot more than pocket change was going to be needed for this new stage of our lives.

Gone were the days when the small amount of money necessary for the occasional soda or bag of chips or a trip to The Harlem Park Movie Theater for one of those delicious movie hot dogs, was going to sustain us. Among other things, we had all suddenly developed an acute interest in our own personal appearance. New clothing was required.

An unexpected, but promising, moneymaking opportunity came along for us in the guise of a strange white man named Mr. Tim. He simply stepped out of his car one day and asked Allen and Bruce, who were sitting on Allen's front steps, if they knew of any boys who were interested in making some money. He worked for a roofing company and he wanted some boys to go door-to-door distributing leaflets, soliciting customers for the roofing business he represented.

He told my two buddies that he would pay them at the exorbitant rate of one dollar an hour, under the table, which was already understood since it was clear that they were underage. They were expected to put in a couple of hours each day during the week and four hours on Saturdays. Of course, my boys said yes, and after a few days, brought me along.

Mr. Tim would drive by Allen's house each day to pick us up and the three of us would pile into the back seat of his beat up car. His car always appeared to be overflowing with stacks and stacks of index card-sized leaflets.

He would then drive us to some distant neighborhood, where the residents actually owned the homes in which they lived. Where there were lovely trees and plants in their yards and the houses were detached from one another. Oh yeah; and the people were all white folk. I expected to see Wally and the Beaver strolling by at any second.

Each one of us would then be dropped off on successive corners and we were responsible for leaving one of the leaflets at each house on the block. Nothing could be simpler. There was, for each of us, the reassuring knowledge that we could expect to see the other guys once we reached the end of our assigned block, in most cases.

All three of us were a trifle nervous about being so far from home, and in a white neighborhood of all places. Also, we really did not know this man Mr. Tim, when you think about it. We knew that we were essentially totally at his mercy way out here, wherever the hell we were. But hey - we were going to get paaaiiid!

Things proceeded fairly routinely during our first few outings. However, upon comparing notes, the three of us realized that we all had one particular problem for which we would have to devise a solution. The problem was dogs. A lot of those people kept a dog in their front yard, or on the front porch, or sometimes they just let them roam freely about the neighborhood.

Now, you can say that we were being paranoid if you want, but we were convinced that those dogs were no more comfortable with seeing some colored-black-negro-child climbing on their porch than many of those white folk. Consequently, we could expect that at least a few times a week, Mr. Tim was going to have to come along and save one of our butts as we dangled from the limb of a tree or were found spread-eagled over the roof of somebody's car, with some mad dog circling underneath snarling and snapping at us.

Our solution for this daily dilemma proved to be an efficient and ingeniously simple one. In our pockets, we each started carrying a strong belt and a few good rocks every time we would go out. Some courage was required for this, because it meant that we must now be resolved to directly confront any menacing dog and somehow hurt him if he refused to back off. This was a possibility that would probably not sit too well with the white owners of those dogs.

Already though, we had discovered that most of the dogs would back down if you were steadfast and did not turn and run right away. Using our belts and throwing the stray rock to ward off those dogs allowed us to continue making some cash to spruce up our personal lives.

Carrying a belt, however, did not solve all of our canine problems. Once, we had to pull Bruce out of a tree where he had sought refuge after a dog had bitten and then snatched the belt from Bruce's hand as he was swinging it at the mutt. Unfortunately, the dogs we encountered were not our only problem.

Eventually we had to deal with a few ignorant white boys; white boys like the three beefy one's I spotted checking me out from the top of that long block that I was working. Quite suddenly, I was reminded of why we hesitated to stray from the brothers back in Harlem Park in the first place.

The boys and I were coming of age in Harlem Park, which was reassuringly nearly 100% Black and racial bigotry was a remote consideration. You hear about it on television and sometimes sense the feelings of revulsion when you go into the stores in downtown Baltimore where all the white people are; but it does not stare you in the face every day as it might in some other settings.

In Harlem Park, practically everybody you encounter all day long, every day, looks just like you. For that reason, the things you find yourself being more concerned with are the minute and subtle acts of bigotry and intra-racial prejudice that Black people are apt to commit against one another. Those negative and even cruel comments and blanket assumptions that might be made about the character of a very dark skinned person, the perception that lighter skinned black folk are somehow smarter or more attractive. There is the concept of of 'good' straight hair, as opposed to bad kinky 'nigger' hair, or pretty light eyes as opposed to plain old brown eyes.

All of those questions of prejudice, race, and self-hatred were shadowy concepts darting around at the edges of our minds for my friends and me. No one was especially anxious to confront these issues yet, but it was something that would eventually shake us all, deep down. The new black pride/black power would be a big part of the change that was creeping over Harlem Park and to a greater extent the entire country.

In my parent's household, I cannot ever recall hearing my parents make any sort of disparaging remark about any white person, nor complain about the oppression of black folk or the dearth of fair opportunities for people of color and so on; and we were about as poor as could be.

They did talk about Martin Luther King Jr., and to a much less significant degree, about that 'crazy negro' Malcolm X. All of this was done in a very non-rhetorical way, maybe only in the context of another bit of small talk in a casual Sunday afternoon conversation after church.

A consequence of growing up in an environment so utterly devoid of any overt racial hostility is that neither my siblings nor I harbored any real ill will against white folk, other than a tacit distrust of them. A distrust born of our observations of the social and economic gulf between whites and blacks down south in North Carolina, where many of my parent's folks were sharecroppers on the properties of the white landowners.

To me, those black folk down there were the very definition of dirt poor. Many had no electricity, and they might not even have their own well, for drinking water. At my grandparent's house, they would have to carry buckets a hundred yards across a cow pasture to the white folk's property to get water from their well.

Coming from the city, I thought the whole business of fetching water was good fun. However, I did feel a peculiar sense of humiliation as I felt those white folk watching us as we stood in bare feet on their porch, pumping water from their well, a feeling I never forgot.

A white woman would come out of her kitchen, wiping her hands with a towel. She would look us over, and speak to my cousin.

"Hey Shirley, how's your Momma? Y'all children mind that you don't spill my water all over my porch."

"Yes ma'am, we'll be careful, my Momma's doin' just fine. These are my cousins from Baltimore. They think comin' over to your house to tote water is fun. By the time we get back to home they won't have much left in their buckets."

"Well, they don't look or smell like much. You tell your Momma I said hey, and Shirley you show them children how to avoid them soft cow chips. It's all over that little boy's feet, he trackin' it all over the place!"

I am reminded of an occurrence in Cherry Hill, back home in Baltimore. As a child, I sat on a hillside and watched the big boys from our side of the tracks literally cross the tracks to where the white folk were and push over some of the house trailers in which they lived. They set one of them on fire.

I was not sure at the time why they felt driven to do this, but I do now vaguely remember someone saying something later about a black guy getting beaten up by some white boys over in the 'Big Woods'. I guess the idea of exacting some sort of revenge is what they thought gave them the right to act the fool.

All of these things tend to make a sort of visceral impression upon a person; and disparately shape and mold one's conscience into a general point of view regarding other people, other races and the country in which we live. Personally, I had no precise reason to fear or hate white boys in any specific way. However, I knew, as any black person does, that whatever relatively innocuous thoughts I may have entertained about white people, I had better watch my black ass if they feel in any way threatened or are maybe just feeling ornery on a particular day. If you did not know them, maintain a discreet distance until you were better able to determine their intentions. After all, Baltimore is still below the Mason Dixon line.

Right now though, here I am alone and aware that my only hope for some assistance lay in the direction somewhere beyond those three ornery looking white boys scowling down at me from the end of the block. I began carefully snaking the end of the belt I carried tightly around my left hand, while with my right hand I was feeling for the rocks I kept in my pocket. I was about midway the block, and they were already heading my way.

What I wanted to do was run, because I did not want any parts of those boys; but running did not appear to be an option. I was sure that they would catch me before I could get back to the end of the block and try to make a dash to meet up with my boys. There was nothing to do but take up a position behind a car and wait for them.

They threw the first rocks at me while they were still on the run. Although one of the stones did bounce off the car just in front of me, the other two whizzed by harmlessly. At that point, I quickly hurled two rocks of my own. I'm sure that probably caught them completely by surprise, but they were in no way even remotely discouraged.

By now they were pretty goddamned close to me, and when they threw their next round of rocks I could feel myself, in what seemed like slow motion, ducking to avoid being hit. However, what I did was to duck right into one of the rocks thrown at me and it caught me just above my left eye. It stung like hell.

Now, angry and desperate, I did the only thing I could do. I tossed a fat rock directly at the nearest car window and shattered it; something I know made no sense at all.

However, confused and once again caught by surprise by all that broken glass, those white boys took off running and I immediately sprinted off in the opposite direction. Then, I took a wide and circuitous route back to where I thought I would run into Allen and Bruce. As it turned out, I had totally lost all sense of direction by that point, but I soon spotted Mr. Tim cruising down the street and all was well.

Quite likely, it was ugly little incidents like this that had Mr. Tim cruising in his car on the hunt for workers in so random a manner in the first place. Allen told me the same three boys had chased him just before they had come after me. All I know is, after a couple of other similar mishaps, me and the boys found some other way to make a buck. I quit first and my boys soon after.

*****

CHAPTER 18 – BAGGING GROCERIES

I began looking around for any kind of job, and after a bit, settled into a job bagging groceries at one of the corner grocery stores up at Edmondson Avenue and Carey Street. Besides bagging groceries, I was expected to stock the shelves, flatten and dispose of empty cartons, sweep the aisles, and sometimes I would pick up a tip by carrying grocery bags to someone's house for them.

None of it was particularly hard work, but it was brutally monotonous and strangely embarrassing for me because I was familiar with almost everyone who came into the store. They would come in and see me standing near the front counter next to the storeowners. As one irate customer said, my job was to stand there and do something 'a trained monkey could do'. She may have been right about that, but it was after all, an honest job.

The couple who owned the store was Jewish, and in my naive opinion, decent enough folk. Outwardly, it appeared as though they got along well with the people in the surrounding community and most of the time the business of buying and selling seemed to proceed in a civil manner by all concerned. But now that I was there all day, I became an eyewitness to an ugly and chronic air of distrust and suspicion that the storeowners and their black patrons harbored for one another.

Sometimes when a customer left, the storeowners would toss about thinly veiled insults, in Yiddish no less. Well... at least the black folk leaving the store assumed that the things said in Yiddish were an insult, judging by the tone of it. It was at this time that I learned the Yiddish word for Black (shvarts). The black folk would respond by letting loose with their own insults, in the most vulgar English at their disposal.

To me, it did appear that sometimes the storeowners were saying things of a derogatory nature, although I can't swear to it because I did not understand Yiddish. There was something to the tone of whatever it was they occasionally muttered that made me uncomfortable at times. Of course, it's just this sort of bullshit that has always made people hate one another.

I saw quite a few verbal confrontations due to the suspicions of the storeowners. Understandably, they were constantly preoccupied with concerns about petty thievery by the neighborhood kids. In addition, there was the ever-present fear of being robbed. There were no bulletproof glass-shields back then. I felt like an unwilling co-conspirator who was unsure about whose side I was on. That was hard to take.

My ambivalence partly manifested itself in a way that was about as pointless as everything else that was going on. I started stealing stuff myself, and of all the things I could have chosen to steal, I picked cigarettes - and only cigarettes. I did not even smoke yet; but I was ready to try!

My father smoked, which was something else a good preacher was not supposed to do. He smoked non-filter Chesterfield Kings. Sometimes he would have me go into Club Astoria to purchase a pack for him, and I never once sneaked a puff from one of his cigarettes. I had no interest, and it seemed to me that Reverend Johnnie Watkins coughed an awful lot. Now, I was succumbing to the cool factor of cigarettes.

More and more, there would be stretches of time where rather than automatically head on up to Allen's house, I would stay in my block and spend some time talking with the older boys who were turning up around Club Astoria with growing regularity. Since I was still practically right at home while on my front steps, I could be out there until two o'clock in the morning when Club Astoria closed, doing absolutely nothing in particular.

The older boys would be drinking or smoking a joint or whatever, and would invariably offer me some of what they had, but I was still only marginally interested. However, I did decide that I had to see what it was like to smoke a cigarette and I finally took one of them up on his offer of a drag. Then, after an hour of coughing, which I chalked up to inexperience, I decided that what I needed were more cigarettes. Pretty damn dumb, huh?

Not only was practicing smoking a new priority for me, but I also got to play the big man because I was willing to share my nicotine bounty with all the nicotine junkies hanging about. If anyone asked me if I had a cigarette, well, I would let him or her have an entire pack! I found myself gaining many new friends.

The whole thing was short lived however, because I simply could not abide the way I felt working in that grocery store. I did feel like a trained monkey. Also, it quickly became clear to me that I was no good at smoking. All I did was cough, and that ruined the visual effect. Plus, there was no chance that I was going to be spending my hard-earned cash for cigarettes, not in this lifetime. Consequently, the job only lasted a few weeks and so did my career as a smoker, thank god.

*****

CHAPTER 19 – FOOLS & DRUNKS & GUNS

Life on the 1300 block of Edmondson Avenue was getting to be more of a frightening adventure every day. Even so, I had gotten to a point where I was almost hoping something crazy would happen; something like a good fight, someone brandishing a weapon or just somebody on the street drunk and making a fool of himself. There was one night on the block when I witnessed it all.

On one Saturday night when the block was jumping with activity, at around 10:30, I heard the noise of what was undoubtedly a fight coming from the entrance of Club Astoria. I walked over to peek in.

What I saw were a couple of men trying to force this chubby person out the door, as he continued to insist upon not leaving. So they just grabbed him by his arms, lifted him up and roughly heaved him out the door, where he landed with a sickening thud on the sidewalk. He was then very pointedly warned by those two men, "And you better not bring yo' big fat black ass back in here."

Poetry...pure poetry!

Anyone could see that the guy was drunk. Staggering all over the place, he clumsily picked himself off the ground and like an idiot he walked back over to the door, where he cracked it open just enough to yell something unintelligible at the people inside. I recognized him as a kid who attended Harlem Park Junior High.

He was a fairly heavyset guy who looked older than his actual age. Already he had a thin growth of ragged tufts of hair clinging to his face. He looked old enough to buy liquor, if the seller were not paying very close attention. I knew him as one of those boys from down around Lexington Terrace.

I watched him stumble around aimlessly for a couple of minutes, until he spotted me sitting on my steps and staggered over, obviously in need of a place to sit down to collect himself. Although I did not know him very well, I did know that I did not like him all that much. From my brief experience with him, I knew that he could be extremely irritating and he talked way too much about a lot of dumb shit.

Almost as soon as he sat down, he jumped back up and began fishing around in his pocket, and yelled out so that everybody on the block could hear, "I need to make a telephone call." I saw him head on up the street in search of a phone. He remained up there talking to someone on the phone for a good long time. Afterwards, he sat down on some steps near the telephone booth and appeared to be nodding off. After a short while, I forgot about him.

About thirty minutes later, I noticed that he was coming back down the street and again, he sat down on my steps next to me. It was at about that time that I was finally able to recall his name, James. Like always, he started running his big mouth, breathing and wheezing the way fat old drunks do.

"You in Andre's class... up at Harlem Park ain't you?"

"Uh - huh," I grunted.

"You see what them muthafuckas do to me...they ain't have to do all that man. All they had to say...was that I had to leave...that's all they had to say...you know what I mean?"

"You all right man? You know you're bleeding on the side of your face...right?" I said.

"Yeah...yeah...I know...muthafucka' hit me in my face with something...muthafucka' had something in his hand... He ain't have to do all that."

Why couldn't this guy just go on home? He was sweating like crazy and smelled bad from the combination of blood, sweat and stupidity.

"That nigga' in there behind the cash register, Tommy... think he can do whatever the fuck he want...don't he? Somebody needs to put a hurtin' on their ass...you know what I'm saying... I tell you what, man...you see a cab pull up...you watch the nigga' with the paper bag... yeah muthafucka!"

At this, I turned and stared at him.

"Watch the wha...?"

As I was speaking, a cab pulled up on the street in front of us and a slim dark skinned guy got out whom I had never seen before. He had an uncombed Afro, was wearing a black shirt and he was wearing cut-off brown khaki shorts and black socks. I remember that there was something strange about his left eye. It was discolored in some way. He was carrying a big brown paper bag in front of him, holding it in his left hand. His right hand was inside the bag. He looked to be a pretty tough boy.

"There he go...I told you man... watch that nigga' with the paper bag."

The guy with the paper bag looked deadly serious and moved quickly, heading straight towards Club Astoria. I couldn't believe what I was seeing, but I sat there and watched him pull the door open and go in. Within seconds I heard the now expected -- Pop...Pop - and I swear, at nearly the precise instant that I heard the shots, that guy came tearing out of that door.

He was running, but running is far too simplistic a description of what he was doing. He was moving - running fast, but he was so unbelievably low to the ground as he made a tight right turn coming out of the door, that he seemed to me to be only inches above the ground.

In no time at all, he had made another quick right turn and disappeared down the alley along the Club, heading southeast, apparently back towards the projects down at Lexington Terrace. The whole thing happened so fast, that it was almost as though he was never there.

At about the same time, I turned to say something to the guy James who had been sitting with me, but he had gotten to his feet and was already walking away in the other direction. I saw him turn the corner at Calhoun Street, and he took off running!

Shortly thereafter, an ambulance arrived and Tommy was brought out on a stretcher. The consensus was that he had been hit good, but it wasn't all that bad. I mean, he was not going to die or anything.

Actually, the next time that I saw Tommy, he had only a splint of some kind on one arm for a short while, but he always walked with a slight limp after the shooting, I never understood why.

This was the first time that I had been this close to actual gun violence. A person getting shot was something you heard about often enough, but it always seemed to happen somewhere else. I know that Tommy's getting shot was not the first shooting in the vicinity of Club Astoria, but it was a first for me, in a second hand way.

Yet, I refused to believe that someone shot Tommy because some fat underage kid in Junior High School had requested it. Even though, I had sat there and heard that fat boy James call the whole thing, as though he were Chuck Thompson doing the play-by-play for the Baltimore Orioles. When the shots rang out, I almost expected to hear him say, 'and ain't the beer cold?'

Surely, something larger had to be going on and that boy shot Tommy for a more serious transgression. Maybe he owed money to someone and that fat boy James had angrily dropped a dime on Tommy; and the two events just happened to coincide with one another in some perverse way. That would make more sense for me anyway.

I did not tell the cops or even anyone around Club Astoria what I knew about the shooting. I told my boys not to tell anyone else what I confided to them about the events of that night. I was scared, plain and simple. If Tommy was shot because he refused to serve liquor to some obnoxious kid, then life was getting pretty damn cheap. I thought it might be a good idea to spend a bit more time up in the 1400 block, where there was some distance between Club Astoria and me.

*****

CHAPTER 20 – MS. ALMA'S HOUSE

What I loved best about Ms. Alma's house was that there was almost an open door policy for those of us who were close to their family. Consequently, there were many times when I would go up to their house and Allen would be nowhere in sight. Yet, I knew that I was still welcome to come in and just hang around. If any of his siblings were in the house, I might sit around with them, or sometimes I might even just chat with Ms. Alma for a few minutes. She was a soft spoken and serene woman. Ms. Alma usually worked at night, so she slept during the bulk of the day and would not very often be around in the evenings.

Usually, her daughters were in the middle room area where they would be doing what young women do, essentially running the house in their mother's absence. Usually that meant cleaning, doing stuff to their hair or cooking dinner.

No matter what the three girls might be involved in at any given moment, it was a sure bet that there would be some good music playing in the background. At odd times during their occupations, when a favorite song played over the airwaves, you could expect to hear any one of the girls exclaim at some point, 'Wait a minute -- ooh that's my song!' Then, let the dancing begin, and Ms. Alma's girls could dance.

Much of the time, my motives for hanging around were not entirely innocent. Everyone knew that I had a thing for Allen's sister Linda. By loitering around their house, I would increase my chances of attracting her notice. Linda was also a very good friend of my sister, Plum, and that association further enhanced the likelihood that we would see one another. She would sometimes visit my house. I was happy just being in the same room with her.

For a very brief moment, Linda and I were supposed to be going together but there was little substance to that assertion, even though I would have liked to believe that it was possible. We liked one another a lot, but it was plainly obvious that I was much too shy and unsure of myself to capture her. She was on the hunt for someone who was moving in a different league than I, even if she were not fully aware of that herself. I am not so sure she would have admitted it, even if she were conscious of it. She was too kind a person to hurt my feelings.

Of Ms. Alma's three girls, I think Linda was most possessed of a slight wild streak, although she expressed it in measured terms. A few times, we kissed. For me it was a memorable pleasure. Linda had the most inviting and excruciatingly soft lips. I thought kissing her must have been a lot like what it would feel like to kiss a cloud. There were many other guys who would have killed to be in my position. All you had to do was to see Linda wearing shorts to understand why. Her legs were incredible.

The idea of anything more between us was fairly out of the question. She was my good friend's sister. I was not bold or mature enough to appeal to her on an adult level. There were many times when I was sure that she regretted that I was so reluctant to press matters more. It was nice to be around her whatever the case, and fortunately this muted passion that we shared in no way interfered with our being just plain friends.

There was also a time when Linda's twin, Brenda and I were a little sweet on one another. Brenda was even shyer than I was, so there was not much of a chance of anything developing between us.

Their older sister Mary had two friends from her 9th grade class at Harlem Park, both of whom were bright girls like Mary. They both happened to be hot as well. They came around quite often, ostensibly to see Mary, but it was clear to anyone with a brain that Janice and Edith were interested in more than simply studying French grammar when they visited.

Both of those lovely ladies had an interest in one or the other of Mary's two fine looking brothers, Glascoe and Hubert. Predictably, these good gentlemen would find some pretext to pass through the dining room, where the girls were studying, while on their way to the kitchen, or so they would have Mary and her visitors Janice and Edith believe.

The dining room was the room where everyone usually got together at Ms. Alma's house. Everybody was out to do it with everybody else, and in such intrigue lay much of the fun of being young and in lust in Harlem Park; anything was possible.

Sometimes I would sit back in a small corner of the room and delight in the good fortune that had me present in a room with such a group of fine looking young women, me feeling completely anonymous while they were in the act of being themselves. I kept my ears open to pick up any tips about the behavior of women that I might use with other girls in other places. Those times in that dining room at Ms. Alma's house were some of the finest of my life. You never knew who might drop in, and I repeat, anything might happen.

In Harlem Park, it was a virtual requirement that you be able to do whatever the latest dance was, as dictated by the Kirby Scott Dance

Show on local TV. Whenever a group of girls got together, it was a foregone conclusion that they would spend time learning, teaching or practicing the moves that would attract the boys and impress other girls with how sharp they were.

The boys and I might come into the room and the girls would be playing some records and dancing with one another. We would each give our best impression of looking silky smooth and self-assured. While the three of us young boys were fine in a pinch, what the girls really wanted was someone like Glascoe, who could dance his ass off!

"I can't get this right...sure wish Glascoe was here...he knows how to do it."

"I thought... you said he would be right back in a little while, right Mary?" Edith would ask.

"I thought...you didn't care if he was here...Edith," volunteers Linda.

"You didn't hear me say that...! Glascoe's not thinking about me... and I'm not even thinking about Glascoe." Edith replies, blushing.

"Y'all think Glascoe can dance so good...but can he do this?" pipes in Bruce, doing something that did not resemble any known dance.

"You better sit your fat butt down little boy.... 'Cause I don't know what that is you're doing." Janice says, in her standard way of reminding us that we weren't grown yet. Although she was always making fun of us, it never prevented us from trying to hit on her.

"Hey.... Janice...Hubert will be with Glascoe when he gets home." Brenda says with a little smile.

"And what's your point, Brenda?" replies an embarrassed Janice.

"Come on Allen ...dance with me so I can try to get this?" Mary asks.

"Go ahead Allen... we all know you can dance...don't try to be shy boy," says Edith.

"I think I hear the door...it sounds like Glascoe, Edith," Allen says quickly.

"Where?" Edith says, with a slight sound of panic in her voice.

"Oh...oh no. That's my Aunt Virginia going upstairs," Allen says, laughing.

"I'm gonna hurt you boy... you play too much."

The truth is - moments such as these were tailor made for a guy like Glascoe. Everyone present was hoping that he would appear soon. It was certainly true that he could dance exceptionally well and it was something that we all looked forward to seeing, especially us younger guys, because you learned a lot by watching Glascoe work a room as he danced.

One of the first things you learned was that you don't walk into a room. You explode into it.

"HEY...HEY...that's my song.... Come on Mary."

That would be Glascoe as he swooped into the room, grabbing Mary and gliding into a dance routine, swing dancing or hand dancing as we sometimes called it. Mary and Glascoe had been dancing like this since they were young kids and it was obvious as he swirled about with her, executing the most complicated turns, twirls and reverses. Mary would be following him as though she were reading his mind.

After a short spell dancing with Mary, Glascoe would also dance with his sister Linda and even Brenda, whose shyness all but disappeared when she was on the dance floor. Glascoe is not going to stop there, because he knows that Edith is watching his every move and he is too cool to pass on so rich an opportunity to set her heart fluttering.

"You're next, Edith.... Come on girl...don't make me come and get you."

Edith is mortified at this, even though we all know she is dying to dance with Glascoe. So, she will stand there insisting that she doesn't want to dance while her girlfriends are trying to encourage her to go on and dance with the boy.

"I can't do that ...Glascoe is too good ...I don't want to get embarrassed."

But, by that time, Glascoe has her and Edith begins dancing with Glascoe and moving in such a way as to completely belie every word of protest that had come from her mouth. Edith could move when she wanted to and Edith fairly oozed sexuality when she was dancing. She often gave the appearance of being very shy, but it was a hard thing to believe when she was swing dancing with Glascoe.

The room will have gotten hot by this time, and the volume of the music was now pumped up to a dull roar to compete with shouts and exhortations of encouragement aimed at whoever was on the dance floor. For that reason, I was the only one to hear the doorbell ring and I had gone to the door to let in Michael Baskerville and Eggy, who were now standing at the entrance to the dining room taking it all in.

"Hey...Michael .... Eggy...come on and help me out...these women have me surrounded. Come on Mike...?" Glascoe would shout as he spotted them.

Michael had a thing for Mary, so he was sure to turn up every now and then. At Glascoe's plea for help, Michael moved onto the floor and he did some dance that I don't know what the hell it was - but damn - it looked good! It was something with his arms, jerking his body with his arms out to the side, and kind of pointing them. It was wild and the girls loved it. Michael made that shit up on the spot, but he sure made it work. It was pretty hard not to like him.

This session was in full swing now. Practically everybody was taking a turn on the floor at some point, including me. For a while, a lot of energy would be expended to find just the right song to maintain the feeling and keep things going. Other people will stop by, and the evening will alternate between, talking, flirting, insults and boasting, with no real intent to harm anyone.

No one ever planned these informal parties. They would simply come together, and whoever happened to stop in was absorbed into the group and allowed to participate in any way they felt comfortable. If you wanted to dance, you danced. If you were too embarrassed to dance, just stay out of the way.

There was no alcohol and no drugs of any kind. Some of those who came by may have done these things before they arrived, but not in Ms. Alma's house. That would have been disrespectful to Ms. Alma.

Many times, Allen's Aunt Virginia would come down from her apartment upstairs. Her role was usually to point out everyone's shortcomings and exchange insults with people. Ms. Virginia had a smart mouth, but she was harmless. Also, Ms. Virginia would have told on all of us if we did anything too out of the way. She also had a big mouth.

Almost always, the real catalyst for whatever excitement there was would inevitably be Glascoe. I tried to figure out just what quality it was that made him capable of forever being the center of attention. I understood that in his own home, he had the support of his sisters and brothers, but he could do the same thing no matter where he was.

On the streets, Glascoe was well known and no one seemed to bother him. Even the outlaws gave him his due. He seemed to be acquainted with some of them. I used to wonder if he weren't actually hanging out with those guys on occasion. He may have been. However, I was convinced that if he were out there jumping guys, Glascoe would be that one guy who would talk the others into taking it easy on the unfortunate bastard.

The guy was an exceptional basketball player and all-around athlete, despite his relative lack of size and height. His shooting touch was uncanny. I have always thought he could have played college ball if he wanted to. Once, I watched him play tackle football, and there was a man observing the game who was fixated on Glascoe, who was a running back. The man kept repeating,

"That boy gets yardage...that boy gets yardage," and indeed he did.

Women loved him. We all used to wonder what it was that he said to them, or what he was promising them that made him so irresistible. He did not have a lot of money or the fancy car, not back then anyway, but women loved him and would do anything for him. Yet, he had a heart of gold. When Glascoe left the dining room, much of the good vibrations left with him. As the excitement began to wane, people would slowly drift away to other parts of the house or outside to the front steps; but wherever we went, the music followed.

It was a time of some magical music, especially if you looked beyond the mainstream music scene at marginal groups like the Moments, the Unifics, Linda Jones or the Marvelettes. The music of these groups was as much a part of the tapestry of the times as were the Supremes or the Temptations. You won't hear much of their music in films or mentioned in books, but down on the streets they were heard loud and sweetly.

Earlier on in the evening, Janice will have already vanished and gone in search of Hubert, who only occasionally participated in our raucous gatherings. As usual, Glascoe and Edith will hook up, and Michael will hang around to make his case with Mary.

The rest of us will take a scaled down version of what went on out to the front steps. We might all be out there until the wee hours of the morning. Those nights were magical. The next day could bring more of the same, or maybe something altogether different.

*****

CHAPTER 21 - THE PLAYGROUND

Although our focus had shifted to girls, parties and nice clothing, the boys and I still enjoyed a good game of softball. Nowadays, we did most of our playing across the street on the blacktop playground at Harlem Park Junior High. There were three softball diamonds laid out on the playground, so it was possible for more than one game to be played at the same time.

The playground was a place where many of the elements of Harlem Park met and sometimes collided. Many of the same guys who always played ball with us would be there, but from time to time some of the boys from other sections of Harlem Park would show up to play.

Further evidence that we had gone through a major shift in our priorities was the fact that we were very willing, and even anxious, to let the neighborhood girls get in on a game sometimes. Of course, those co-ed games would not be very serious games.

Since Ms. Alma's house was directly across the street, Ms. Alma, her girls and Ms. Alma's sister Ms. Virginia, could watch us from their front steps. Seeing some of the other neighborhood girls playing with us would prompt Ms. Alma's girls to head over.

On a couple of occasions, the entire family came over to the playground and surprised us by asking to be allowed to play, including Glascoe and Hubert. For us boys this was great, because it was a chance to show off our skills in front of our women.

The game would often be the boys against the girls. All the guys would be their most macho and condescending, and the girls would cheat like mad. Try as you might, you could not convince them that a foul tip on a third strike that wasn't caught was not a strikeout, at least not when we were at bat.

"That's three strikes, get your fat butt outta there boy," one of the girls will say.

"Naw, Naw, I tipped it. It's not a third strike unless your catcher catches it, and it's not my fault Ms. Virginia can't catch.

"They cheatin' Mom. When we're up, they always say we're out once we swing at the ball three times… or something like that they say."

When they were batting, they refused to believe that a foul tip on a third strike, that went higher than six feet, and was then caught, was an out.

They would be screaming.

"Foul tip…Foul tip…Foul tip…like y'all said!"

A lot of the time, they would grab and hold us to prevent us from running to a base or they would demand more than three strikes when they were at bat.

When the girls were at bat, no one wanted to play catcher. I'll tell you man, those girls would always sling that bat in any direction once they had managed to hit the ball. If you were behind the plate, you stood a good chance of a black eye.

I even recall Ms. Alma stepping up to the plate for a turn at bat. All of us guys would move way infield to let her know that we did not expect her to hit the ball. It was an insult, but she laughed it off and she was actually able to make contact with the ball. It was good to see her so relaxed and girlish. She so obviously enjoyed spending time with her family. In many ways, she was a second Mom to several of us and she was shown considerable respect.

The playground could be a scary place as well. There was a guy named Dinky, whom I knew to be a heroin user. His situation was an example of the darker-side of the neighborhood playground. He was the guy who I used to see nodding off with his girlfriend across the street near Bozy's house. Dinky worked part-time at the recreation center adjacent to the playground.

He was working there one night when they were having a dance for the community. While many of my friends attended the dance, especially the girls, I did not. Later that same night, everyone was talking about how Dinky was shot and killed at the dance.

Apparently, one of those boys from up around Gilmore and Lanvale streets asked Dinky to hold his watch for safekeeping, only God knows why. At the end of the night, Dinky can't find the watch. The guy leaves and comes back with a gun. He confronts Dinky outside of the recreation center and shoots him in front of everybody.

Everyone who was there kept zeroing in on one detail, how Dinky keeps begging the guy, "C'mon man, please don't shoot me man. Please! You ain't got to shoot me man. I can get you another watch," but the guy shoots him, point-blank, anyway.

Dinky takes off running up an alley and collapses in someone's yard, a whole crowd of people following him. Dinky dies from a gunshot wound, over a wristwatch, and the guy who shoots him goes to prison.

I remember Allen was over at the playground one day when a couple of strange guys tried to take his watch from him. Allen's brothers were nearby on the playground at the time but they did not notice what was going on; no one did. Somehow, he managed to talk his way out of giving up his watch and later told me what had happened to him.

Not too long after that incident, Allen and me were sitting on my front steps when, standing across the street, Allen saw one of the guys who had tried to pull his watch from his arm. Allen went into my house and got my BB rifle. Then, from the cover of our first floor hallway, he shot the guy. When the guy was hit, he started jumping around and screaming, "Got-damn...somebody shot me...they shot me, man...somebody shot me."

Meanwhile, we were across the street practically rolling on the floor laughing. I mean, for crying out loud, he was only shot with a tiny BB.

*****

CHAPTER 22 – THE NEW JOEL FINNEY

I was now the new smartest kid in the school, the new Joel Finney. Joel had left Harlem Park and was attending a private school. Now, I was the kid that other people would point out and say, "See that tall dude over there. He's like the smartest guy in the school."

Our school was involved in a national scholarship-recruiting program called A Better Chance (ABC). Harlem Park had already sent a number of students to private boarding schools around the country. Mrs. Fing started introducing me to previous participants in the ABC program when they returned for a visit, so I assumed she was looking at me as a potential candidate for the program. This faint ray of hope remained in the back of my mind.

For the first two semesters of the eighth grade, I once again maintained an A average, with what seemed to me little or no effort. It almost seemed as though all I had to do was to show up and I would get good grades, so I made sure to show up for school every day. However, a subtle change in my attitude was pretty evident to anyone who was watching, although at first I did not notice it myself.

The third grading period that year was a wake-up call. My average had slipped to a B, and for the first time since coming to Harlem Park, I did not make the Distinction Role. In addition, I was starting to get into a wee bit more trouble in my classes. I wasn't paying attention in class and I was beginning to clown around more. It was nothing to be too concerned about, I thought. I was only a little bored.

Fortunately, for me, someone was watching. Mrs. Fing, our guidance counselor, hauled my ass into her office before things got too out of hand. Mrs. Fing encouraged me to apply for and take the test to determine my eligibility for a scholarship to a boarding school. She explained that there was a fee of eight dollars to take the test. I told Mrs. Fing that I was hesitant to ask my parents for the money because even that small amount was a hardship for them. She told me to go home and ask, because the test deadline was in about two weeks. I stalled for a couple of days, but I finally brought it up.

"Mom, remember me telling you about how some of the kids at Harlem Park got scholarships to go away to school? Well, my counselor at school wants me to take the test, to see about getting a scholarship."

"A scholarship? That's sounds good. When did this happen?"

"The thing is, I need money to take a test, and it's coming up in two weeks."

"How much is it?"

"Mrs. Fing said it will cost about $8.00, but look, I know that's a lot of money and if we don't have it, it's ok. Chances are I wouldn't get the scholarship anyway.

"Lord Child! I know we don't have that much money to spare. We use the stove to heat up the house now 'cause we can't afford any oil for the furnace. Where are they talking about sending you?"

"I don't know Mom. Don't worry about it, there's enough stuff to worry about. I'm probably not ready for it anyway. Most of the kids who get it, don't go until they're in the 10th grade. I can try again next year."

"I don't know child!"

"Don't worry about it Mom. Next year will be better."

I was determined that she was not going to have any trouble from me.

"Maybe next year." she said, and she looked unbelievably sad.

I understand how much she must have been hurting inside at that moment, especially now that I am older with a son of my own. I hated asking her for that money. I wanted to spare her that defeat. Mrs. Fing paid for the testing herself.

She suggested that I also apply to a local military school and arranged a visit to the campus. Once we got there, it only took a short while for me to decide that I did not like the place very much, what with the uniforms and an overwhelmingly pervasive atmosphere of severity about the place, which is exactly what they were trying to project I guess.

I do think they were going to admit me, but their intentions became a moot point after I received a letter of interest from a New England boarding school I had never heard of. It was located in Concord, New Hampshire and called St. Paul's School. It was nothing short of a miracle. I had put all my money down on the education hustle and it looked as though it was going to pay off.

Like many disadvantaged kids who grow up in the inner cities of America, I had assumed that I would be lucky if I made it to adulthood alive and well. Of course, it wasn't something about which you spent sleepless nights obsessively speculating, or crying. You just figured the odds were against you.

What happens, I think, is that American culture drums it into your head that you are disadvantaged, that you are an 'at risk' youth, and we simply conclude that it must be true because everyone, including our own people, keep reminding us of it. Meanwhile, all we are endeavoring to do is to get from one day to the next in whatever place providence has seen fit to dump us. For better or worse, that becomes your life and you live it as best you can.

Now, something akin to the miracle of lightning had struck me. Except for the recent talk with respect to boarding schools that I had heard at Harlem Park, and a recollection of a drawing in a comic book of the Kennedy's playing volleyball at a prep school called Choate, I was oblivious to anything regarding private schools. New England may as well have been a black (or maybe white) hole in space. I had heard of it, but just what exactly is it - and where? However, based on what I saw in that comic book, I knew that you were supposed to play a lot of volleyball there.

The truth is, none of it mattered really. I would have gone anywhere, anywhere at all, even to that military school. Intuitively, I knew that I had a window of opportunity opening for me that might not ever open again. This was no time for fear, and I felt none. Nothing that I might encounter could possibly be tougher than where I was growing up. I was all in.

I did not even ask my parents if I could go; I informed them that I was going and they of course said, "Fine." As relatively unsophisticated as they were, and neither one of them had gone beyond 11th grade, they recognized a miracle as well as the next person.

The exit plan was that I would finish out the school year in June, and then sometime in July 1968, I would go to Dartmouth College in Hanover, New Hampshire. There, I would receive six weeks of intensive instruction in reading and mathematics. In the fall of 1968, I would go to Concord, New Hampshire where I would begin enrollment at St. Paul's Preparatory School, on a full scholarship.

When the scholarship people at St. Paul's School asked me how much my family could contribute to my education on a yearly basis, Mrs. Fing and I decided on the princely sum of $20.00. She thought that we should put down something to show an investment in this undertaking. Nevertheless, I was not to leave Baltimore before the city gave me one last unforgettable impression.

*****

CHAPTER 23 – 'AND BALTIMORE IS IN FLAMES'

When I would take the #23 transit bus to downtown Baltimore, I would see the Soul Shack from the window. On the front of the building was a brightly colored sign with African symbols. Supposedly, it was a place where a part of the Black Power movement held its meetings. I did not know anyone who actually went to any meetings there, or what it was they really stood for. I was, however, aware of the National Black Panther Party, since they seemed to be in the news more and more.

The older teens and young adults in Harlem Park were somewhat more politically aware than they had been just a couple of years before. Typically, this put them somewhat at odds with their parents and grandparents, who had far more conservative views. The Black Power movement frightened many of them.

On April 4, 1968, everyone's worst fears were realized when Dr. Martin Luther King Jr. was assassinated. There was immediate speculation about the possibility of race riots occurring in cities across the country. The wait was not a long one, just two days.

Dr. King died from an assassin's bullet on a Thursday evening. The next day, there was no school. Around the city, many of the merchants who did not already have steel gates to cover the fronts of their businesses spent the day boarding up the fronts of their establishments with plywood.

If the business happened to be Black owned, they used paint to scrawl the words 'Soul Brother' across the front of the store as a sign of solidarity for anyone who might not be aware that Black people owned the store. On the streets, the feeling was that something was definitely going to happen, and the weekend seemed the most likely time.

The day after the assassination was eerie. People seemed to be listening and watching to see how other people were going to react. It almost seemed that everyone was feeling that something big and bad must happen to show the country that it could not kill someone so revered, and then afterwards everything was just going to be business as usual. Other cities had already broken out in violence

From Black community leaders there were appeals for calm. That was going to be sufficient for those who were older and more mature. What the city, and the country, had to be concerned about were the young people, who had already decided that they did not care about anything anymore. They were waiting for 'it' to start. Listening to some of the talk on the streets, it appeared as though the young people felt it was expected of them to act, to make a symbolic statement, like maybe burning this city to the ground.

The thing is, for many of the older folk, there was a distressing sense that the threatened violence was going to have very little to do with how these young people felt about Dr. Martin Luther King Jr.; but was only an excuse to loot and burn. I suppose it came down to being a bit of both, but the violence that ensued was senseless no matter what the motivation.

That Saturday, just when and where the first brick or bottle is tossed, is probably buried deep down inside some dusty and obscure police file. However, when people started hearing about scattered violence around the city, the people on the streets knew that it was on!

My block, the 1300 block of Edmondson Avenue, was sure to be a focal point for looting. We had the grocery stores, the drugstores, the hardware store, and a couple of miscellaneous small businesses that were undoubtedly going to be targets. Then, there was the coveted 'plum' of the block, which was only about four doors houses down the street from my house - The Pawnshop.

Looting the grocery stores came first. My mother and father wouldn't allow me to go out on the street, but I had an exceptionally good vantage point from which to see the action from my mother's second floor front bedroom window. I watched a small group of people strain together to pull off the plywood nailed to the front of a store. Next, was the sound of breaking glass as they smashed the windows and doors. Once they gained entrance, it was a free for all.

Women, men, teenagers, and even children rushed in, and I watched them come running down the streets clutching boxes of candy and pre-sweetened breakfast cereals in their arms, sodas, cartons of cigarettes, you name it. You had to be first inside to get cigarettes because they disappeared quickly. I saw some of the looters gleefully run home to drop off their loot, and then boldly return for more.

Now that the ice had been broken, so to speak, parts of the crowd moved across the street in order to be the first to get inside the other grocery store. As word spread, and the word went out quickly, I could see people on the run coming from far up Edmondson Avenue, desperate to get a piece of the action. At this point, no one had much fear of the police. The word was, all the cops would be downtown guarding the larger White-owned department stores and surrounding businesses. The smaller neighborhood businesses were somewhat expendable.

Yet, it did not take long before the police arrived, maybe 10 or 15 minutes, but in that short time, everything was gone. The police officers that came were able to arrest one or two stragglers. After securing the area, they would leave one officer on the scene and speed off to the next emergency.

By this point, all over the city, the violence had escalated. Businesses were now being looted and then torched, and there were reports of gunfire being directed at the police. The shit was getting way out of hand and this was still only the beginning.

Before you knew it, the police officers left on the scene were hopping into their cars to go to some other hot spot. Almost as soon as they left, the looting started all over again, except now it was obvious that people had taken some time to consider how best to do this thing. The next places looted were Caplan's drugstore and Adam's drugstore, with their shelves filled with drugs - of course. They also sold watches, radios and jewelry, the kind of items that were very portable and therefore valuable.

Both drugstores had licenses to sell liquor. With that in mind, people were now bringing bags and even shopping carts to cart off more loot. Now they were running away with bags, boxes and carts filled with hard liquor. Some people started acting as lookouts, to warn the looters of approaching police. They were organizing this thing!

Soon after Caplan's drugstore had fallen to the looters, the hardware store was next. For me personally, that was one of the saddest parts of it all. The old Jewish guy who ran the Hardware store was such a kind person, and funny as hell. I liked him. He had this bushy moustache and he was always smoking a pipe. The floor in his store was rough and splintered, and it was beyond me how he ever found anything in there with everything piled on top of everything else. I liked to go in there and look at all the different kinds of nails he kept stored in woodbins.

After another round of looting, the cops would return and there would be a couple more arrests. That would restore calm, and a momentary peace would ensue. Of course, now everyone knew the city cops would likely leave again. A very orderly dance was in play.

I could see, and feel, the collective anticipation for the inevitable assault on the Pawnshop. At first, a small group of men went up to the imposing steel gates and gave them an exploratory shaking. I watched this from my front steps; by now my Mom and Dad would allow me to go that far, but under no circumstances was I to go any further.

They were not going to allow me to participate in any looting, and to this day, I am not sure whether I would have done so if my parents were, less present. Sometimes I think I would have. I really wanted to get in on all that free/stolen stuff.

Even I could tell that those steel gates on the Pawnshop would come down easily enough if enough people put their weight to bear on them. Those boys on the street saw the same thing, and shortly after their first tentative effort, they returned in numbers.

A crowd of twenty or so, men, women, boys and girls started shaking those gates back and forth, until the bolts securing them broke from the walls. Even before the gates completely came off the wall, a couple of the people had scrambled over the top and slid down through a small opening. From there, they proceeded to push from the other side, and the walls come tumbling down. Glory Hallelujah! They were in.

There was a roar of glee from the crowd that was as joyful a noise as you were ever going to hear. It was like the sound children make at Christmas in that instant when they first see their toys. The speed with which I saw more people descend on the Pawnshop was breathtaking. My Mom and Dad made me come inside the house.

In the ensuing weeks, people justified what they did by saying; it was because of the somewhat predatory nature of the Pawnshop. When you were in dire need of cash, they took your most valued possessions, gave you far less in cash than it was worth, and then charged you a little more to get it back, if you were ever able to afford to get it back.

Moreover, it was felt that the Pawnshop owners bought items from known thieves, who preyed upon the community, with very little crisis of conscience in patronizing these criminals. Everyone understood that the owners were just doing business. It was the nature of the conduct of some of that business people found objectionable. For these reasons, even people who had avoided any participation in the earlier looting were now showing up to loot the Pawnshop. Looking almost directly down upon the scene from my mother's bedroom window, I watched in envy as I saw people strolling out with musical instruments, clothing, tape recorders, radios, color televisions and even huge sofas.

The faces of many of the people were very recognizable to me, but I did not feel any measure of disapproval of their actions or pass any judgments. I only wished that I could have gotten one of those televisions, or a shiny brass coronet, which would have been nice. After a short while, a couple of small scuffles erupted in front of the pawnshop when more than one person was interested in the same merchandise.

This time, when the police showed up it happened much more suddenly, and to me they seemed a little more ticked off than before. The police arrested more people this time, and the cops exercised a good deal more force as they made the arrests. Not a very comfortable situation when you have a lot of angry Black people yelling 'Black Power'!

However, one dude got a big laugh from onlookers, and even the police officers, as he insisted that he had only gone into the Pawnshop to take a piss. To underscore his point, he kept trying to zip up his fly as they were leading him out of the rubble.

The city police left several officers holding rifles and shotguns to guard the pawnshop, and there was a sense that these cops were going to stay for a while. There were guns, rifles, and ammo missing from the pawnshop, which raised the level of concern for the police and everybody else. Night was closing fast.

Another interesting development was that the owners of Club Astoria and a few Club loyalists had decided to form a human barrier around the entrance to the Club. This was a show of force for anyone who might be getting any dumb ideas about taking out their establishment. They were somewhat discreet about it when the cops were around, but several of them were packing guns, which they occasionally brandished as a clear warning.

Club Astoria was Black owned, a fact that should have assured them of inviolability against looting. However, they understood, as did the people on the streets, that the allure of alcohol would surely take precedence over the fact that they were Soul Brothers.

Essentially, things had gone as the Black merchants had hoped. Those businesses that were Black owned had made it through the day intact for the most part. The artifice of spray-painting the words Soul Brother across the front of a store worked well. One story that quickly made its way around the neighborhood, involved the dark skinned Pakistani storeowner who sought to protect his store with a sign declaring him to be a 'Sole Brother'. The misuse of the word 'Sole' sealed his doom.

By the next day, things had calmed down considerably in our immediate area, but there was still a fair amount of violence in other parts of the city, largely in the form of fires. I was in Allen's block that afternoon when I saw smoke in the distance, somewhere up towards Lafayette Avenue where Harlem Park Elementary School was located. Allen, Bruce and me ran up there to see what was going on.

What we saw was another recently looted grocery store. It was just across the street from the school, but this one had also been set afire. The blaze intensified quickly because of the debris inside. We sat across the street on a metal rail alongside the school and looked at the thick flames. Some of the kids sitting near us were eating boxes of black and white good 'n plenty candy they had just looted from that store. One of the kids kept throwing the black pieces of candy on the ground. They sat near us, peacefully consuming their goodies, while the store burned to the ground. I used to buy candy in that store when I went to the elementary school. That small corner store was Black owned.

That afternoon, the National Guard arrived and there was going to be a dusk to dawn curfew, but that did not stop the madness completely. That night, I was sitting on my front steps when a Black National Guardsman, in full combat gear, came over and asked if he could sit with me. We began talking about all that had been going on. He told me he was there to protect Club Astoria.

"Are you in the army man?"

"I'm in the National Guard little guy."

"Looks weird to see real soldiers dressed up for combat here in Harlem Park." I said.

"Yeah well, it looks strange to see people running around screaming Black Power while they're burning down their own community. People should think about that."

"I don't think they care," I said.

Just then, we saw a flickering flame across the street, and it was moving - fast! Before the soldier could get up to investigate, a guy came running out of the alley, crossed the street and tossed a flaming Molotov cocktail at the entrance to Club Astoria. He then continued fleeing down the alley alongside the Club, and was gone.

The guardsman ran to the Club's entrance and managed to stamp out the flames, which was not difficult because the bottle the arsonist used had bounced from the wall of the club, before shattering, and the flames spread over the sidewalk. Another soldier came down the street to help him out, so it wasn't even necessary to call the fire department. Things quickly settled down, and the streets were again silent.

Maybe an hour and a half later we heard a loud – BOOM. The soldier jumped to his feet, and while checking his weapon and heading up the street, he yelled at me to go inside. Of course, there was no way I was going to do that. I heard the sound of police sirens, and very quickly, what seemed like an army of police and National Guardsmen descended on our block, with searchlights and rifles trained on a house up the block.

After a brief standoff, the police brought out a shoeless and shirtless man, wearing black pants. They were shoving and knocking him around pretty good. He was shouting the Black Power slogan, and he continued screaming it until they took him away in a police vehicle. The loud booming sound we'd heard was that shirtless guy firing a shotgun at a guardsman stationed across the street, but he missed. You had to wonder what was he thinking, and what would have been proved had he shot the guy.

Sunday was markedly quieter than the day before and the rioting appeared to be on the wane. Now, the time had come to clean up the mess and reflect. On Monday, a couple of the storeowners cleaned up their establishments in an effort to try to reopen on a limited basis. Others simply came down to board up what was left of their businesses, salvage what they could, and return to their county residences.

The already tenuous bonds of trust between them and this Black community were forever shattered. More than a thousand businesses were lost, looted and burned. Most of them left the community for good. What else could they reasonably be expected to do? There were fears that the summer would bring more rioting, but that did not happen - enough already. The community was devastated, and sadly, it never fully recovered.

Much of the aftermath of the rioting is a blur to me. At the time, I was preoccupied with my impending journey into the larger world, far beyond Edmondson Avenue and Harlem Park. Several weeks later, my father and his pastor gave me a ride to BWI airport, where I found myself taking my first flight on an airplane headed for Logan Airport in Boston, Massachusetts, then on to Hanover, New Hampshire via bus and finally arriving at Dartmouth College.

THIS - WAS DIFFERENT!

*****

CHAPTER 24 - DARTMOUTH

We came from all over the country, a bunch of inner city black guys, Latinos, country boys, poor whites, Asians and Native-Americans, all of us brought to Dartmouth to be spit-shined a bit before we assumed our places in some of the finest private schools in the nation. Looking at us, you had to wonder, had anyone really thought this thing through.

These guys were unlike any boys I had ever met. Some of them had huge Afro hairstyles or a bush as most of them called it; and they were wearing African styled dashikis, giving them that bad ass Bobby Seale or Stokely Carmichael look.

They seemed to know more about all manner of things than I did. Some of them looked and sounded almost foreign to me, almost like we were not from the same country. Many were from the Deep South, from places like Yazoo, Mississippi and Augusta, Georgia.

They had accents so thick that I couldn't tell what they were saying, and for the first time I became aware that I had a strange accent of my own, which they found equally baffling and even amusing. If I was asked where I was from and I responded in my typical Baltimorese by saying, "I'm from Baldimore." their reaction was generally, "Baldimer?" Where the hell is that?"

Some of them were from Chicago, Detroit, New York, and from out west, places like California and Oklahoma. Like me, many of them had arrived here having recently seen their own hometowns torn up by rioting.

What was nearly strangest of all for me was that a good number of these guys were Native American, from actual tribes living on reservations. I mean - man! I had never met any guys like this before.

When I was taken to this dormitory called Cohen Hall where I was to stay, I was greeted by another surprise when I was introduced to my white roommate. He was from a place called Lebanon, New Hampshire that was not very far from Hanover; and he was already fully settled into the room.

After we were left alone, I noticed something I had not especially noticed in the flush of my first sight of him. The boy had a huge Confederate flag draped on the wall above his bed. Probably seeing me staring at that flag, he cautiously said, "Look at this!" and he pulled up the flag to reveal a wall plastered with nude pictures of Playboy bunnies. That was pretty cool, and we never had any problems with one another.

All of us boys were divided into smaller groups in our respective dormitories, and the groups held informal meetings so that we could all get acquainted. In our group, each guy was asked to give his name and any nickname by which he would prefer to be called. I listened as four boys gave their name and a nickname. *

When my turn came, I gave my name, but on the spot decided that I would give myself a new identity. I gave my whole name but said that

I preferred to be called Woody, which everyone agreed sounded like a nickname anyway. So, on the very first day I reinvented myself.

Right away, I made a few friends, mostly among the guys in my immediate group. I got along with Scott (Scottie) and Thomas (Tommy). There was this other kid named Augustus (Gus) that I really liked. He was the most naive person I had ever met, I mean even more naive than me. He was from down south somewhere and he had this thing about not using cuss words, something I could distantly relate to. So, instead of saying fuck you, he would say things like, "Bull manure on you," - who the fuck says that?

Later on, in one of the other dorms, I met two other guys who were also slated to attend St. Paul's School. One was a little guy from Brooklyn named Jose Wiltshire and the other was a big guy from North Carolina named Michael Shivers. We did not hang out together very much that summer, but both of them seemed decent and it was comforting to meet two other people headed for the same school as me. In a new and strange situation, it never hurts to have a friend or two.

Dartmouth was a revelation. It was an Ivy League College campus, which meant nothing to me at first, but a fact of some significance that I very soon learned to appreciate. They were feeding us food that I considered to be outstanding. There were showers in the bathrooms, color televisions in the lounges and there were no muthafuckin' roaches. Was I in heaven or what?

Everything seemed so green and clean, and except for those of us in the ABC program, everyone was so White. So, one started to wonder, where were the local Black people? Very quickly, I learned that the nearest concentration of Black folk was about an hours drive south, around Boston, and we were not going to be getting anywhere near those parts for the next six weeks. Perhaps there really was a method to this madness.

Our days would consist of reading, writing and mathematics; and to round us out; we would learn something about as many different sports as possible. Therefore, for the first time in my life, I learned to play soccer and I loved it. I briefly tried lacrosse, a fast and aggressive game, and I liked that too.

I was taught to swim - I mean really swim. We received swimming instruction in what I was told was an Olympic sized pool. That state of the art pool was an incredible sight for me at that time. We were shown how to play tennis, and once I even went out to the golf course to knock around a few balls. Golf is not as easy as it looks.

There were some good basketball players there. Two of the better basketball players seemed to me to be as rough as the hardest guys I'd seen on the streets of Baltimore. Later that summer, I saw the faces of those same two bad guys in a photograph in Ebony magazine showing them as they were being detained for looting in the riots that occurred in Detroit. They did look like two rough boys!

A disconcerting and even humiliating surprise for me was the degree of difficulty I had coping with the academic requirements of that summer session. We were asked to do a lot of writing, and the English teachers were demanding that we dig deeper than many of us were accustomed. They were looking for us to be more comprehensive, more descriptive and analytical in our book reports. I was not used to having my first efforts rejected as not good enough.

I balked at their demands at first, but this English teacher I had, Mr. Marshall, was able to convince me that he was looking out for my best interest. He explained, in a way that got through to me, that much more would be required of me when I got to my college preparatory school.

For the first time I was surrounded by guys, many of them, who were smarter than me. Mr. Marshall had me look at the study habits of the very brightest boys and I could see that their success was the result of a disciplined approach to studying. I was going to have to work on that.

That had me thinking, and I was now even more determined that I must satisfactorily complete this summer program and take my place in one of those schools. I began to try a bit harder and I soon started to understand his point about the value of hard work better. He had me read The Autobiography of Malcolm X, which made a lasting impression upon me. Mr. Marshall was a good guy. He was one of my very first white teachers!

Math was even more difficult, and what really knocked me for a loop was the amount of homework that we were expected to complete each night. It was more than three times what would be required of me at Harlem Park Junior High. I thought that I was really applying myself to the task, but it was a struggle every step of the way. While I was not exactly failing, I was far from the top of the class. It appeared that I had risen to my level of incompetence.

Then, to exacerbate my feelings of incompetence further, I had this kid in my math class, a Native-American, who appeared to me to be some sort of math genius. I was continually astounded by the ease with which he seemed to perform in class, and by the scores on his test. He was also one of the nicest and most humble people you could ever meet. You wanted to hate him, but it was impossible; at least it was for me. Some of the others had no trouble at all hating him.

It was much easier than I thought to let go of the idea that I had to be the smartest guy in the room. For one thing, I was seeing irrefutable evidence to the contrary; and there was no sense in arguing with it. Although, I figured, at least I did make it up here with all these smart guys in the first place.

I had never fully bought into the gifted boy idea anyway. I really wanted to be that well-rounded guy, who had a nice balance of street smarts and book smarts. In addition, I had learned from Mr. Marshall that an awful lot was dependent upon just how much I elected to apply myself. I could do better, if I wanted to.

I needed to embrace fully the idea that I would have to work harder than I ever had before. Malcolm X had written of the same kind of focused work ethic in his autobiography, and Malcolm X now represented more to me than that crazy Negro - as I had once heard him described. My work improved but I knew that even more effort would be required.

Many of us at Dartmouth that summer suffered with painful pangs of homesickness because for most of us it was our first time away from home, but the Native-American guys took homesickness to a whole new level. They really seemed to suffer, and I can recall one guy who totally flipped out. He threw a heavy-ass lounge chair through a (no kidding) plate glass window in one of the 2nd floor lounges, and had to be forcibly subdued by four or. five guys who pinned him to the floor.

He just kept repeating, "August 15...August 15...August 15...!'

On August 15, we boarded jets and flew home.

*****

CHAPTER 25 – GOODBYE, HARLEM PARK

For us kids, other than a few more boarded up buildings blighting the streets, there was little evidence of the riots that had occurred in Baltimore only four months ago. Shopping for food from day-to-day had become a bit trickier in the neighborhood because most of the corner stores were gone, making it necessary that we travel farther when sent to the store to get milk or bread. Otherwise, I found my boys playing ball and hanging out, as before.

I wanted to think that essentially I was the same person who had left barely six short weeks ago, but oh, man was I kidding myself. Everyone looked at me a little differently, and I have to admit that I looked at them in a new light.

I did feel that I had some responsibility to be a different person than the kid who had left. It is a part of my nature that I tend to soak up new experiences like a sponge and quickly assimilate what I have learned into my daily life. Those six weeks away felt like six years to me, and I had much new information to process, so my mind was overflowing.

One of the first things I did was to go to Jesse's barbershop, and for the very first time I simply had my hair 'shaped up,' rather than getting a complete haircut. Jesse asked me if I had learned to be a Black militant when I was away.

There was some truth to that! I was trying to affirm my growing political awareness by adopting the corresponding look. The funny thing about it was that my hair was genetically programmed to grow little more than about 1/8 of an inch, so I had a little Afro, but at least I felt like I had an Afro.

"You not plannin' to go up there taking over buildings and burning things down are you? Jesse asked. "'Cause if that's what you want, you see you can do that right here."

I said, "The brothers got carried away Jesse. They weren't thinking."

"Black brothers? Shoot man…those weren't nothing more than a bunch of thieving Negroes taking advantage of a bad day." Jesse added.

Someone pipes in, "You got that right Jesse. Half of them young niggas out here tearin' up, couldn't even spell King."

"Some of the brothers I met this summer say that what we need now is somebody else strong and intelligent like Malcolm X was, to take us to the next level." I said.

"You go on and get that education son, come on back. That's what we need," says Jesse.

Someone else tells me, "If you smart boy, you'll get as far away from here as you can, and stay away. Ain't nothing here for you."

Things were changing. There was no denying that.

One afternoon I was sitting on Allen's steps just playing around with one of the girls and she kept slapping at my head,

I yelled at her, "Yo', stop hitting me on the head!"

Our friend Butch, who was standing nearby, laughed and said to Allen,

"We have to be careful around him, because he don't want anybody to touch his head. He's trying to be all proper and talking like a white boy?"

The point he was making was regarding my pronunciation of the word head. Instead of using the Baltimorese ('hid'), I was now pronouncing the word properly. After six weeks at Dartmouth, listening to all those varied accents, my own speech pattern was changing. My first real clue about this was the wisecrack made by Butch. It bothered me a lot, a whole lot!

It then became clear to me that I was literally going to have to work consciously at modulating the changes within myself, here where I had grown up. Frankly, I was warned to expect this by ABC students like Joel who had gone before, but I naively thought that it could not happen to me.

In retrospect, I see that I should have relaxed more and kept a lower profile. No one was prepared for the drastic changes they were seeing in me. I made some dumb mistakes, but the world was beginning to look differently to me and I was expressing it in my speech and thoughts. I had to stop showing off.

Since I was only going to be home for a few weeks before taking off for St. Paul's School, I tried to get around and see as many friends as possible. Allen's sister Linda made me feel good by allowing me to spend more time with her. That was a boost to my fickle confidence, and when I again left Baltimore, I left thinking that we really had something going. I thought I was in love.

I also started to feel more entitled to hang out late at night with some of the older guys, just as I had at Dartmouth. My Mom and Dad were extending me more latitude with coming in and out of the house. I wasn't going to try staying out all night, but I was out there until two or three in the morning.

Guys like Tony Stewart and Michael Baskerville and John (Eggy) Reese were unbelievably encouraging and supportive of what I was about to undertake. They seemed to have a sense, as did I, that no matter the outcome; going away was not the worst thing that could happen to a slightly weird young kid like me.

Maybe they understood because they were a couple of years older, and at our ages of 13, 14 and 15 years old, there can be a great difference in what you understand about life with even only one year separating any two guys. At that age, so much of real grownup life is coming at you so fast.

This was the age at which guys like us are fully expected by everyone to contribute something to our respective households, to get some kind of part-time job and help our Moms and Dads with some household bills, or at the very least to stop being any sort of drain on the family's resources.

This was the age where you knew your conversations with folks should contain references to how much money you are giving to your mother to help out. I felt a little bit guilty that I would not be around to get a job somewhere and do something to help my Mom with some money, now that I was getting old enough to help. That's the eldest boy's duty.

I figure guys like Tony, Michael and Eggy were just beginning to assess their own prospects in this world, from the somewhat bleak perspective of the tough neighborhood in which we lived. They could see that a person had better grab at any promising opportunity, with both hands.

I mean, you're a teenager and you want girls, good times and nice things and you start to see that no one is going to walk up and give you the things you covet. You had better find some sort of hustle that will bring some real money your way.

To them, this private boarding school thing seemed like a good hustle. They already knew me well and had seen my talent and hunger for education, so they understood that this was my likely destiny. They might be average boys from the streets, but they were all far from stupid and I had often learned a lot about life and being a man from them. They joked with me about all the white pussy I would get. Michael Baskerville in particular kept messin' with me.

"Keep an eye out for those big tough white boys up there who might try to fuck you in the ass, like in jail," he says. "They may be rich and look all nice and dumb, but those are the ones you have to watch out for. Them boys will hold you down and take your shit!"

Ah, the unfettered truth.

I was beginning to feel sentimental about these boys and all my boys, their families, and my friends here in Baltimore. They were the sum total of my life until now, as were these streets, homes, and even the burned-out buildings and the alleyways.

Nevertheless, I was unabashedly eager to say goodbye to this familiar haven, headed for some unimaginably gleaming white ivory tower called St. Paul's School, in Concord, New Hampshire, where they say knowledge of the world was contained. I envisioned the school (in occasional flights of fancy) sitting on a floating white cloud in the frozen white north - New England.

Oh, I wanted this.

#######

CHAPTER 26 – PACKIN' UP

There was no noticeable change in our household surrounding my inevitable departure. In other words, nothing was different and everything was different. I know it consumed my Mom, but she did extremely well not to show it.

Of course, my Mom knew that this was a good thing for her boy. For so many years, she had been in the uncomfortable position of deferring some of my needs to the needs of the family, for the sake of peace. My role had been to help her out. I did that by asking for very little from a family with severely limited resources.

I am sure she was proud that I had done the 'manly' thing and rescued her from some of her worries for me. I had stumbled upon something that could make an enormous difference. This would give me a fighting chance, and she would see her first-born son do better than she did. She could relax a little about me. Now that I have a child of my own, I know what that does for a parent's peace of mind. Mary Jane was bursting with joy, but she was quiet and content, not at all fretful or boastful. I understood my Mom well. She did not have to say anything. I could see.

Otherwise, in our house you would have thought that it was perfectly normal for a poor Black teenager to head off on his own to god knows where, to do only god knows what! There was almost no talk about it, no extraordinary preparations, no one running out and buying things, no parties and no parting gifts.

In September 1968, the night before I left for St. Paul's School in Concord, New Hampshire, I packed our family's one big suitcase, which we only used for family trips south. It was a large gray and black vinyl suitcase, large enough that a child could climb inside. We used to sometimes put my brother Anthony inside it and zip it up. He got a kick out of that.

My brother Anthony was about the only one who seemed to be even remotely engaged with what was going to happen. I suppose that was mainly because we shared the same room, and at night, before we went to sleep I would share with him some of my vague dreams of the future. I would tell him how this move would guarantee that I would be an important man in the world and have a good life like the rich people we had seen on television and in movies.

They were grand ideas, yet vague. I did not know enough to fill in the details. I was trying out these grand ideas before a safe audience – my loyal but naïve young brother. Anthony did not have much to say about any of it. He was simply glad that he would have our room to himself.

Although I have never been comfortable with it, I am aware that my brother absolutely idolized me and probably missed me a great deal when I was gone. The thing about that is - it has always made me a little nervous whenever anyone looks up to me. I have gotten better about that now.

We had grown up watching the television show Leave it to Beaver depicting the daily life of an American middle-class white family, with me taking the part of Wally the older nurturing brother, and my brother Anthony being the hapless Beaver. We loved that show.

We liked to think that our lives in Harlem Park mirrored their seemingly idyllic lives. I mean, we did live in a two-parent home like them and we were boys sharing a room and trying to grow up in a sometimes-baffling world. Unfortunately, that is where the similarities ended.

While I never spent a whole lot of time hanging outside in the streets with my brother, I would sometimes allow him to stick around when my boys Allen and Bruce came over, and sometimes we would let him hang out with us in the back alley lot. There wasn't much to do back there, so we would pass the time by picking on my little brother. However, what was chiefly important was that Anthony and me had put in countless hours as brothers sharing the same room and we had a very close bond.

Therefore, there were no warm and wistful protestations from my family of 'I'll miss you,' 'I love you,' other than one instance from my older sister Plum who could be such a drama queen. We didn't roll like that in my family, although I will say that the aloofness we all shared changed later in life, after our parents were dead. By then, we had mellowed with age and come to terms with our shared heritage and values.

As much as I have always felt like an outsider in my family, we do share certain unmistakable traits. Thanks to our parents and our upbringing, none of us was particularly demonstrative with our feelings and none of us was especially racist or bigoted. We had reasonably good vocabularies and we liked all kinds of music; Gospel, R&B, Rock n Roll, including and especially the Beatles.

Even though my family was aware that something grandiose was about to happen to me, there was no way any of us could truly fathom such a fortuitous event. Let's face it; no one around us on Edmondson Avenue in Harlem Park would have the faintest idea about what lay before me. That thought gave me cause for concern - for about a split second.

Reverend Johnnie Watkins was largely absent from what little discussion there was of my impending departure, at least in my presence he was. I learned from my mother that he bragged loudly and often to all of his friends about his son who got a scholarship to a fancy private school. I don't remember him saying much to me. She says she often admonished Johnnie for bragging about my accomplishments, but never doing anything concrete to help me. I noticed the same thing. That's how he was.

I did not have many clothes, so packing took about ten minutes and that's because I was dragging it out. I had about five pairs of pants, jeans, some shirts and one black suit jacket, a clip on tie and a real tie, one pair of black shoes, a pair of sneakers and a small black radio.

The only thing extraordinary was that I had bought more t-shirts and underwear using the little money my parents could give me. It did feel good seeing those few nice new white cotton articles of clothing in my suitcase. It made the whole occasion a little more special.

No one else offered me any help. My uncles, aunts, family friends and the folks from my parents' respective churches were all proud of me, but that was as far as that went. Those church folk might pass around the collection plate for a kid like me – someone doing something special - but that did not happen in my case. I don't like to admit it, but I found that disappointing.

All of my life those people had looked at me as the one child in my family who did not need any extra help, because as they said, "He so smart!" They figured that if I could get a scholarship to a private boarding school at thirteen years of age, how much help could I need from them.

During the summer, I had made a few dollars by doing odd jobs. With the last of my money, I purchased this cool looking, very cheap black trench coat that was not very warm, but it did look slick with belts and buckles and epaulets. It would be my winter coat and I fancied that I would put it on and cruise around St. Paul's with my collar turned up, carrying books about deep and scholarly subjects. I couldn't wait to wear it, thinking I would be the envy of everyone at St. Paul's School. I'm sure you're thinking, 'Could I have been more clueless?'

My parents did not own a car and they did not have money for the long cab ride to Baltimore Washington International Airport, so my father had again arranged for his pastor, Bishop Clifford, to drive me there.

Bishop Clifford was a very good-looking man, slender, neat, and possessed of a preacher's mandatory soulful voice and a head of fine wavy hair. That made him irresistibly attractive to the (predominately) female members of his congregation, and quite likely to a few of the men as well. Ferrying around members of his congregation was part of Bishop Clifford's duties as a pastor, which to my mind was only fair since it was probably my nickels and dimes in the collection plate that paid for his nice car.

This time, neither one of my parents were going to be able to get off from work to accompany me to the airport, so I was to be ready and waiting for Bishop Clifford when he showed up at the house in the late-morning.

Very early on the morning that I was to depart, my mother came into my room and sat on the side of my bed, next to me. She rubbed the palm of her hand down my face to awaken me.

"Good morning. I was just sitting here looking at you. Did you get all your things packed? I wanted to make sure you didn't forget your new underwear."

"What are you doing here Mom? Shouldn't you be on your way to work?"

By this time, my Mom had begun working at a Senior Citizen's Home as a nurse's aide.

"I'm going to work now. I wanted to be sure that you know I would be going with you to the airport if I could, but I can't lose any time from work. You know how we need every penny right now."

"Yes ma'am I know. There's no need Mom. All I need is for Bishop Clifford to get me there on time. After that, I'll be fine. Don't worry about it."

"How much money do you have?" she asked tentatively.

"I won't need any money. I have my plane ticket and when I get to the airport in Boston, there'll be buses to take us the rest of the way to Concord. Once I get to St. Paul's, they said that I would get spending money as part of my scholarship. I should be all right." I insisted.

"That's a long way you're going. You should have some money, in case you have to get back home."

"Relax Mom. This is me. I'll be fine."

She then grabbed my hand and placed some coins in it, closing my fingers over them.

"This isn't much, but you can't leave this house with no money in your pocket."

She had given me .47 cents, much of it in pennies.

"I won't need it Mom."

"You take it," she said.

It was important to her that I accept the money. She had probably searched all over the house to scrap it together.

"Ok, thanks," I said resignedly.

She again rubbed the dry scratchy palm of her worn hand down my face as she always did. It was our thing. Her hands were always dry and cracked. With four kids and a husband, she had to wash many clothes and she often washed them by hand, saving the money she would spend in a laundromat.

"Be good. Call us if you need anything," and she left as quietly as she had come.

"Yes ma'am," I said.

*****

CHAPTER 27 - ST. PAUL'S SCHOOL

I hauled that big 'ol suitcase from my room and down the three flights of stairs to the front steps, and then sat next to it waiting for Bishop Clifford to drive me to BWI airport. My father said the Bishop had gotten a new car and was driving a yellow car now. I kept peering up and down Edmondson Avenue looking for any yellow car moving.

While I waited, I walked across the street to Mr. James's luncheonette and bought a soda, chips and a couple of Tastycakes for the trip using the very last bit of my money. As usual, Bishop Clifford was late - an hour and a half late. When he finally showed up, I watched him hurrying to get out of the car, before he rushes over to me,

"C'mon baby, don't be dragging your feet. Bishop Clifford has got a lot to do. I think poor Mother Clara is about to pass away any second now...," and he continues past me and gets back into the car. I had to struggle mightily, all alone, to get that big suitcase in the back seat. I swear! Preachers are always late, and I know why. It's because they can never shut the fuck up!

I missed my flight, and of course, Bishop Clifford was very long gone. I found out from a lady at the information desk that there was nothing to do except wait for the next flight, which was not going to create too much of a problem, or so I thought. The next flight was in a couple of hours, but it too ended up arriving late.

When I landed in Boston, I was to look for signs directing me to the buses for SPS. Looking around I saw nothing, no signs and no buses. There were other kids around in jackets and ties who looked like the students I'd seen in the SPS brochures but I wasn't about to ask any of them anything. After that rock-throwing incident with those three white boys back in Baltimore, I didn't exactly fear white kids, but I trusted them a lot less.

Who knew what kind of crazy guys might be hanging out at the airport?

I walked around outside, dragging that heavy-ass suitcase looking for something or someone who might be connected to SPS. I saw nothing that stood out. I was in a major metropolitan airport where everyone is pretty much sporting their best attire, so everyone looked very much the same to me.

Of course, I probably stood out a good deal, with my screaming bright purple double-knit pants and purple nylon knit shirt, but had you asked me at that time, I would have been certain that I looked as well-dressed as anyone else. I went back into the terminal and sat down. It was nearly dark and I did not want to be stuck in Boston. This was a bad start.

In my pocket, I had a card that had come with my SPS admissions package. On it was the address and telephone contact numbers for the school. The night before I had placed an envelope containing the information card, my SPS bus ticket, and an SPS school brochure in the side pocket of my suitcase where I could reach them easily if I needed them. This morning I decided to place the telephone number in my pants pocket, in case the suitcase was lost.

I called the school collect and asked for the only person I could think of, the Rector. It took some time for the person at the other end of the line to get someone who could help me, but finally the school Rector, Matthew Warren, was located and informed that one of the new students, who had missed the bus, was on the line. Mr. Warren was a tall, gruff man with that dignified old school authority and a face that was weathered and stern.

"Hello son. Where are you?"

"I'm here at Logan Airport. I missed the buses and I have no idea how to get to the school." I said.

"Where did you fly in from?"

"From Baltimore."

"Ah yes, I remember who you are now. Our staff made your travel arrangements. What happened? Did you miss your flight?" he asks.

"Yes sir. My father's pastor was late picking me up."

"Well hold on son, while we figure out what to do here," he tells me.

When he gets back on the line, he seems to have a plan.

"All right son, this is what you will do. Go to a taxi stand and get into a cab. Use your own money to pay the fair and we will reimburse you later. Go to the bus terminal and we will…"

"I don't have much money on me Mr. Warren." I tell him.

"Not much money…you didn't spend it all did you?" he asked.

"I haven't spent any money." I told him.

"Well, I don't believe your parents would send you this far with no money. How much money do you have?"

"I think I have about .47 cents on me." I say.

"Good Lord!" I hear him exclaim. "Hold on son."

The tone of disbelief in his voice was unmistakable, and he probably later felt terrible about it. At that moment, I remember feeling unspeakably poor.

I could hear him talking to someone else, and after some time he comes back on the line. "I want you to find a comfortable place in the terminal and sit tight. We're sending one of our people to get you. It will take at least an hour because he will have to drive from here to Boston, but that will be best," he says.

"Who should I look for?" I ask.

"He will find you and he will know your name and your mother's name."

"OK, thanks. I'll wait."

I was impressed that these people would go to such lengths to make sure that I arrived at SPS safely.

When the guy who was to pick me up arrived, he had no trouble finding me, a very destitute-looking Black kid alone at Logan Airport. During the ride to SPS, he told me he was a groundskeeper. He said he loved working at the school and stuff like that..., and that he had volunteered to pick me up because he liked helping out in any way he could. He was also picking up one other kid who had missed the bus.

I had seen this other white kid sitting nearby but we did not talk, so I had no idea he was also going to SPS. He was blond with a crew cut, wore braces and his name was Sam Johnson. We later became good friends when we ended up playing on the same Delphian club football team for a couple of years. Sam had a little size to him and played the position of offensive lineman to my running back. Good 'ol Sam knew how to blow open a hole in the line for a guy. Our Delphian team lost only one game that first year, and was undefeated the second year we played together.

It was dark when we finally got to the SPS campus. While I could not see very much, I had the feeling of having reached the country, like being in the back-woods of North Carolina when I visited there with my parents during the summers, with a strong smell of water, plant-life and earth. It was a little creepy.

My time spent in the woods around Cherry Hill back in Baltimore was a distant memory and although I had recently spent those six weeks on Dartmouth's campus, it seemed quieter here and felt more remote than Dartmouth.

I was a city kid now and accustomed to concrete, brick, asphalt and the incessant but oddly comforting street sounds of the inner city. This place had some kind of stream running through it. When I got out of the car I could hear rushing water, like a waterfall.

We made a quick stop to check-in at the Rectory. This was the residence of the school Rector and I thought the place looked like a mansion, just not a very big mansion. It reminded me of the large Victorian houses that dotted the campus of Dartmouth, except this building was more compact and statelier. I used to stare at the facades of those lovely homes and try to imagine what the daily lives were for the obviously wealthy people who resided in such affluence. Could they imagine how wonderful their lives might appear to someone like me? Would they even care what I thought?

The Rectory was bustling with students shuttling in and out, standing about, sitting on fancy leather furniture, sprawled on the floor, on the stairs, some of them drinking tea from what looked like real china (like I knew the difference?) and engaged in polite conversation with one another.

Most of those present at that hour seemed older and they looked sophisticated, like the people you see at grand dinner parties in films. Yet, I was pleased to see guys drinking cans of Coca Cola and munching on chips, pretzels and cheese and crackers like normal people.

I guessed that they were upperclassmen, all of them wearing a jacket and tie; the better-dressed boys in blue blazers, charcoal grey slacks, penny loafers or suits. The more casually dressed wore shorts with a blazer and sneakers. That looked ridiculous to me at first, until you begin to see, it's done!

Even at Dartmouth, I had not experienced anything like this because all of the guys there were at risk kids like me. I mean, how can you be sure how to behave in such a setting? More specifically, how does a guy like me behave in such a setting? For now, I decided to approach things by simply remaining laid back and observant. I wasn't being neurotic, just slightly wary.

However, I did notice something that interested me. I saw that when some of the boys left the Rectory they would surreptitiously stuff sodas and snacks into their jacket pockets. As I saw it, either they were ripping-off Mr. Warren, or this was the Promised Land where everything is free. It looked to me as though they were swiping his stuff, while Mr. Warren and his wife stood around smiling and shit. When I asked Sam Johnson about it, he told me, "You're not supposed to do it without permission, but it's done."

I thought, "Very interesting."

After I had checked-in and briefly met the rector and his exceedingly kind and almost suspiciously solicitous wife, the groundskeeper who had picked me up in Boston dropped me off at a dormitory called Simpson House, part of a quadrangle of ivy-covered buildings.

That sound of rushing water I'd heard was much louder here, so the source of it must be very close, something that was of some slight concern to me. I could swim, but trying to do so in unknown waters and in the dark did not appeal to me.

Let's face it; essentially I was a young Black kid alone at night somewhere out in the woods with a bunch of white folk, who were strangers to me.

*****

CHAPTER 28 - UNPACKING

Arriving at Simpson House, I met Mr. William Kellogg who said he was the Housemaster and a member of the History Department. He introduced me to his wife and young daughters, all of them smiling and standing there in this 'family portrait' pose as though they expected me to take a photo of them. They were all so warm and incredibly friendly, and they were as pale and Caucasian as they could possibly be.

I figured that they had to be a bunch of phonies standing there grinning at me like that, but it was quickly apparent that they were not. It turned out that they were only very kind people, although I wasn't too sure about that 'Housemaster' title thing. That reeked too much of the old South for me - but I did eventually get used to it.

Soon this longhaired guy named Greg Vail showed up. More than once, he referred to Mr. Kellogg as, 'Sir.' I'd heard the same sort of thing at the Rectory. I wondered what that was all about. Growing up, I was taught to say 'Yes sir,' and 'Yes ma'am,' but this seemed different, more formal and almost ceremonial.

Mr. Kellogg then explains that Greg will show me to my room. Greg grabbed my suitcase and began leading the way to my room, which turned out to be at the end of the first floor hallway, then through a doorway, where my room sat near the bottom of a staircase that went from the unoccupied basement to the occupied upper three floors. It was a dimly lit area and it was noticeably isolated from everyone else.

I wondered about that for a second, because on our walk down the first floor hallway we had passed several robustly occupied rooms, from whence bright lights and music blared, with guys lounging in the doorways, laughing a little too loudly. There was a party-like sense of expectancy in the air as guys were setting up their rooms, renewing acquaintances and making new friends.

So, why was I stuck out here alone, away from everyone? It gave me pause, but I decided it wasn't worth mentioning. The room seemed ok and I saw no signs of a roommate. I didn't want a roommate. Maybe this isolation is the best thing, or maybe this is where they put the poor people?

Greg seated himself on my oak desk and explained that he is my Old Boy and his job is to help me through my first year at SPS, blah, blah, and blah. I suddenly remembered receiving a letter from him during the preceding summer welcoming me to the school, but I paid little attention to it since I didn't know who he was. I think I may have written a short note back to him, but I'm not sure.

He was a senior (sixth-former) and had come to SPS from some place out west. I thought he said he came from Vail, Colorado, but I think that is only because his last name was Vail and I am confused. At first, he didn't appear very comfortable as he talked to me, but I thought I liked him. He was funny, soft spoken and appeared progressively decent as he sat there and talked.

Among other things, he told me about the many sports programs at SPS. Ice Hockey was huge here and he asked me if I could ice skate.

That gave me a good laugh. I had never even seen a pair of ice skates. He did tell me something that I thought interesting. He said that the game of hockey actually began at SPS and then spread to other schools. No wonder they took it so seriously.

Greg insisted that I would learn to ice skate before I left the school and he even gave me a pair of hockey skates the next night. I accepted them to be polite but there was no way that I was ever going to use them. At the time, I did not actually know they were hockey skates or that there were any other kinds of ice skates.

These skates were heavy, black and burgundy, and pretty beat up around the toe where they were worn to a grey color, but I did like the feel of them in my hand. They were probably expensive and this guy had given them to me at no cost.

I wondered why he made such a point of encouraging me to learn to ice skate. He was either looking for a good laugh or maybe it was some sort of experiment for him, to see if he could change this inner city kid's (black) spots, so to speak. I put them on and tried to stand in them. It felt weird and I decided there was no way a person could balance on that single blade for very long. I threw them into the closet.

Once I was left alone, I began unpacking, which did not take very long. My closet still looked empty after I was finished. My room was nice, but after seeing the rooms of some of the other guys on the way down the hall, I was aware that even after unpacking all of my things, my room looked no better than a maximum security prison cell, and I have to tell you, it remained that way for the longest time.

It was a corner room overlooking the quadrangle commons. The windows in the room were interesting to me because they were leaded glass and seemed so fancy and upper class. For the time being, that would be enough ornamentation for me.

There was not much in the room, a bed, bureau and desk and there was a small walk-in closet, but the room was clean and warm and it was my room, no roommate and no roaches! This whole thing felt a lot like my experience at Dartmouth, but there was more of a feeling of permanency for me here.

Sitting on the bed, atop two folded heavy-wool blankets, was a bundle wrapped in brown paper and tied with string. It contained some sheets, pillowcases, towels and washcloths. Greg had explained that I could put my bed linen and clothes into a bin in the hallway each week. The following week I would get it back, wrapped in a neat bundle. If you did not want to pay for the laundry service, there were a few washers and dryers located in some of the dormitories. I would start out paying for the laundry service.

I was going to be here for a while, I thought, and so far, this wasn't so bad. For a while, I simply sat there in my heavy wood desk chair, looking around at my drab and empty room. Later on, I planned to relax on my bed and enjoy the soda, crackers and cheese I had lifted from the Rectory, and then try to rustle up some real music on my little black radio.

The value of the six weeks I had spent at Dartmouth College now loomed very large for me and I realized that the good people at the ABC program had a pretty good idea of what would be necessary for kids like me to acclimate themselves to a boarding school like this.

Everything I encountered was relatively new to me, but not overwhelmingly so. My time spent on that Ivy League campus had had the desired effect; to give me some of the flavor of life on a New England boarding school campus, and now, while I was not completely at ease, I did not feel any sense of panic so far from home.

I heard a knock at my door and I opened it to see this very small, pale blond kid standing in the hall. He seemed surprised to see me, and it appeared as though his surprise had left him speechless.

Since he couldn't seem to spit anything out, I spoke first.

"What do you want man? Say something."

"Hello…Bonsoir. Have you som'sing su eet?" he asked.

"Huh? What are you saying?" I asked.

"Je ne parle pas …my English is no good. J'ai faim. Do you speak French?"

"Oh …you're French. You're…'J'ai faim?' …You're hungry?"

I had taken French at Harlem Park, but of course, there were not a lot of opportunities to use it on Edmondson Avenue. With this little kid, it appeared that I probably knew more French than he did English, and that was bizarre. Mademoiselle Boone, my French instructor at Harlem Park Junior High would have been proud, even though she once made fun of me and called me a geek in front of the entire class, which didn't help anything.

Before I'd left Baltimore, I stashed a couple of chocolate Tastycakes in my suitcase, and I offered them to him.

"Voila, c'est pour vous, d'accord…pour manger? I said.

I wasn't sure if he could make out my French, and I mimed eating food for him.

"Merci," he thanked me.

I think he understood me. It was basic stuff. The kid seemed so happy to get something to eat and I felt good for having helped him. I imagine helping him made me feel like less of an outsider, like a good American, I suppose.

The French kid was an exchange student, part of a program at SPS called Schoolboys Abroad. He did not stick it out very long at SPS. He became very homesick and left after only a few weeks. I have often wondered if he remembers his encounter with the black kid from the 'hood'.

Later that year I signed up for the same program, to go to France, but I bailed out when I heard that I would have to remain in France for the entire school year. Of course, now I wish that I had kept my nerve.

Before the little kid could walk away with his Tastycake, this other sandy- haired guy who looked like a benevolent sheepdog, with his sort of mop top haircut falling over his eyes, came bouncing by knocking on doors. He seemed very excited. His name was Karl Methven.

"You guys hungry? Come on down to the lounge. We're gonna have a zafeed."

"We're gonna have a what?" I asked.

"A zafeed, come on, hurry up!" and he rushed through the door and down the hall banging on doors.

"Yo', what's a zafeed?" I yelled after him.

I knew that what he was saying was English, but I had no idea what a zafeed was, but it couldn't hurt to look. The French kid and I followed him to the student lounge where there was a bunch of guys scattered about chatting in small clusters and sprawled around a TV.

They were all my age. I learned that Simpson House was a dormitory for (what were called) third-formers. A first-former was a seventh grader; a second-former was an eighth grader and so on, until you reached the sixth-formers who were the seniors.

The whole form thing seemed a little silly to me, and still it was somewhat cool. I learned that some of these boys had started at SPS as first-formers, a fact that begs the question, "How can their parents afford SPS for five or six years?"

That was hard for me to fathom. Just who were these people and what sort of money did the parents of these kids have to make to be able to lavish so much of it solely on their kid's education at a place like SPS? The cost of SPS was extraordinary, more than most colleges, and yet, here these young teenaged boys were with their fine clothes, refined ways, and as I was soon to observe, keen minds.

When Methven's parents appeared, carrying several boxes of pizzas, I finally understood what za was. I thought it curious that at SPS, in all of this affluence, the guys lived for these 'feeds', when free food was served up. Rich or poor, I guess everyone likes getting something free. When you're rich, that's one way to ensure that you stay rich. When you're poor, it is a way to survive.

I had never had pizza, and that night I decided it was pretty damn good, sausage or hamburger with extra cheese! Whenever the evening meal was not very good, guys would have pizzas delivered from Chuck's Pizza in town, especially when the dinner was shepherd's pie, which everyone detested.

I wondered how these guys could afford to throw away money on pizza, night after night. Since I had never had any money, such a cavalier attitude towards it was simply impractical, yet to my eyes, they appeared not to give their money a second thought.

As I later learned, these guys do not stand around talking about how to go about making some money, like many of the guys I knew back home did constantly. Back home, guys were fixated on finding a way to make some big money, but here, it just wasn't something they ever talked about. It just was! I suspected that there was something careless about how these SPS boys were; but that did not stop me from wanting to be a part of it all the same.

Here, they talked about everything else instead, as if any talk of money was in poor taste. They talked ideas, events, sports, girls and anything else rather than – money, but on this particular night, they were all interested in showing off how much they knew about SPS and the people who lived here.

I understood enough to know that the young boys scattered about this student lounge were from some of the oldest and most privileged families in America and beyond. They were the sons of politicians, judges, industrialists, Fortune 500 CEO's and other movers and shakers in American society.

Their parents ruled America, and I was amazed at how beautiful they were, how enormously eloquent they could be, how strong and self-assured they seemed at so young an age, yet they were just boys, probably posturing most of them, but they carried it off well. I had a certain level of confidence about myself, but these guys spoke and behaved as though they owned the whole damn store – and in some cases, they probably did.

I did not say very much. As confident and almost cocky as I could be at times, as I had come to feel while at Harlem Park, I did begin to feel slightly intimidated. A couple of them were especially sharp, a guy named Graeme Boone being one of them.

He was very slim - almost painfully so - with dark hair and sharp features. When he was engaged in conversation, he never seemed to back down from anyone. He had a sly smile and a biting wit. He struck me as pretty smart and edgy, but never dangerous. Back in Harlem Park, a guy like him, with all that mouth, would have to do a lot of fighting.

When these boys engaged in conversation, it almost seemed combative. It brought to mind watching those teen girls fight back in Harlem Park, when nothing less than the complete humiliation of the other person would do.

Each boy seemed determined to subdue the other with words alone, summoning a barrage of facts to back up his position. You lived or died based on how smart you were, how much you understood of the world, how articulate you could be.

Right then, I knew that I would not want to take any of them on, unless I was sure about a thing. They seemed to enjoy humiliating one another and everything reeked of cruel juvenile sarcasm that was sometimes jarring, but I was surprised to see that everyone seemed to hold their own essentially. No fights were breaking out.

Besides me, there were three other black guys in the room. Seeing them there, I was sure that someone thought it might be a good idea to group four of the incoming black boys in one dormitory so that they would not feel isolated. They too seemed so much more polished than I, yet like me, they were also in their first year at SPS.

One was a kid from around Pittsburgh named Mike Nelson; there was a guy from Rhode Island named George Turville and a guy from the Eastern Shore of Maryland named Michael Russell (Mike).

Mike later told me that the instant he saw me walk in wearing those bright purple pants he knew that I had to be the guy from Baltimore he had heard about. At the time, I wasn't sure if he was making fun of me. Mike smiled a lot and talked a lot. He appeared to be bright, everyone seemed anxious to know him, and he seemed (to me), very comfortable with the whole thing.

I thought the other three black boys carried themselves very much like these white boys in the way that they dressed and spoke. Looking at them and listening to them speak; I felt that I was decidedly much rougher around the edges than they were, but I was not going to allow myself to feel inferior in any way. I may not be as well dressed as them or have that 'upper-class' lilt to my voice, but I knew that I had a few things up my sleeve to recommend me.

My first impression of the kid Turville was that if I had only heard his speaking voice, I would have sworn that he was a white boy. Nelson (with that odd Pittsburgh drawl) and Mike (with his ever so slight southern inflection) were both close on Turville's heels in that regard, but Turville was really working that Rhode Island sound, whatever it was. I can best describe it as a cross between Bill Cosby's whine and surfer dude cool – very strange!

The kid named Nelson was very quiet. Nelson even had an

older brother at SPS, Charlie, who was in the fourth form. That was something I would not have expected, two black guys from the same family at this exclusive school. From what sort of background did they come?

I found myself not speaking very much to the black guys either. My instincts commanded me to listen. Some of these white boys were returning for their second or third year at SPS, they had a lot to share, and I was looking for some clue to getting along here. I listened and began to hear what I was in for.

There was a good amount of the usual immature and derisive talk about particular teachers, whom they called Masters. I heard about the daily requirement of attendance at morning chapel. There were an intramural club athletics program and the inter-mural athletics program; predominant were hockey, football, crew and lacrosse.

Jackets and ties were required for all classes and for the more formal seated meals that were scheduled a couple of times a week. There were even classes held part of the day on Saturday, a fact which was a bit startling to me. I didn't remember picking up on that detail in the brochures I had received from the school. I got an earful and it was a lot to absorb. They appeared so matter-of-fact about everything, but I was trying to imagine how I was going to fit into such a foreign environment.

After sitting there and listening to them laugh, joke, belittle one another and horse around, I began to view them with a more critical eye. I could see that they were just another bunch of boys, not all that much different from some of the boys that I encountered my first year at Harlem Park.

If I could survive that, when I was literally concerned about life and limb, then this couldn't be all that bad. That is to say, I couldn't imagine a situation arising where I would have to end up punching someone in the chest for spitting on me, the way I had done with Andre.

I began to remember things that I had heard during those six weeks at Dartmouth College, and some of what other ABC students told me when they returned to visit Harlem Park. They said that it would be intimidating at first, until you caught up, "…but know that you can catch up!" I was comforted by the thought of those six weeks. Life at St. Paul's would still be a major adjustment for me, but that experience had removed some of the edge.

Most of these guys at SPS came from families that were on solid ground in the grand scheme of America, and some of them would likely one day rule it, among them were some very keen minds. At the same time, I saw that some of these guys were not so smart, some were jerks and some were hopeless punks, some of them were actually not from a lot of wealth relatively speaking, but all of them were solidly upper crust.

Each one of them was seeking some kind of edge, just like me. They were all probably insecure in some way, just like me. They were just another group of boys. However, if these boys represented the cream of the crop, well then, I think I just might be able to survive.

I was not going to fear them, or worry in the manner of one other black guy who later confided to me that, "When I arrived on the SPS campus, I was just wondering from behind which tree the white boys were going to come when they jumped me." It was easy to see that none of these guys was threatening in any way.

Like my boy Tony Stewart back home in Harlem Park, I was going to be calm, careful and confident. From hanging out with Tony, I'd seen how people respond to that sort of quiet confidence, as long as you could back it up when it was time for action.

These boys were intelligent but did not generally strike me as tough, and hell – I was intelligent?

*****

CHAPTER 29 – INSIDE THE PEARLY WHITE GATES

St. Paul's School for boys is neat, ordered and civilized. It is the substantial result of well over a hundred years of refinement of a concept for educating and otherwise preparing well-heeled young men to assume positions of leadership in the world. It is no joke. They have this thing down and it runs efficiently, with the school always continuing to remain out in the forefront of the educational continuum. The curriculum has its roots in the Classics.

It sits upon 2,000 acres of stunning grounds, with athletic fields, lovely woodlands and meadows, streams and ponds. The buildings on campus are generally stately, dignified, ivy covered monuments to educational excellence, a considered and homogenous mix of old and new architecture.

It is an exquisitely beautiful place. There is even a small picturesque waterfall at the sluice, where water from the Library Pond drains.

Another name for the surrounding campus area is Millville, this warm embracing New England community that is a picture postcard in the fall, whited-out in winter, lush wet and green in the spring.

The school's philosophy is to attend to the complete boy, mind, body and spirit. In a few years time, you will sharpen your ability for critical thinking; learn to think and communicate clearly, precisely, and attempt to temper one's judgments with some modicum of compassion. You will learn how to listen, and seek to empathize with the other man's point of view by using your head, your senses, and to some extent – your heart.

It is through total immersion in academics, sports, the arts and service to the community that one absorbs these lessons. It sounds quite simple actually, but it is deceptively simple. It is ingenious how the school works you, shapes and molds your powers of critical thinking, helping you to discover the best that you are inside, and the worst. Personal responsibility was paramount. You had the responsibility to self-regulate your own worst parts - freedom with responsibility.

The day after I arrived, I had to meet with a guy in the business office for financial aid who explained how I was to manage the scholarship money set aside for my daily expenses, books, sports paraphernalia and incidentals. I had a school checking account with a fixed sum for the entire year, and had to write checks to pay for things; everyone at SPS did this. He was very pointed in communicating that managing this money was my personal responsibility.

Of course, maintaining a checking account was something new to me and once set loose, predictably I struggled against the urge to buy-out the school store. No one had ever given me hundreds of dollars at one time before, but I was able to manage my funds reasonably well, and when I eventually did run out of money earlier than expected, I discovered that they would give you more money - but you knew not to go crazy!

Checkbook in hand, I was now armed and ready to see what I could do here. I now had the funds to begin purchasing the tools needed for a fighting chance at this place.

Some faculty members at SPS served as Housemasters and advisers. In Simpson House, a very quiet man named Mr. Adams, who was a slight man with a sort of bullet head and dark thinning hair, supervised me. He spoke softly and wore large black framed glasses that made his eyes look big and round, like an owl.

His face was often flushed red and it appeared to me that he was a drinking man. More than once, I remember him nursing a drink when I went to visit him to consult about my academic schedule or grades. It was curious to see someone in his position drinking in front of me, but on reflection, it all seemed to be on a par for this place. He did nothing to conceal his drink. It wasn't at all like public school. There was considerably more expected of you here.

Later on that year, I had to go to see another of the Masters about an Ancient Civilization's paper, and he too came to the door holding a drink in his hand. What surprised me in his case was that he was wearing a clerical collar. Interestingly, seeing him holding that drink led me to re-examine what I thought about religion, thereby making the required Ancient History course at SPS more relevant to me, personally.

Many of the preachers I knew back home surely drank alcohol, but there was no way that they would ever knowingly allow me to see them doing it. However, because I lived with a preacher who drank, I saw him and his preacher friends drink all the time, on the sly. Could it be that imbibing strong drink did not assure you a place in hell? Were there other things I learned in church that were not necessarily true? My mind was reeling.

L. T. Woody

Mr. Adams let me know that I could come to him with any problems, which of course I never did. Stupidly, when I was in trouble I always waited until they came to me, and by then it was already too late.

*****

CHAPTER 30 - WADE IN THE WATER CHILDREN

The first day of classes, I almost overslept because I did not have an alarm clock, but the sound of the chapel bells saved me. I awoke suddenly and for an instant, in my gut, I felt that stabbing sense of suffocating panic when you think you've gotten up late for something important. In my two years at Harlem Park Junior High, I had not once been late or absent. I'd have to remember to put an alarm clock on my list of things to buy with my money.

Sitting up in bed, I could hear the sounds of early morning campus dormitory life: doors slamming, running water, guys talking and horsing around, and footsteps pounding up and down the stairs.

The noise level was high and I knew that meant a lot of guys were still around in the dorm getting started. Had it been quiet, I would have known that I was probably late. As I discovered while at Dartmouth, that slow build and then recession in the noise level of a dormitory in the morning can talk to you. I had time. I was glad for those chapel bells.

Housing those bells is the Chapel of St. Peter and St. Paul, an English Gothic chapel. I had never seen anything like it. It is an imposing and majestic centerpiece of the SPS community. Inside, it is a cavernous structure, all fine wood and stained glass, with an enormous pipe organ. It is the sort of spiritual sanctuary designed to inspire noble and ambitious prayers. I could easily imagine some kid sitting in his assigned pew praying, asking to one day be president of the United States, and feel that it was entirely possible. Most certainly, it was nothing like the tiny and cramped storefront Pentecostal Holiness Church I had attended with my family back in Harlem Park, where prayer expectations were likely more... modest.

The sounds of the chapel bells were one other soothing aspect of life at St. Paul's, much like the sound of the rushing water at the sluice. They rang out four notes every quarter-hour, and then the appropriate number of peals on the hour. The sound of those bells at St. Paul's never leaves you.

Somewhere beneath those bells, all over campus, guys would be getting up, getting dressed and preparing to hustle over to breakfast at the Upper School. Today, it was my turn to get into the game, and I determinedly waded into the stream of the time-tested, daily routine of St. Paul's School for boys.

Wearing my one black suit coat, my clip-on tie, and my new black trench coat and carrying a few notebooks, I struck out for breakfast at the Upper. The Upper (School) was this massive old building sitting atop a hill. It was a student dormitory for fourth, fifth and sixth-formers. It also housed the school's two dining halls and a formal dining room (where we had seated meals) on the ground floor,

In all of my time at SPS, I never felt comfortable in the Upper, and whenever I was there, I rarely left the ground floor where the dining halls were. It was too easy to get lost in The Upper's many floors, corridors and staircases. It never appealed to me as a dormitory in which I would want to live because it seemed so ancient.

Of course, many of the buildings at SPS seemed ancient, and I could live in an old building back in Harlem Park. I preferred the relatively more modern dormitories. After third form year, I would have a choice about where I wanted to live on the campus. I knew that one of the older black guys lived somewhere in the Upper, but the one time I went in search of his room I couldn't find it.

In order to get to the Upper from Simpson house, most third-formers would take the path behind Library pond, although sometimes that way could be damp and muddy, but it seemed quicker. Then you had to climb the hill that lead to the entrance of that imposing building called the Upper School.

Entering the first hallway, one of the first things encountered would usually be Mr. Potter's enormous St. Bernard dog lolling about at the door leading to Mr. Potter's quarters. Brennie had great sad eyes and drooled like crazy, but she was a tame dog, although on occasion she could be fucking scary. I once saw her rear up and let out a good warning growl when she was disturbed while eating.

She would sometimes submit to petting, but I wasn't going to try it. I was always afraid that Brennie might decide to devour me whole in that quiet hallway, and no one would ever know how I disappeared.

The hallway that led to the dining halls had coat trees, hooks and benches where we could deposit our coats and books. Carved into the wood walls along the hallway were the names of all the members of all the former graduating classes for what seemed two hundred years ago. St. Paul's School was founded in 1856, so you can imagine the numbers of names!

I would sometimes stop to look at names from year's past and wonder if I would make it to a day when I would see my name on those walls. I also considered that when my name was on the wall, I would then have become one of those tired guys from two hundred years ago. It was hard to wrap my mind around that possibility.

Contrary to what I had heard from the returning white boys, the food in the cafeteria seemed good to me. Given where I had come from, it was hard to argue with three easy square meals a day. Moreover, you could go back for seconds and even a third helping of food if you wanted; so how was it possible that anyone could have a problem with that?

I can't remember ever harboring any serious complaints about the food, except for the Shepherd's Pie, which looked like something that you would feed to Mr. Potter's St. Bernard dog, and that might be an insult to dear sweet Brennic.

Breakfast was always very good. It's hard to mess that up. However, it was in the breakfast cafeteria that I experienced one of the first false notes of life at SPS. I observed that some of the white students did not always treat the people who worked in the kitchen, all of whom were white, nicely.

A few of the white boys referred to them as wombats, which is an Australian creature that looks something like a rat. I never found out why they picked that particular animal. I'd heard people using the term, but at first, I wasn't in on the joke. However, I could discern that the offending people deluded themselves into thinking that referring to them that way was only a harmless (juvenile) joke.

What they were doing was calling the kitchen staff stupid, plain and simple. Some of the boys had even made up a derisive tune. They would begin on a high note and progressively lower their voice singing,

"Heeeeeeeyyyyyy Wombat!"

You'd hear them singing it for anyone to hear on the pathways and laughing.

"Heeeeeeeyyyyyy Wombat!"

They were careful to avoid doing or saying anything when faculty members were present, but it was a tacky, tacky thing to do. Had any of the kitchen staff been Black, I'm sure I would have been outraged – but none of them was. This was rich white boy against poor white boy - class warfare.

The boys usually insulted them very slyly and in an ambiguous way, sometimes by trying to confuse them when ordering their food, using foreign accents, the usual adolescent bullshit. At times, I could see some of the kitchen staff (usually the younger men) appear to perceive and then noticcably fume at the insult; but largely I thought they exhibited commendable self-constraint. They probably did not want to lose (what was likely) a decent job.

I know that I was sure that it was risky business, and downright stupid, to insult people who prepare and serve your food every day; but most of the kitchen staff appeared to be kind, cheerful and dedicated people, to me.

Sometimes, upon leaving the Upper dining hall I would stop in the Lower dining room to look for my boy Jose Wiltshire, who was supposed to eat in the smaller and separate Lower School dining room. He hated it in there. He was the only black guy in the first and second form, and would sometimes come and eat his meals in the Upper School dining room with the upper formers.

Rarely would any of the older guys object. After all, Wiltshire was Black, cool and he knew how to handle himself among the white guys, who found him engaging. I always admired the easy way that Wiltshire had with all people. It was so New York! I wonder if he could have imagined then that he would one day become president of his class.

Wiltshire was relatively short and slight in stature, but he had a killer smile, an ingratiating charm and he was very knowledgeable about sports. He had been at Dartmouth with me. He was my age and was supposed to enter St. Paul's as a third-former, but for some reason he had to come in as a second-former. It likely had to do with what had (or had not) been covered by the curriculum at the school he attended in NYC, and he just was not ready for the third form at SPS.

It was a goddamn madhouse in the Lower school dining room where the first and second-formers had their meals. It was fascinating to me how young and immature the kids in the Lower School appeared, even though they were only a year or two younger than a third-former. I was glad that by entering SPS in the third form, I did not have to endure the indignity of the Lower School.

A couple of times I went into the old dank and forbidding Lower School building where the first and second-formers lived and it felt like I was in a scene from the film Apocalypse Now, the part where they have traveled upstream to Cambodia and stop at that out-of-control American outpost.

Just as in the film, here there seemed to be no one in charge, things were flying through the air, occasional screams and shrieks would rise above the constant din. The only thing missing was the gunfire. Everyone seemed to be having a real good time.

The lower schoolers lived in cubicles of sorts, so there were no private rooms per se; rather it was like a prison cellblock or maybe an army barracks, without any doors, so there was no real privacy.

I met one young kid, who had managed to buy porn magazines in town and then rent the mags' to the other kids in the lower school, which I thought was ingenious. There was an enormous market for those books.

It occurred to me that with no doors on the rooms, the purpose for which the guys rented the porn magazines (masturbating) was extremely restricted. Later I learned that they didn't care about the lack of doors or any possible audience. I told the kid I might come back to take a better look at some of his stock. He also traded in other coveted and forbidden goods, like cigarettes and beer.

Their dining hall boasted the same kind of insanity as the dormitory. Those little kids could be unbelievably gross, throwing food at one another and leaving the tables in the dining hall in a salt, sugar and butter covered ooze, however, to be fair, some days in the Upper School – same thing!

Just before 8:00 am, we would begin to make our way to morning Chapel. Attendance was required at morning chapel service but it was a relatively simple affair. Most mornings, we read a prayer, sang a hymn and waited for the Rector to read special announcements, which he sometimes did outside the chapel when the weather was not god-awful.

We all had assigned seats and faculty members were responsible for groups of boys, for whom they were to account each morning. As one's status (form year) grew at St. Paul's, one's seat in the chapel progressed to the higher pews.

Some guys skipped breakfast and chapel in order to sleep late. If you did that too often, you were going to hear about it. The one time I skipped chapel, I spent the entire time lounging on my bed afraid of someone coming in and discovering me. Some boys would sleep in their closets. Hiding in my closet seemed so pathetic to me. I was exhausted from studying late the night before and I wanted a few extra minutes of sleep, but I couldn't sleep because I was listening for any faculty patrolling the halls looking for guys skipping chapel. It just wasn't worth it.

At first, the idea of having to attend chapel each morning was distressing. I imagined that it would be too much like having to attend my father's Holiness church back home in Harlem Park, which I hated.

In the crowd that I ran with back in Harlem Park, I was the only one who had to go to church on Sundays on a regular basis. Bruce and Allen would be hanging out, having fun, and I was stuck inside a hot storefront church listening to some guy preach about what an evil sinner I was. Fortunately, chapel at SPS bore no resemblance to that experience. It was little more than a morning student-body gathering, and relatively painless. I can't say that I hated it.

There was no finer moment in morning chapel than those occasions when the Rector would announce a surprise holiday. Once or twice a year he had the discretion to grant a surprise school holiday and there would be intense school-wide speculation on when the Rector might choose to do so.

It is hard to say how, but everybody generally knew what day was picked, often by the morning of the day selected. On the appointed morning, there would be 450 boys sitting on the edge of their seats in desperate anticipation of a surprise holiday.

We were listening for a particular bible verse. It contained the words, 'And the streets of the city shall be filled with boys and girls playing in the streets thereof.' At that point, a joyous drone from all the boys drowned out the rest of the prayer and I have no idea how it goes.

Morning chapel eventually became just a minor annoyance for me. I enjoyed hearing that great pipe organ grinding out hymns like; A Mighty Fortress Is Our God. The sound was grand and powerful, not at all like the blues-tinged Hammond organ gospel-boogie that Bishop Clifford played in his Pentecostal Holiness church, and that sound was coming at you through an amplifier.

We also had to attend chapel on Sundays and that was a longer and much more comprehensive service, which I could not learn to appreciate. Sometimes there might be two services on Sunday, both of which we were all required to attend. Those Sunday services did feel something like 'church.' I thought that I had left that stuff back in Harlem Park with Reverend Johnnie Watkins.

*****

CHAPTER 31 – CLASSES

Classes began after morning chapel and were primarily held in the Schoolhouse building where the general atmosphere was much like what one would encounter in a busy school building anywhere in the country; a bustling stream of noisy students and faculty racing in the halls from class to class, followed by 45 minutes of quiet. Science and math classes were in separate buildings nearby.

Inside the Schoolhouse there was a distinct hint of days gone by in the wood paneled hallways, polished floors and those heavy oval tables sitting in classrooms that reeked of the history of the school and gravitas; oval tables that had countless names and other graffiti meticulously gouged and scrawled into their surfaces. This building, these classrooms, had a long history.

Each boy at SPS selected his required classes much the way a college student might, fashioning our own individual schedules, with faculty adviser assistance if required. Most classes took place in a round-table forum; 9-12 boys seated around one very large oval-shaped table. I now know this is a particular style of teaching called the Harkness Method. This meant that we were all essentially facing one another when we spoke. For me, this contributed to a kinder, more personal learning environment than the large unwieldy public school classes of 30-40 students sitting in loose rows, to which I was accustomed.

At SPS, there was no place to hide. If you were not prepared, everyone would know. Right away, I struggled academically, particularly in math and science, but I did reasonably well in the humanities courses. I knew enough about myself to know that I had reasonably strong verbal skills and so-so math skills. At this school, I would need to bolster both - a lot.

Latin was a pleasant surprise for me. I began to feel that Latin was one of the great secrets that the rich kept to themselves. It's not that hard really; and studying one of the primary roots of the English language deepened my understanding of the English language. There's no doubt about it, every kid should be required to take it.

I had a hard time with French. I quickly found out how much I did not know, and I had taken two years of French at Harlem Park. Monsieur Billet, my French I teacher at St. Paul's, was not amused.

"Monsieur Laurent, I will say it in English. Please conjugate the verb for me, en Francaise. You should have studied this!" He shouted - actually.

I would get it wrong repeatedly and it would drive him mad. He would pull at his hair, flush red and bang on the table.

"Are you mad? Are you insane?" he would plead.

Monsieur Billet was an actual Frenchman. He was short, mustached, with slick plastered hair and pockmarked skin that was predisposed to flushing deep red, and I am guessing that he had not encountered many inner city black kids. It was funny sometimes.

"Monsieur Billet, I am trying to make sense of the verbs but there seem to be so many exceptions. I'm trying to find a logical way to remember them."

He exploded.

"There is no logical way to remember it! You simply have to know it!"

"Wait a second! You're telling me that I have to try to remember all of the exceptions. You do know there are lots of them, right?" I said.

"Yes!" he sighed. "You must sit down and study them all, learn them all."

I had excelled at Harlem Park using lots of mental tricks, and because of the school curriculum's reliance on the constant repetition of facts, for which I had a good memory. This guy seemed to be saying that he wanted me to really absorb this, know it well, viscerally. At Dartmouth, this must have been what Mr. Marshall was getting at, and I guess I did not entirely believe him. I wasn't used to this.

"No one ever told me that." I said. "I thought French was like math, with plain logic to it. I thought everything was like that?" I told him

"You must sit down and study." he repeated.

That lesson learned; things improved for me academically - slightly.

Incrementally, I was seeing that I would have to dig more deeply than I had before, study more in order to tap into that well of knowledge that was surely submerged somewhere deep within my mind; some vast pool of intellect that these people were convinced was within my reach.

I would have to try very hard, but I was beginning to believe that I could find it. Here at SPS, I was daily getting a glimpse into what it looked like, so I was beginning to understand what was required a little better.

There were kids in my French I class who were first-formers. Most other third-formers were already taking French II or III. Mike Nelson was taking French II and he seemed to be doing fairly well. He had attended an academically challenging school prior to coming to St. Paul's School.

Mike Russell was in French I with me and he too managed to perform well in class. At SPS, you were in the appropriate class for your level of accomplishment, regardless of what your form was. Plainly, I was a bit behind these kids.

There was a second-former named Sheldon in my French class whom we called Maisonblanche, because his last name was Whitehouse. He was the go-to kid in our class, the one who could most be depended upon by Monsieur Billet; much as I had been while at Harlem Park where I was 'Monsieur Laurent, the man with all the answers.' Now, those days seemed a long time ago.

Often, Monsieur Billet would ask Whitehouse to "please conjugate this verb pour Monsieur Laurent," when I was being inordinately thick. Whitehouse was nearly fluent in French, an impressive little kid and he knew it. Sometimes he could appear to be a little condescending, which annoyed me because he was younger.

He had pale skin, a freckled face, and he was always doing that annoying head flick and sweeping motion with his hands, to keep his hair out of his eyes. His French accent was very good and he spoke very fluidly. Someone told me that his family had a French housekeeper or something, and that is how he learned the language.

At first, it was humiliating being in a class with younger guys, but I wasn't the only one, and it quickly began to make sense to me. At this school, what mattered was how much you know!

I'll never forget the feeling of utter failure and disbelief that my first report card engendered in me. It was something like a B, two Cs, and a couple of Ds and maybe an F, in math. I had to sit down with Mr. Adams, my Dormitory Master, and discuss my grades, which he was holding in his hand on a plain-looking slip of paper from a computer printout.

There was nothing very encouraging in what we had before us, but he didn't beat me up about it. My bad math grade was the thing that concerned everyone. They worried that I would fall too far behind.

Mr. Adams marked it down to a matter of adjusting to the curriculum and he asked if I felt I needed any help. I told him I did not, and that my next report would be better, and it was - slightly.

My grades were humiliating for me, and the only redeeming feature was that no one from my glory days at Harlem Park, just a few months ago, was there to witness it.

The struggles I had endured academically during my six weeks spent at Dartmouth had already deflated my ego somewhat, yet these grades were still devastating to me. I was not sure what I could do to turn things around, but I was not yet ready to turn and run. I knew that I wasn't stupid. I simply had to figure this thing out, find an angle.

*****

CHAPTER 32 - LOUIE

It was at about this time, the end of the first grading period; that I first became better acquainted with Mr. Louis Grant, a new Black faculty member in the history department. He was planning to offer some Black history courses to round out the SPS curriculum for the brothers.

He and I had met briefly and talked on a few school social occasions, usually when I was in the company of Mike Russell, but I had not had a whole lot of contact with him. He seemed nice enough. Eventually I wanted to enroll in one of the Black history courses he would teach.

He casually approached me one day when I was alone in front of the Post Office, and began asking me how things were going, and whatnot. It looked to me that SPS faculty were always doing that. There was nothing ominous in his approach; he began with a simple, "How's it going?"

He was very soft spoken and seemed almost shy. His demeanor was pleasant, and at first, it appeared his only concern was that I do well, and that I know he was available if I needed any help. However, I felt that by talking to me, he seemed to be discharging an unsolicited chore.

I thought that he did not seem especially comfortable talking with me, at least not in quite the way that he appeared at ease with someone like Mike Russell, Charlie Nelson, Tony Hairston or even the white kids. I noticed with them he joked, and could be seen laughing aloud and roughhousing.

Conversely, at other times he would stand apart from everyone, alone, looking sullen and professorial - but that was all right with me. Until now, we had nothing to discuss. I hoped it would stay that way.

He didn't try any small talk or probing questions about my life in the 'hood or anything, but he was obviously well acquainted with what my grades were and I felt strongly that he was not pleased, but neither was I.

I thanked Mr. Grant for his concern and assured him that I would do better. I was never sure who put him up to coming to see me. I think someone thought that Mr. Grant might be able to better relate to me than say Mr. Adams or Mr. Kellogg, my Housemasters. They were mistaken.

I do remember thinking that it must have been tough on him being one of only a couple of Black faculty members, and although it was none of my business, for some reason I could not help wondering what he did on this godforsaken campus when he wanted to be with a woman. There did not appear to be many women around who were not married to someone.

He seemed nice, but I didn't like something in Mr. Grant's tone. He struck me as sneaky. I'd have to keep an eye on him.

*****

CHAPTER 33 – LIKE MIKE

Me - I preferred to avoid close contact with any faculty members, even those that I liked. I never felt that anything good could come out of it and many of them seemed to be trying too hard to be a pal. They were that way with everybody.

The faculty members that intrigued me most were generally those who seemed to be most consistently themselves, whatever that happened to be, even if it meant they were surly and unsocial. There were some good strong men there at SPS, outstanding examples of what it meant to be fair, firm, respectful and human. Their influences have remained with me to this day.

I noticed Mike Russell seemed to enjoy bantering with the faculty and they actively sought him out after dinner or after classes, and the truth is there was nothing wrong with that. He seemed to have a good time. If I happened to be hanging out with Mike, like after a seated meal, and I was in one of those annoying social situations requiring polite talk and sparkling conversation, I would find some way to get through it. Much of the time, I listened, and watched Mike dazzle them.

Seated meals in the old (formal) Upper dining room were a couple of times a week. Jackets and ties were required and we had assigned seats at assigned tables headed by a Master (faculty member); often his family would be there as well. It was a good opportunity to practice one's best table manners and to practice the art of polite dinner conversation. For that reason, many of us avoided sitting at the end of the table nearest the faculty, where you were almost obligated to join in the conversation.

All of us had to take turns serving as waiters at our assigned tables. You waited in line in the kitchen for the food, loaded it on a tray and carried it to your table where the presiding Master served it. I hated being a waiter because I felt (being Black) that I must look especially subservient carrying one of those giant trays. It may have only been my own paranoia, but I'm sure (subliminally) many of those people thought, 'ah yes - the black servant,' when they saw me transporting a tray. I know that I did, whenever it was my turn to be the waiter.

However, the meals were generally very good, with roast beef dinners and the accompanying dessert of apple pie being a particular favorite for me and almost everyone else. When the dessert was strawberry shortcake, nobody missed a seated meal. The interval before the start of the evening seated meals, and the period immediately following dinner were a time for greetings and small talk with members of the SPS community.

Most of the time I would arrive for a seated meal as late as I could, and then cut out of there as soon as I could, but sometimes I might stay for a short time when something interesting was going on. People were doing their best to include me and the other black guys into the community, and they often sought us out after dinner.

When I was in Mike's presence, it was easy for people to ignore me, particularly if I was silent. I usually was. That suited me fine and I never held it against Mike. They were usually there to see him. Everyone always seemed to know Mike's name. My name might slip their minds.

That first year Mike Russell and I managed to remain very good friends. His room in Simpson house was in the first floor main corridor just on the other side of the door outside of my own room. In the beginning, we talked a good deal, usually about music or our families. I think Mike liked me because of a certain urban chill factor he sensed in me, which appealed to his small-town bred curiosity. I liked him, because I like almost everybody.

A few times, we attempted to study together, but with my inconsistent study habits, I was not in Mike's league. He generally studied with some of the more brilliant boys, like Locke Bowman who was in our Latin I class, and who by our senior year was teaching a beginning Latin I Class for his Independent Study Project.

The friendship between Mike and me took off during an early third form picnic when we had to run together in a three-legged race. We easily managed to synchronize our movements and flew across the field. All day we absolutely crushed the teams from the other third form dorms in that race and other athletic contests. That demonstrated for us that together we were a formidable team.

During that year, we chased girls and danced with them at the Tea Dances. We would excitedly share any information we had about the latest Motown songs. The two of us auditioned for the SPS chorus, with both of us singing first tenor. I soon quit but Mike continued for the rest of the year. Often we ate lunch together and were on an obvious track to eventually room together the next year.

Mike was a kind, generous and considerate guy and reached out to everyone. It was no secret, Mr. Grant thought highly of Michael Russell, as did practically everyone else. Their relationship almost seemed more peer-to-peer than Master-to-student. They were always laughing when they were together. Mr. Grant appeared to enjoy Mike's company, but what was not to like about him?

Academically, I struggled much more than I thought possible that first and second semester. Yet, there were things that went well during my first year. Socially I fit in reasonably well. I had forged some relationships with many boys, mostly those in my dormitory, and a few others that were older and younger than I was.

I had some slight success in sports. I played club football, club basketball, and varsity track and I learned to play ping-pong in the basement of Simpson, although I sucked at it. Besides that, I had some exposure to a number of other sports. Playing pick-up games of hockey at the Gordon Hockey Rink was the most fun. I played goalie at first and I sucked, but I was fast and aggressive and my skating skills progressed rapidly, so soon I was on attack. Skating backwards came easily to me, making me an adequate defenseman. With a stick, my backhand was good, but I could never hit a decent slap shot.

Now, whether I was to succeed or fail academically, well I suppose that was still to be decided.

*****

CHAPTER 34 – SPORTS & DAILY LIFE

In the afternoons, participation in sports was mandatory for everyone below the fourth form. Once you reached the fourth form, you could take one semester off from sports, two in the fifth form. By sixth form, you could dispense with participation in sports altogether and instead pursue some other course of study of your own choosing.

As much as I loved sports, I couldn't wait for the time when I could take a semester off. I had no idea what I would do with so much free time, but I wanted it just the same. Probably all I would do is sleep, like everyone else. I never seemed able to get enough sleep at SPS.

Each boy at SPS was on one of three intramural sports clubs, the Delphians, Isthmians or Old Hundreds. You were also in one of two boat clubs, the Halcyons or Shattucks. I was a Delphian/Halcyon.

At that time, everyone said that the best combination was Old Hundreds/Halcyon, but that was not entirely true, although that year, the Old Hundreds Club did include some good athletes school-wide. Mike Russell was an Old Hundreds/Halcyon.

As a Delphian, I played club football and basketball. That kid Sam Johnson, who was waiting at the airport with me, was also a Delphian and played second team Delphian football with me.

Our club football team sucked at first, but it was my first opportunity to learn the rules of the game and play on an organized team with coaches, equipment and referees, and I excelled at the game.

We lost our first game, and I won't ever forget one humiliating play where I was attempting to tackle a guy named John Dodderidge and he managed to drag me for several yards into the end zone. Mike Russell and some of the older boys were watching and that gave them all a good laugh.

However, after that day, our Delphian team did not lose another game for the next two years and I became the star of the team. I discovered humiliation could be a great motivator sometimes.

Of course, many of the guys playing club football were scrubs who couldn't or wouldn't play on the varsity teams, so if you had any modicum of athletic prowess, you could romp over most of them, and I did. I had a strong desire to excel at sports, but unfortunately, I was painfully skinny, not yet physically strong enough to get out there with the big boys. Better and stronger athletes like Mike Russell (who was sufficiently physically developed) were already playing with the older guys.

I never had any interest in crew, but I did attend one boat race and that was because an English teacher, Mr. Prudden, allowed me to follow the race as a guest in his speedboat. He even let me take the controls for a short time, which was neat.

If you wanted permission to participate in crew or to go swimming at SPS, you had to pass a swimming test in the Lower School Pond. Since I had learned to swim at Dartmouth the previous summer, I decided to go for it, if only to prove to myself that I could really swim. All that was required was that you swim about 100 meters across a section of the Lower School pond, but I began to get cold feet when I approached its cold murky waters.

Dressed to swim and with everyone watching, it was hard to suddenly back out of the swimming test, so I found my nerve and eventually dove into the murky water. I was about half way across when I began to get tired and then panicked; soon I was gasping for air. I was flailing about pathetically and yelling, "Little bit of help?" More humiliation - does it ever end? It was a lot harder swimming in the Lower School Pond than that nice calm Olympic pool at Dartmouth.

There was a rowboat stationed out in the water to pick up the guys who couldn't make it across and I made a desperate dash for it. They towed me to shore where I was supposed to rest a bit and try again - yeah right! I left. After nearly drowning, I decided that I was never very interested in swimming anyway and I never went swimming at SPS again - ever. There were plenty of other (safer) activities offered by the school on dry land – plenty of them!

*****

CHAPTER 35 - MILLVILLE

Undoubtedly, the center of campus life was the old post office building, a tiny brick structure with a distinctively round and pointed roof. It was located roughly at the center of campus. We all had a post office box, but I did not receive very much mail. The people I knew back in Harlem Park did not write letters and my letters to them only put them on the spot.

Occasionally I wrote a couple of people anyway, like to my boys Bruce and Allen, but they rarely responded. I wrote a couple of letters to Linda Pope, but that ended quickly. I envied the guys who always seemed to have a mailbox stuffed with mail. It must have been nice to be acquainted with people who had the time to sit around writing letters.

Stopping in to check for mail was one way of bumping into guys who might not live in your dormitory or your area of the SPS campus, which was somewhat spread out, yet intimate at the same time. On nice days there were always guys loitering outside the post office socializing, just as people hung out on the block on Edmondson Avenue outside Club Astoria, but here you did not have to worry about any of these guys pulling out a pistol or shotgun and clearing out the corner.

It didn't take long to learn how to get around SPS. At first it was only necessary that I know a few pertinent buildings, the Schoolhouse, the Gymnasium, the Rectory, the Upper, the Lower School where the first and second formers lived and where the school store was, and the Sheldon Library which was perched near the Library Pond and effectively represented by the very gracious Ms. Locke, a school librarian. She was pretty cool.

Bit-by-Bit, I branched out to learn every corner of SPS: Hargate where we went for instruction in the arts, the Squash Courts, the Gordon Hockey Rink, the Infirmary and Memorial Hall where plays, films, musical instruction and graduation were held.

There was nothing to be afraid of anywhere in Millville. It was a good place for quiet contemplation, long moody walks, communion with the earth, all of which (unknowingly at first) I was inclined to do. Standing and looking around at such a beautiful place, you can't help thinking, "This is not Harlem Park."

Listening to music turned out to be one of my greatest comforts during my first year. The occasional sounds of familiar R&B artists helped to make me feel connected to Edmondson Avenue and all my friends back in Harlem Park. I wanted to evoke the basement house parties and hot nights spent sitting on those cool, white, row house marble steps.

I knew that I was now a very changed person and what I was experiencing here at SPS would substantially change the direction my life would take, but for now, I still fervently loved my old neighborhood. Living there had made me strong. I would need that strength to get on here.

Third-formers were required to be in bed with lights out at 9:00

p.m. I never got into the practice of sneaking around the dorm or the campus at night, looking for mischief like some of the other boys. Therefore, at 9:00 p.m., I was about ready to crawl under the covers.

Outside my window, it is brutally quiet with no hint of traffic noises, no echoes of gunfire or people yelling and fighting in the distance. It always seemed to me to be freezing cold, with a blanket of deep snow carpeting everything. Yet, my room at SPS was always warm and cozy. I had seen heavy snowstorms back in Baltimore, but when it snowed heavily here, it could be formidable, as well as breathtakingly beautiful.

Ensconced in my warm bed, I think about the many cold nights that I had to endure inside 1315 Edmondson Avenue when there was no money for heating oil. I would then consider that my family was still dealing with such privations while I was here, warm and well fed. That thought gives me some degree of discomfort.

Nearly every night I lie in the dark on my stomach, chin in my pillow, my fingers turning the radio dial, scanning for some Black music, anything. At that time, I thought listening to so-called 'White music' was a precursor to becoming 'White', and I wasn't going to fall for that, no matter how much I liked the song.

There was very little R&B music to hear so far north, and the nearest Black station, in Boston, was too far away to be picked-up with my cheap radio. Sometimes I might hear some Johnnie Mathis or Ray Charles. They weren't my favorites but I was grateful for anything.

Drifting off to sleep I ask myself, "Is this the better life?"

*****

CHAPTER 36 – NELSON

Early in that first year, I began hanging out with Mike Nelson, the black guy from Pittsburgh. Nelson was a smart guy too, maybe even as smart as Mike Russell was, but I found him to be much more irreverent than Mike Russell and therefore a lot more fun. Generally, Nelson was a year ahead of both Mike Russell and me in several subjects.

He told me he had been at another private day school before coming to St. Paul's School. Nelson was very light-skinned and had the fluffy kind of hair that could be fashioned into a big round Afro encircling his soft round face. He was surely smarter than I was, but I was a lot meaner and tougher than he was.

We competed in everything. Typically, Nelson won the mental games and I won the physical. Sometimes I might score a win in the mental games, but Nelson was almost never able to beat me in a one-on-one physical match-up. When we played one-on-one basketball, I don't remember him ever beating me. I would not allow it.

Everyone would get a good laugh from the way Nelson and I walked.

We both walked quickly and bobbed from side to side, making us look like penguins when we were walking side-by-side. I was always making fun of what I perceived as Nelson's clumsiness. He, of course, did not see himself that way.

During the winters at SPS, you were always walking on an underlying layer of ice on the grounds because we got lots of snow and it was often cold. Nelson and I decided to hold a contest to see who could fall the fewest times during the winter. Nelson was out of the contest after only one snowstorm. I did not fall very much.

It was Nelson who taught me how to fashion a knot in my one tie. That was after he made fun of me for wearing the clip-on tie. During the first week of school, Nelson also recommended that I read The Catcher in the Rye. He told me that it would give me a good idea of what the boarding school experience was all about and he was absolutely correct.

I devoured The Catcher in the Rye in only a few days, and for the first time I felt I had a clearer understanding of the big picture at work in a place like SPS. Varying shades of all the characters that Holden Caulfield described at Pency Prep were present in the boys that I was seeing here at SPS, with quite a few originals here, to boot.

Of course, Holden Caulfield was a sick puppy, but I loved his story nonetheless and I almost felt as though his story could be my story. When I was no longer a student at St. Paul's and looking back on my time here, I wanted my SPS story to be as original and funny as Holden Caulfield's story was. If nothing else, Holden's story was a cautionary tale on how not to become too self-absorbed, the way I felt many of the boys here were.

It also gave me a hint into what their lives at home might be like. I thought it was interesting that Holden's family lived in an apartment. That was a different idea of wealthy people for me, choosing to live in an apartment when you could easily afford a house. I suppose that when you're wealthy, you can do as you please.

After reading The Catcher in the Rye, I resolved to avoid letting anything here at SPS make me crazy, to maintain my sense of humor and most importantly, to never be afraid to leave. Pency Prep, the prep school that Holden Caulfield described, sounded like a nice place (as SPS is a nice place), but it didn't suit Holden.

I would be watchful in an effort to be certain that this school, this experience, was suitable for me. Thus, I gave myself the freedom to fail, which was liberating and took away some of the fear of failure, although I was reasonably confident that ultimately I would not.

After that book recommendation, I trusted Nelson's judgment a good deal, but not blindly. The next book he recommended, Fahrenheit 451, did not appeal to me after the first few pages, and unfortunately, to this day, I have yet to pick it up again. I followed-up The Catcher in the Rye with A Separate Peace, thus rounding out my 'books about private school' reading, for the time being.

Nelson was thinking about going out for the SPS cross-country team, and he mentioned an annual cross-country race called the Thanksgiving Turkey Crawl, in which anyone could participate.

"You don't know why they call it the Turkey Crawl? That's a dumb name. Why would they call it that, everyone will be running ...right? So like...are you supposed to lose or something?" I asked Nelson.

"I don't know man, but anybody can run. It's only like a couple of miles or something"

I asked him, "You planning to run in it?"

"Maybe," he replied.

"Shit Nelson, I could beat your slow ass." I told him.

"Yeah but it's not about speed. In cross-country you have to have mental toughness, so your ass would lose," he countered.

"I've never run cross-country, but I bet that I can beat most of these boys here, and even if I can't beat some of them, I know that I would definitely place higher than you Nelson." I said.

"It looks like we're going to have to run that race then?" said Nelson.

"Looks like!" I nodded.

The day of the race, about 140 people gathered at the starting line, students, faculty, families, SPS staff, and even dogs. This was the sort of community event that the people here at SPS lived for. Here, in the cathedral of the great outdoors we could all commune together in a wholesome, healthy way. Looking around at them, I was certain that I had a chance to win this thing - while they were all standing around communing.

If you were one of the top finishers of the race, the prize was a specially baked cake - Free Food! McDonald, a white guy, who was the star of the cross-country team and expected to win, did not look like so much to me with his long stringy dark hair, his sweaty bandana and skinny frame. I figured that winning this race would be a good way to begin making a name for myself at this school.

At the sound of the gun, McDonald and the other cross-country boys jumped off the starting line – smokin', and I did not see any of them again after that. I found myself with the main pack of runners practically sprinting for most of about 200 yards. Then there was this slight upward grade in the road, a deceptively long and hard stretch that wore a lot of us down.

We were all breathing hard and losing ground and we had likely not even run a half-mile yet. Nelson was right; this was largely about mental toughness. I was beginning to realize that I was a sprinter, not a long distance runner. It was brutal.

I kept trying to make myself run, but my legs were so fucking heavy and like many others I would simply walk a lot, still I knew that there were a good number of people behind me. However, there was about a foot of frozen snow on the ground and once we left the plowed main road, we had to slog through this long unplowed meadow in the countryside, which was even more brutal.

Near the finish, you had to run through some pine trees and down a very steep narrow path. Muthafuckas' would come staggering out of the woods and exhaustedly slide down that steep incline on a bed of pine needles, and then with aching muscles, struggle to their feet for a sprint to the finish.

Once I crossed the finish line and stopped, cramps hit me in back of both thighs at the same instant and I collapsed to the ground. In trying to break my fall, I stretched out my arms and caught cramps in my arms. All around others were doing the same, it was pretty comical and I guess, pathetic.

When I was finally able to get to my feet, so that I could sit down safely, I threw up all over the snow. It was fucking ugly, but - I knew that I had beat Nelson.

Later, when they posted the results, I saw that I had placed 59th in the race. Nelson placed in the 90's.

"I don't want to hear shit, I kicked your ass!" I gloated with Nelson.

Those white boys were a lot tougher than I thought, too. McDonald did win his cake. When they presented it to him at a seated meal in the dining hall, he looked fucking happy about it.

It wasn't going to be as easy as I thought to find my niche here, but I was sure something else would come up. That race helped me to see that I was not as physically or mentally tough as I imagined, and I acknowledged that I was going to have to work on that if I was going to make any kind of noise here.

*****

CHAPTER 37 - FOOLISH PRIDE

Simply coping with the New England winter helped to make me tougher, mind and body. Some days the wind coming off the Lower School Pond would howl and bite ferociously when you were on your way to morning chapel. The wind-chill factor could cause the temperature to register an incredible 50 degrees below zero, and that winter I was running around SPS in that thin black trench coat.

It must have been difficult for people to see me so inadequately dressed for such severe weather, but I did not complain. Since many of the white boys would be outside in only a sports coat on many of those cold days, I suspect many people comforted themselves with the thought that I was only someone else who enjoyed a good brisk day.

To make matters worse, that trench coat kept tearing in various places. I learned how to sew because I had to repair constantly the almost daily rips and tears that would develop; I fix the right arm and the left one rips open. There would be no point in writing home and asking for another coat.

One day my old boy Greg Vail and his roommate Sergio Uribe came to my room carrying a green wool winter coat.

"One of the guys just got a new coat and he said you could have this one if you want. Don't argue with me, you are going to take this," said Greg.

"So you are just going to tell me what I'm going to do," I replied.

"Yeah, we are," said Sergio.

I looked the coat over. It was a nice wool coat, a little preppie, but well made, probably very expensive.

"I don't know if it's my style fellas."

They were doing their best to help me but I wasn't making it easy for them. I can't imagine where I picked up such traits. My parents were never the type to declare, "We don't accept charity." If someone was willing to lend us a hand, we knew how to accept it graciously.

Greg and Sergio stood there looking at one another, seemingly at a loss as to what more they could do or say to convince me, without offending me. Many of these boys up here had no experience dealing with black folk on a daily basis and their discomfort was sometimes amusing to me.

Finally, Greg said to me, "Well, you do with it what you want," and they left.

I did not ever wear it. Even now, I cannot say why. They were only trying to help. Soon after that, Greg brought me a couple of very nice sport coats that he got from one of the other sixth-formers, and later a few ties. Those I did wear. It helped me to save face. It was becoming uncomfortably embarrassing having to wear the same things to class every day.

However, that business with the coats was clear evidence that there were some very decent boys among the white boys. Greg was a good old boy. I did not spend much time around him, after all, he was a sixth-former, but it was obvious that he had kept his eye on me.

Sometimes I would stop by his room with some of the other third-formers for a chat, but not very often. Those older guys had a way of ganging up on you, making you feel really dumb, and I didn't like that. There were already enough things for me to feel stupid about at SPS.

*****

CHAPTER 38 - THANKSGIVING

I chose not to go home at Thanksgiving. I told everyone that it seemed (to me) like too much traveling for only four days. The transparent truth was, had I gone home for the four-day holiday break, my parents would have had to pay my airfare. That was a part of the scholarship agreement. I was not going to ask my folks to do that.

It was a deserted campus practically, with those of us remaining behind all crammed into one or two dorms. Luckily, one of those dormitories was big ol' Simpson House, so I did not have to stay in a strange room like some of the others. Nelson was one of a couple of other black guys who also remained at SPS. Practically everyone else had gone home or gone to visit at someone else's home. Mike Russell was able to afford to go home.

With nothing specific to do, Nelson and I roamed the campus, played basketball, waited impatiently for meal times and sometimes listened to music in Bill Woodward's room. Woodward was a sixth-former. I liked him a lot. He had a biting deadpan wit, yet he was really mellow, not at all a mean person.

He was always telling me that I had a lot of mouth, but he seemed amused by me. When he graduated at the end of that year, he signed my copy of the yearbook with one line, 'To – the mouth!' That made me proud.

He had a nice stereo and he had given me permission to use it over the Thanksgiving break. Nelson and I would sit around in his room listening to his records. Nelson taught me to play a card game called Setback, the only card game that I have ever enjoyed and we played it constantly. He usually won.

Alone, I would sometimes stop to look into guys' rooms, which was a violation of privacy and contrary to school rules, but all I did then was to stand in the room and look around at their things and maybe open a drawer or two. The very fine quality of their many possessions was impressive; gold watches, 100% wool blazers, silk ties, rich leather loafers and complete sound systems. I owned nothing of such quality craftsmanship, and these were the things that they casually left behind, laying about.

I even took a long look in Mike Russell's room. Mike had some nice stuff. My feeling was that his parents had probably gone out and spent a ton of money once Mike got into SPS, to ensure that their boy did not have anything to feel ashamed of at that fancy boarding school. His things were good quality stuff. Much nicer than anything that I owned. I wish I'd come from a family like his. They could afford airfare to bring him home for Thanksgiving.

Being on the campus during the Thanksgiving break wasn't so bad. The place was quiet, serene actually. I was learning to appreciate the beauty of the grounds and autumn in New Hampshire, the smell of cold damp country air. It was a chance to get a sense of the place without the distractions of the people and the constant buzz of activity that was the norm when school was in session.

There was an area below the dormitories, a large flat kind of meadow near a stream, which sometimes flooded and froze over. It was a place where you could ice-skate with no fear of breaking through what was a relatively thin layer of ice over solid ground, something that kept me away from the Lower School Pond skating rinks. There was no way I was going skating over a deep pond no matter how thick or safe they said the ice was.

Caught up in the whole preppie thing, I had already tried out my hockey skates at the in-door Gordon Hockey Rink before the hockey season was underway, when you could still get in there, but I couldn't yet skate very well. However, once the school put some hockey-boards on that ice in that meadow, Nelson and I spent the holiday ice-skating, pushing around hockey sticks and pucks. Nelson had talked me into trying it. We had it all to ourselves.

Turville, the black kid from Rhode Island came out to skate with us on the final day of vacation and we played a pick-up hockey game. Turville wasn't especially athletic and left complaining that I was too rough because I kept smashing him against the boards. The speed and the physical contact in hockey were very appealing to me. I was shoving Turville all over that ice. I did the same thing with Nelson. Nelson even skated clumsily, I thought.

At the end of the short break for Thanksgiving, I could skate very well. I think I liked the idea of going back to Harlem Park and telling people that I could ice-skate; a skill that very few people in Harlem Park could claim.

Being able to stop on the ice was a big issue for me and for a couple of days I fell on my ass until I figured it out. Now, I could stop on a dime! I was becoming a real Paulie. Greg, my old boy was right. This was pretty sweet.

With Thanksgiving over, everyone streamed back onto campus. The few short weeks we now faced before Christmas break were more of the same, a succession of routine days consisting of classes, study, sports and meals, nothing particularly outstanding. I was learning everything; everything was new, but other than my struggles with class work I sailed through those few weeks without notable incident.

A single room in an isolated corner turned out to be a good thing for me. I probably needed the solitude. At SPS, you must study diligently because study is the essence of life here. I wondered how someone had divined that I would need a certain amount of seclusion, or was that a fluke.

I thought that I was studying hard. However, I now know that I was not studying effectively. Holed up in my room, I was reading the study material, putting in the time, but my instructors were telling me that there was no real reflection in what I was doing. I was falling into my customary habit of only trying to memorize and then restate facts, neglecting the less obvious clues surrounding an issue, the information that might prompt a deeper understanding.

Here they repeatedly wanted to know specifically what I thought about a thing, how did it make me feel and why? I would receive papers back with the same comment, "Tell me what you think."

Here, they were asking a good deal more of me and it was frustrating. In my work, I needed to learn to express what was in my gut. I wasn't used to foraging that deeply inside, and while I did feel anxious about the possibility of failure, I was sure that I was not yet overwhelmed. I was going to be ok. I could do this.

Nonetheless, after a few weeks, when the next big holiday (Christmas break) finally came around, I was anxious to return home.

*****

CHAPTER 39 – CHRISTMAS BREAK

All semester I had been looking forward to Christmas break and returning to Harlem Park the conquering hero. I had hoped to be looking and sounding as polished as the ABC students I had seen the two years prior. I'd made a promise to myself to maintain a profile of low-key sophistication, thus avoiding the mistakes I'd made after returning from summer school at Dartmouth.

This time, I behaved like the perfect Paulie. It worked well. The school administration at Harlem Park welcomed me and gave me the run of the school, as did my former teachers. That felt good. It now seemed that I had a lot more friends at the school than I remembered.

Mrs. Fing, my former guidance counselor was full of pride and overjoyed to see me. I went to see her first. You would have thought that I was her own son; she was so excited. She was a good barometer for determining how much of a change my short time away had wrought. Mrs. Fing thought that I had matured considerably, and even I could hear it in my voice as I spoke with her. I felt confident, and I felt grateful to her. I would not let her down.

My former classmates were much less impressed with my being around, something that I expected. It didn't matter. I remained humble and quiet. Most of the day I accompanied the guys from class to class, and except for the fuss every teacher felt compelled to make on my initial entrance into their classrooms things proceeded well enough. One of my former teachers did create somewhat of a strain on my attempts at a low profile, but Mr. Williams always did have a penchant for stirring things up.

He was a gym teacher, and guys had nicknamed him Tittie-neck, because of some rolls of fat at the base of his neck. Despite the jokes about him, Mr. Williams was beloved in a macho kind of way, even by the many boys he popped on their naked ass with a towel.

He would also wait at the entrance to the shower, and randomly select guys as they came out. Holding a clean white towel, he would grab a guy and vigorously rub the kid's neck and upper back with that towel, and if any dirt was on it, he would send your ass right back in the shower repeatedly until you came out clean.

However, here I am again inside Harlem Park's familiar funky-assed wrestling room with my former classmates, who like me were now in the 9th grade. Mr. Williams is managing the class using his trademark growl.

"All of you boys have a seat on the mat...and we will finish going over the rules of the sport of golf."

That's when he finally noticed me sitting among the group.

"Well. It is nice to see you young man... How are they treating you in that school up there? What's it called...? Oh, Saint Paul's School - all boys... you look good young man...you look good. Now...I want the rest of you boys to take a real good look at this young man...Here's a young man who has made up his mind to make something of himself...

230

This is a young man with discipline and a respect for himself and other people..."

Meanwhile, I am trying to find some space underneath that stinking wrestling mat where I can crawl and hide, while the other guys are groaning and cursing me under their breath, but there was going to be no relief for any of us.

"...And I hope that all of you boys here will learn from the example of this young man and begin to work harder at improving your minds and your bodies so that you can..."

As usual, once he got started Mr. Williams could go on this way for a painfully long time; however, thank god it finally did come to an end.

"...So if I can continue with our discussion of golf, I would like someone here to tell me what we call it when a golfer is one stroke over par... Does anyone here know...?"

"That's called a bogey... I think." answers Ricardo, who is still a troublemaker, but like I said, he was a pretty smart guy otherwise; especially if it involved mathematics.

"That is correct young man...it is good to see that someone has been paying attention. Now can anyone here tell me what we call it when the golfer is two over par on a hole...anyone can answer...? I am sure someone here knows what this is called...anyone...anyone at all...a one over par is a bogey...what is a two over par?"

"It's called a booger," blurts out Andre with his finger stuck in his nose. That sets off a torrent of laughter.

"Now this is an example of what I have been talking about...here is a young man who is not going to make anything of..."

I could feel that I was changed. Now, it was even relatively easy to deal with wise guys like Andre and Quentin. They were tough guys and they got the girls, but now I had something very good going for me. They were no threat to me and I posed no threat to them. I could simply enjoy them now.

I spent several days of my long Christmas break hanging with my former classmates at Harlem Park Junior High. I even went over to Harlem Park Elementary School so that they could gush over me as well.

*****

CHAPTER 40 - TURVILLE,
SCRIBNER & TEA DANCES

During Christmas break, I purchased a couple of posters to hang on the walls of my room in Simpson House. My walls had remained bare during that entire first semester, a fact that had not registered with me until one day Turville came sauntering into my room.

"Thank god you put something up on your walls? It's was always so depressing in here, and why don't you open the windows and let some light in."

"Why don't you take your muhfuckin' ass back to the third floor, Turville," I responded.

Of course, he was right. My room was still as drab and nearly as empty and unadorned as it had been on my first day, it still looked like a dreary prison cell. I was fairly conscientious about spending the money allotted to me by my scholarship. After paying for books, the laundry service, sports equipment, etc. and the occasional pizza from Chuck's, there was not much money left for sprucing up my environment. The occasional pizza was a priority.

Turville was an oddity to me; he was a black guy from the state of Rhode Island. It was hard for me to imagine that there were any black folk in Rhode Island. Of course, I'd never been there and until I'd met Turville, I'd barely recognized that state's existence.

Turville asked me, "How come you're so hostile all the time? Why do you have to talk like that?"

"That's because every time you come in here, you come in with that superior attitude, always criticizing everything."

"Wait a second, that's not true. When did I ever criticize you before?" he asks.

"You embarrassed me man, showing off." I replied.

"When, what did I say?"

"You don't remember the day you walked into my room with Scribner and Van Dusen, and you yelled out, 'God it smells in here!'"

"Ah come on, I was kidding. You know I was just kidding," he pleaded.

"Yeah well, everybody didn't grow up playing drums in Up With People in Rhode Island like you Turville." I'm not sure where I was going with that remark.

Up With People was a feel-good multi-racial musical act that had received some national attention. Turville played drums with them. He was an excellent drummer. I once saw him play a drum solo in the basement of Memorial hall and he was amazing, the crowd was gyrating.

"What do you mean by that?" he demanded.

"Look, I'll admit that my socks and sneaks may have been kickin' a little bit, but I don't have all the clothes you have Turville. Sometimes I have to wear things more than once to save money on the cost of laundry. It's not like I'm behaving like Nick Davidge down the hall, with a big poster of a pig on my wall and my room looking and smelling like a dumpster, " I explained.

Nick Davidge was infamous for his carefully cultivated pigsty of a room and was somewhat of an annoyance when I had to inspect his room in the mornings. By this time, I had become one of the people who inspected the other boys' rooms in the morning, a rotating responsibility for those of us who generally passed inspection, which I usually did. I mean, there was nothing in my room to inspect. All I had to do was to be certain that I swept my room every day.

"Well, c'mon. You know I'm not like that. I wasn't trying to make you look bad. Hey, I'm Black just like you. Sometimes I just say things."

"That's exactly what I'm saying," I fired back pointedly.

"Hey, I'm sorry. That's not how I am. C'mon, you know that." he countered, sounding like Bill Cosby.

"Yeah, but you're careless and carelessness can get a person hurt. You were trying to impress them, but you need to consider other people's feelings."

This was a useful lesson I had learned from time spent around dangerous people: It is important to be conscious of how you talk to people; words have power and can get you killed if you encounter the wrong person.

While I understood that there were few dangerous people here at St. Paul's School, I did not want to let my guard down. I wanted to maintain that razor's edge, and that meant that I could not allow Turville to get away with showing me disrespect.

Turville and I had had several such moments of discord between us but I basically liked him. He was just a little uptight and needed to learn how to deal with the brothers. He was Black, but it didn't appear that he'd had very much experience with that.

One of the posters I purchased boasted an image of Malcolm X, looking stern and determined above the slogan 'By any means necessary!' The other poster showcased the singer Dionne Warwick. It showed her performing, her curvy frame encased in a tight fitting sequined gown. Dionne Warwick was not as soulful as say... Aretha Franklin, but her voice had a certain something that I found sexy.

One evening when I was in my room studying, Blair Scribner walked by my door, and then back peddled to peek in. I liked Scribner a lot. He was from a high-powered New York publishing family but he was very unassuming and had an endearing way of always seeming slightly confused, but I suspect he never was, really. We talked often.

He was unabashedly curious about my life, my speech, anything, everything, but he was never insulting or condescending. He was secure enough in himself to even make fun of me when it was just the two of us – although never publicly, even when sometimes I deserved to be made fun of.

"Wow man, is that your Mom?" he gasps.

"What the fuck are you talking about Scribner?"

I now cursed liberally, especially after I learned that these white guys, with all their alleged sophistication, used profanity all the time. They used some of the words differently, but they used them often. That one kid Graeme Boone had used the word shat for the past tense of shit. That was a new one for me.

"No really, is that a picture of your mother on your wall?" Scribner says excitedly.

"Wait a second Scrib'. You mean that black and white poster on the wall?" I can't believe what I'm hearing. Did he really believe that anyone kept a poster-sized picture of their mother on their wall?

"No, I mean, yes, I mean – I 'm not trying to say anything sexy about your mother. I'm just saying that if that is your mother, she's beautiful."

'You're fuckin' kidding me, right?" I asked that the way the white guys said it.

"It's a compliment," he said defensively.

Scribner knew there was always a chance that I might decide to punch him or grab him in a neck-hold. I got a kick out of roughhousing with Scribner, and Clint Van Dusen and Nelson. I could nearly handle all three of them at once.

We would wrestle in the hallways on the second floor of Simpson and the three of them would try to take me down. I would always give them a good fight; after all, I had spent countless hours wrestling with tough guys like Tony Stewart and Alfred back home. These guys were a pushover, and just as Tony Stewart would do to me, I would occasionally issue them a little serious pain, to let them know who was boss. They thought I was nuts, punching them in the chest or slamming them to the ground, but we had fun.

"I only wish that she was my Mom Scribner, with all the money she must have. You don't know who she is?"

He studies the poster more closely and says, "Who is she?"

"That's Dionne Warwick muhfucka'. She's a singer. Obviously you have never heard of her?"

"Oh yeah, I think I've heard about her. I thought she was white?"

"Youse a stupid muhfucka' Scribner."

"Why do you talk like that?" he says suddenly.

"Because you thought Dionne Warwick was my mother." I reply.

'No, I mean you're always going around saying stuff like, 'Youse a liar.' 'Youse a liar.' You don't really talk like that – do you?"

"Shut up Scribner."

Scribner, with his tussled hair and whiny nasal voice was a funny guy. It's hard to say why, but I was never uncomfortable around him. I was always glad to see him. He was a very decent fellow. I felt Scribner liked me, and unfortunately for him, that meant he had no choice but to put up with my aggressive behavior.

He was the sort of white boy I was encouraged to get to know, by all the good people in Harlem Park responsible for me being here. The assumption being, that he was one of those upwardly mobile social contacts that would translate into a 'cushy' job later in life. I mean, Scribner Publishing, are you kidding me?

Scribner always kept cash sitting in a mug on his desk in his room, and I would sometimes come in and ask him if I could have some of the money. I would take some of it no matter what he said. He complained, but he usually allowed it.

Despite such indignities, he respectfully tolerated me and all the other black guys, generally. I sometimes wondered how he really felt about us, but I never dwelled upon it too deeply. At the time it didn't matter all that much, since he had no power over me. I just knew that I liked the guy.

It was much the same with Clint Van Dusen, except Van Dusen thoroughly embraced all the black guys. Van Dusen was the son of some influential judge from Philadelphia who had been involved in some landmark local desegregation decision, and later nearly made it all the way to the Supreme Court Bench.

Van Dusen was always coming around and hanging about the black guys. You felt that he found us fascinating, which probably had something to do with the occupations of his father, the judge. Van Dusen had a strange awkward manner about him. He seemed so unsure of himself, yet so good-natured. It was impossible not to like him. I remember hearing that after Van Dusen had graduated SPS and gone to Princeton, his first girlfriend there was a black girl. Go Van Dusen!

All in all, living daily among these very privileged kids was fun. No one was overtly racist in my presence and I felt that my inclusion in campus life was limited only by my own personal reservations. There were many opportunities to get to know some of the guys reasonably well and I did make some friends when I wasn't keeping to myself, something that was becoming a habit with me. I was becoming a loner.

There was only one time during that first year when I might have questioned whether I wasn't being insulted. That was when three of the white guys came to me and asked me to help them put together a dance routine for a campus talent show. For a moment, I questioned if this wasn't a case of the stereotyped idea that all black folk gots rhythm. However, they insisted that they had only seen me dancing at one of the Tea Dances and figured that I could make them look good. They were going to lip sync to a song and wanted some cool soul-group steps to compliment the song. By then, I knew the three of them well, and of course, I would help them.

I had a blast teaching them those dance steps even though none of them could dance very well. When they performed the routine before an audience, dressed in dark suits and sunglasses, they were a big hit and I was proud of them. They let everyone know that I had helped them.

In a way, I was pleased and not a little surprised that they had asked me to help them, rather than Mike Russell. I liked to think I was the better dancer and since I was from the 'hood in Baltimore, I was supposed to be.

When there were Tea Dances at SPS, Mike Russell and I both looked forward to them, even though there were hardly ever any black girls present and we had to dance to rock and roll music, rather than rhythm and blues. Mike and I both liked to dance and both of us could dance so much better than most of the white boys at SPS. That did not require much.

All the white boys would dust themselves off, slick down their hair and await the arrival of the girls, who arrived on several buses from a number of different private all girl schools. Lower Schooler's could not attend.

The dances were, generally, stiffly pathetic affairs and took place in the Gates Room, which was a bi-level trophy room and lounge attached to the Gymnasium; not a bad room for a dance actually. Yet, tea dances were fun in a very wooden sort of way.

There were plenty of chaperones and no one could leave the vicinity of the Gates Room with any of the girls, but the older boys found ways to get around that. The Gymnasium/Gates room/Athletic Cage was a big complex with lots of nooks and crannies where the guys and gals could sneak away for a prohibited smoke or grope.

It was such a pleasant surprise when one or two black girls were in attendance. If a black girl showed up, there was the chance that Mike and I might get a kiss and a grope during the evening. Lots of the white girls who came to the tea dances were eager to dance with us, but little more than that. That was good enough for us. We just wanted to have some fun.

At one of those tea dances, I met this incredibly beautiful black girl by the name of Kelly. She and Holly, her equally stunning older sister, were from a very well to do family. Both of them had lovely hair and petite curvy figures. Back in Harlem Park guys would have been tripping all over themselves trying to get with them.

Kelly was very smart and sophisticated, highly sought after, and it was too much to hope that we would be attracted to one another; but we were. We danced together several times, sat down and talked and ended up exchanging addresses at the end of the evening. There was no goodnight kiss or anything, a detail I would rather no one knew. I was a little in awe of her, and I knew that Mike Russell fancied her as well.

Some time after that evening, she wrote to me. It was a very sweet letter telling me about her days at her boarding school, but there was not an ounce of sentiment in it. I suppose that disappointed me, and I wrote to her complaining of the blandness of her letter to me. It was unbelievably pushy of me and I have no idea what I was thinking, but I really ticked her off!

She then sent me this letter in which she wrote about "the hot breathless nights she spent dreaming of me, and she didn't know how she had survived without me all these years." It was dripping with indignant, sticky-sweet sarcasm. I did not get any more letters from her, but I did see her around at other tea dances occasionally. Mercifully, she never mentioned my lunacy. She was very classy.

CHAPTER 41 - MIKE AND LOUIE

A place like SPS is all about academics. People spend a lot of money to send their children here and nothing is more important than learning, which one understands after any time here. We were constantly fretting about our grades. In my case, so much of my personal angst surrounding my grades at SPS was a result of my interactions with two people, Mr. Grant and Mike Russell.

Mr. Grant held Mike up as an example of what I should be doing as a student at this very elite school. Mike, rightfully, was trying to be the very best student he could be and was succeeding spectacularly. They were both doing their respective jobs – but they were killing me.

Before I had arrived on this campus, back home in Harlem Park, I felt that I was capable of the kind of impact that Mike was making, but I soon learned that such a thing was not possible. I did not have the proper temperament or talent. Such a realization did not particularly discourage me, but my self-confidence had admittedly taken a beating. However, I now knew that success for me would look very different than it would for a guy like Mike. Somehow, I would have to find a way to fashion something that was uniquely mine.

I had none of his considerable ability to connect with adults, for one thing. At Harlem Park Junior High that was not necessary. The sheer size of the student body at Harlem Park severely limited any substantial contact with the teachers, and then, at the end of the day, everyone went home. Here at SPS, I felt as though I was 'on stage' 24/7, school was never out.

When I got here, I was looking around, sizing up people and fantasizing about being this incredible black guy who shows up on the campus fresh from the inner city and dazzles everyone; a star athlete, scholar and all around swell guy. I continued believing that until the moment that I went outside onto the Quadrangle commons and observed a pick up game of touch football in progress. Right then, the adjustments to my fantasy began.

My first acquaintance with Mike Russell's substantial athletic ability came on that second day at SPS, when I asked to play in that touch football game. His team was throwing off to mine to start the game and Mike threw a high arching pass, which I caught. At that moment, I was thinking I would show these guys some of my speed, until I looked up to see something startling.

Before I could gather any steam to evade the oncoming rushers, I saw Mike Russell's athletic frame bearing down on me. It scared me. He was coming at me so fast and hard, that I knew I had no chance of eluding him. He looked like a charging bull and I was really worried lest he crash into me at that speed, which could only result in me being hurt. Right then, I knew that I would not be the fastest guy at this school, and I was pretty fast. I was counting on that. I would have to find something else to grab some attention here.

Mike had all the requisite tools. At 14 years old, he was nearly 6' tall, about 165 lbs, fast and coordinated. His skin was very dark and he had perfectly white teeth, a good-looking guy. He had come to SPS a week before the start of school to train with the varsity football team. Not a lot of third-formers were developed enough (physically) to play with those older guys, but Mike was invited.

My first night at SPS, when I saw Mike in the lounge of Simpson House, the Housemaster Mr. Kellogg had us all play a game of charades, another first for me. Mike was giving the clue, and he stood before us and beamed a great big toothy smile. Instantly I guessed, 'The Shadow of Your Smile' and that was the right answer.

With Mike's dark skin and that smile, it all came together for me. I had played that song on trumpet at Harlem Park. He couldn't believe that I got it so quickly, but I was thinking something else. I was thinking that the white kids may have known the answer, but did not want to risk offending the nice (and very dark) black man, by associating him with the word 'Shadow'. That same thought had occurred to me.

Mike and I hit it off, but that did not mean that we would hang out together all the time. Mike studied a good deal and moved on a different plane than I. He was much more of a social being, so he spent more time than I ever could with a variety of people, even faculty members.

He was in great demand and just the sort of black person the white folks hoped their children would meet, if they had to meet some black boys. He was safe, civilized and completely non-threatening.

Mike and I could not have been more different from one another. He was from a tiny rural town on the Eastern Shore of Maryland. His was a small close-knit family; and while they were not wealthy, they seemed so when compared to my family and me. Like I said, Mike had some nice things, some nice clothes and his folks sent him frequent care packages full of food, clothing and other goodies.

As I've said, he was highly motivated, intelligent, poised and this quickly made him the darling of the faculty, coaches, student-body, everyone. Louis Grant, who is black and a member of History Department as well as de facto faculty adviser to all black students, was very pleased with Mike. Mike received good grades, followed the rules and was polite and respectful of everyone.

It was my opinion that Mr. Grant was a black man who, despite all his outward black-revolutionary trappings, was probably not truly comfortable with his ethnicity. Outwardly, he seemed to be the personification of the self-aware, committed-to-the-cause kind of black brother, teaching the rest of us about our people's history and obligations, but I never believed any of it.

The more I saw of him the more I thought he seemed kind of tortured, being often sullen and angry one minute, manic and playful the next. I knew nothing of his background but I wondered where he was from and how he had grown up. Of course, I was only a young black boy, but for some reason deep in my gut, I just did not trust him. He seemed angry about something.

In a creeping sort of way, Louis Grant was becoming an imposing presence among us. It was his job to keep tabs on all the black guys and as the year progressed, he discharged this duty with an oppressive efficiency, taking advantage of every opportunity to remind those of us who were not doing so well (mainly me) that we needed to work harder - and he seemed so nice at first.

He looked every bit the scholarly Black revolutionary with his afro hairstyle, bearded goatee and African dashikis that he sometimes wore. He had a habit of clearing his throat before speaking, as a way of ensuring that he had your complete attention.

He spoke softly and rapidly, and exuded moral and intellectual superiority. I began to see that Mr. Grant was very arrogant, and when challenged he could get mean. He had no patience for anyone he considered lazy, and it was becoming apparent to me that he thought of me as lazy.

The thing is, except for me and maybe Wiltshire and Shivers, all of the other guys were doing about as well as one could expect. However, Mr. Grant appeared to like most of the other black boys, including Wiltshire, but it was becoming increasingly clear to me that he did not especially like me.

It appeared to me that the more Mike Russell succeeded, the less Mr. Grant liked me. Mike Russell was the standard against which Mr. Grant measured all other black students. While he was usually careful to avoid comparing the rest of us to Mike specifically, we all knew how he felt.

I'm no psychologist, but any idiot could see that there was something out of whack here, but I never thought about complaining to anyone in authority about it. That would be acting like a punk.

When he was annoyed with us, he would often launch into diatribes during the meetings of our fledgling black student group. He would remind us of the great opportunity we had before us and of our responsibility to make the best of it, and how we must be mindful not to let our people or ourselves down. His examples of what constituted appropriate behavior always seemed to sound, suspiciously, exactly like Mike Russell's behavior.

That was particularly irritating for me as I struggled to make the grade, but I did not resent Mike for it. It was Mr. Grant who was the problem. He had that very silky learned voice, but he had a way of slyly belittling a person. He would likely have argued that he only had our best interest at heart, and that would have rang hollow for me. Mr. Grant was mean.

At Harlem Park, I had been a star and all the teachers, counselors and administrators were anxious to instruct me and impart their wisdom to me. I felt no such love emanating from Louie Grant. Louise Grant was the first educator I had who did not seem to adore me. That was a rude awakening for me, especially since Mr. Grant was Black. I guess

I thought that his being Black meant he might cut me a break, but I was so wrong!

I knew that I needed to develop disciplined study habits to cope with the demands of the SPS curriculum, but Mr. Grant's censure sometimes seemed more personal than constructive. For some strange reason I was more vexing to Mr. Grant than the others. I know that even Mike had trouble with some subjects, but he and some of the other black boys obviously handled it better than I did.

All of us were doing our best to behave ourselves that first year, doing our best to be like Mike, but except for me and Jose Wiltshire from NYC, the black guys who were at SPS at that time were not really hardcore inner-city guys. When I look back at the small bunch of ten or so black boys at SPS that year, Wiltshire and I were the closet thing to straight-up, inner-city, so-called ghetto niggers, but Mr. Grant seemed able to tolerate Wiltshire, despite his bad grades. He soon had no use for me.

None of this bunch of boys was bold enough to stand up against Mr. Grant and that includes me. Mr. Grant had a mean streak and I did not stand a chance against him alone. Knowing that he was not particularly enamored of me, I retreated into myself as a means of insulating myself from his judgment. That probably did not help matters.

My disdain for Mr. Grant, while not overt, was understood by nearly everyone. He could not have been happy about that. Quite enough of the other guys, white and black, found me likable enough and my refusal to bend to Mr. Grant surely served to undermine his authority. For some of the guys I was a kind of hero for my ability to get under Mr. Grant's skin. That did nothing to make my life any easier.

My powers of observation were honed by years of living in the uncertain environment of the streets of Baltimore. To get by, it is critical that you stay aware of the people around you, so that you can pick out those few who might be dangerous. It is a basic survival skill.

I observe people, and when Mr. Grant looked at me, I saw in his eyes an inexplicable loathing. I could see no reason for it, but that is how it can be. Some people don't like you because they just don't like you. Therefore, I was uneasy around him. Back home, I would not let him stand behind me at a party.

I am sure Mr. Grant had good reasons for disliking me, but I was not smart enough to understand them. Therefore, I did the only thing I could do to get back at him - I ignored him. I behaved as though he did not exist, and I know he hated that coming from me.

By the end of that first year, the grading system at SPS had changed from A's; B's; C's etc. It was now: Unsatisfactory, Pass, High Pass, Honors and High Honors. Mike was essentially an Honors and High Honors student. I was a Pass and High Pass student.

I finished the year reasonably certain that I could make it through the next three years to graduation. If I could do that, it would be an accomplishment, and now that I had been allowed to survey the field, I saw it as an achievable goal.

That is, if I could stay out of Mr. Grant's way and pass trigonometry.

*****

CHAPTER 42 – BACK IN HARLEM PARK

At St. Paul's, one of my first acts upon arrival had been to write Linda Pope's name on my desk in my dormitory room using white gauze tape. I thought that was a very romantic thing to do because it demonstrated that I was pining over the girl I had to leave behind.

Arriving back in Baltimore for the summer of 1969, I made a jolting discovery. Linda had met a guy – no, check that - Linda had met herself, "a man honey!"' At least, that is how I heard her describe him to someone at the time. Her man was a fellow who was soon heading off to Vietnam, so he was a soldier as well. There was no way to compete with that. Not to mention that after meeting the guy, James, I had no choice but to admit that he was the finest kind of human being. I liked him.

If there was any doubt in my mind that Linda was completely taken with the guy, it was erased on one hot afternoon while I was in the dining room of Linda's house and she and her man came in because he had to use the bathroom.

As Linda sat down to wait for him, we could all hear the sounds of him urinating because it was quiet and the bathroom was nearly right there in the dining room. It was somewhat of an awkward moment that became hilarious when Linda said,

"Y'all listen to that...listen to that big pee."

She was sure in love with her man. I suppose it was a good thing that I did not bear the two of them any ill will, because they were soon engaged and Linda arranged with my father Reverend Watkins to officiate at the ceremony.

Had I been a drinking man I probably would have gone out to get drunk.

Maybe not so coincidentally, my first real drink was just around the corner. Allen had a cousin who would sometimes stay at his family's house. Pete was a thin gangly fellow, with a prominent over-bite that gave a kind of goofiness to his appearance. He also had this loud giggly sort of laugh that was endearing in an odd way. Pete had a tendency to drink a good deal and he was not the most industrious person I had ever met. He was also clumsy and accident-prone.

Pete was interested in this girl across town. Once, when he went to see her, there was another guy there at her house that also liked the girl, and he and Pete got into a fight over her. Pete came out of the fray beat up, and with a broken arm. Pete then had a hell of a time getting his arm treated because he had run up hospital bills all over town in the past, which he admitted he had no intentions of paying. Eventually he found a hospital to set the arm and put a cast on it. Long before his broken arm had properly healed, Pete grew tired of wearing the cast and decided to remove it himself. He then went back to the same aforementioned girl's neighborhood, where he again got into another fight over the girl, and ended up having his arm broken, again.

My boys and I had made up our minds that we were ready to try our hands at drinking. We had spent some time hanging out with Pete at the house and he always seemed to be so funny when he was drinking; and what the hell, we figured we were not young boys anymore. At the time, everyone was drinking a new wine on the market called Boones Farm Apple Wine. It was cheap and sweet, just the right thing for a group of young guys looking for their first drink, almost like drinking soda. Pete was glad to help us out by going down to Club Astoria and getting us a bottle, one bottle, which we had pooled our money to buy.

We went down to Allen's basement to drink, and spent the rest of the evening doing a lot of giggling and staggering about. None of us ended up throwing up or anything; so I would say we handled it as well as one might expect. Now – we thought we were men.

In an effort to confirm my manhood, I continued to spend more time hanging out with a few of the older guys, like Tony, Eggy, Michael, Alfred and Wine. It was somewhat of a delicate balancing act for me as I tried to be careful to avoid any real trouble, yet not look like a total pussy either. Tony, who was willing to let me hang around, made things easier for me. He saw me as someone who was trying to get ahead, but I always felt that he was making sure that I avoided any real trouble.

Tony and his primary partner Kenard were both becoming deeply immersed in the drug culture on Edmondson Avenue. I would see Kenard up around Fulton and Baker Streets, a notoriously brutal corner known for hard-core drugs. There were some mean boys around there. It is no place I would ever be, other than just passing through.

Wisely, Kenard saw fit to keep a low profile. Whenever I would see Kenard, he was moving fast with a very businesslike attitude about him. By this time, I was certain that Kenard was dealing a little heroin and some weed. Tony was a part of the business, but mostly the weed end of it. Tony confided to me that their supplier was this guy named Maurice, who would come around driving a white Camaro.

Tony came by my steps one night accompanied by Alfred and Wine. Alfred had a new pistol he was showing off. It was a .25 caliber pistol, a small handgun. Tony was just itching to fire it. He suggested we all go up to the back alley behind Allen's house, so that he could shoot off a round.

Tony said, "You wanna come with us man, we're gonna go fire one off, test it out, smoke a joint."

"You're gonna fire that gun now...where?" I said with some interest.

"Out back on the playground man, where you think?" said Wine.

"Come on and smoke a joint." Tony said.

"That nigga too scared to come." Alfred threw in.

Then Wine adds, "If he get scared and start screamin' I gonna shoot him man."

What Wine said didn't even make sense.

"Anybody gonna get shot, it's gonna be one of y'all, 'cause I got the gun." Tony tells them.

Here was a textbook example of me about to step across a potentially dangerous line, and I was perfectly aware of it at the time; but I really wanted to see him fire that gun and they were obviously going to let me tag along.

Back in the alley, the four of us sat down on one of the metal rails and smoked a joint while passing the gun around to be examined. I took a few hits off the joint but it was a struggle to keep from coughing, so I didn't pull too deeply. I knew Wine and Alfred would laugh at me hard if I started choking. Alfred handed the pistol back to Tony, who cocked it, pointed it into the air and pulled the trigger.

I had heard gunshots many times before, but this time was different because I was sitting right next to the guy who was firing the weapon. I could not believe how loud the noise was, and even I was aware that this was a tiny gun, as guns went. At the time, I was struck by the thought that it must take nerves of steel to be involved in a gunfight and keep a grip on one's self with all that noise. It was an explosion.

In addition to hanging out with Tony and his boys on the 1300 block of Edmondson Avenue, I had found another activity that was to bring me into even more frequent contact with them.

We were all really into basketball, and since Allen and Bruce had only a passing interest in the sport, I found myself spending much less time with them and more time on the basketball courts at Harlem Park. This also brought me into closer contact with Allen's older brother Glascoe, an outstanding basketball player himself.

Basketball had become something of a passion for me at SPS, where I had tried out for the varsity team in my third form year but did not make it. I was determined to make it my fourth form year.

The year before, I had played Delphian club basketball. Now, it should be understood that (all of the stereotypes about blacks and basketball aside) during my first year at SPS I had no real skills at the game. Where I had come from in Harlem Park, we were much more interested in softball. At Harlem Park Junior High, I had played on our class basketball team, but I sat on the bench most of the time. The real players were all those boys in my class who were from the projects.

On the Delphian Club basketball team, I was not very good at the start but I got by on the strength of what I believe was a sort of 'stereotyped expectation' on the part of the white kids I played with. They seemed to assume that I should be able to play basketball well and that gave me some relative freedom to take some chances, to be on the court constantly and therefore incrementally learn the game. I was fast and could jump well but I needed to develop a good jump shot.

Most of us playing Club ball were the scrubs that couldn't make the varsity or even junior varsity teams. My coach Mr. Dunbar, and Richard Lederer who was the coach of the Old Hundreds, both worked with me after regular practice sessions to teach me a jump shot.

I guess they saw that I had some potential since I had speed and a little height. All I needed was to gain some weight and learn to shoot a jump shot. They were both good men but they always seemed to be in disagreement on the relative importance of hesitation on the jump, as opposed to back spin when shooting a jump shot. I ended up using a combination of them both.

I worked my ass off and improved my game and after a summer of playing on the courts in Harlem Park with Tony Stewart, Glascoe and those older boys and then running with these new guys at SPS, I was much improved. This year I would make the varsity, as well as a few of the other new guys. Mike Russell was also on the squad, but he had played on the varsity his freshman year when he was the only Black on the team.

*****

CHAPTER 43 - FOURTH FORM, NEW JACKS

There are moments now, in my adult life, when I wonder if it might not have been better if things at SPS had remained much the way they were that first year. In my fourth form year, a great change happened, and regrettably, I would never again spend much time with any of the white kids.

My first year at SPS, there was only about ten black and Hispanic boys enrolled in a student body of about 450 boys. We started a black student organization representing all of us, and called it the Afro-American Student Organization, with Mr. Grant serving as our group adviser.

There was nothing especially militant about our group; still three of the older black guys at SPS wanted nothing to do with it, so we had a membership of seven, which is not exactly the sort of number to cause anyone to circle the wagons, but it was a beginning.

My second year at St. Paul's School the number of black and Hispanic guys on campus nearly doubled, and St. Paul's School was never quite the same. I felt an immediate connection with a few of the more outspoken of them. Like me, they were full (or almost-full) scholarship students who came from housing projects and assorted urban badlands. The big difference was that these new guys were not quite as passive as the group of us who landed on the SPS campus my first year.

Some of them came bearing the wildest fashions popular in the Black communities of their respective cities with crazy hats and loud colors; provocative Black and Caribbean music, and many of these boys were crazy for basketball. It was party time! That Fall, whenever possible (usually Sunday mornings) we would all meet at the Gym to hang out and run ball. Everyone on campus knew the gym was where you could find most of the black guys on Sunday morning. It would be safe to say that Louis Grant was not fucking amused. Surely, some of us should be in our rooms studying.

The year before, I had arrived on the SPS campus wearing bright purple knit pants, and while I continued to wear them that year because that was essentially all I had, I admit that I did so somewhat self-consciously, on a campus where blue blazers, khaki slacks and penny loafers were more the norm.

During the summer, the Rector Matthew Warren sent me a check for fifty dollars, which he directed that I use to purchase some additional clothing. My struggles contending with the SPS dress code and last year's New England winter had not gone entirely unnoticed. That was very kind of him. It helped.

My second year, I arrived in Millville with not much more clothing, but decidedly warmer clothing. I had gone to an army-navy surplus store in Baltimore and bought a heavy corduroy jacket, a couple of warm sweaters and more jeans, underwear and socks. I needed a few more of the more standard things to augment my wild-thing colors.

Now I had some guys around who wanted to shake things up. Oh it was on now baby! We couldn't wear some of our flashier stuff in classes, but we could and would on our own free time.

I had the same big old suitcase but it was heavier this time around. This time, there were other personal items from home packed in with my clothes. I brought with me some photos and other assorted boyhood crap, things to make my room more of a home away from home. Some of that weight was my B.B. rifle, which I was able to fit into my suitcase diagonally.

I knew I wasn't supposed to bring any kind of weapon to SPS, but I couldn't resist. Given my reputation among the other guys for a certain urban toughness, I almost felt obligated to bring it. I kept it hidden away at first. I certainly didn't let my roommate Mike Russell know I had it.

Mike Russell and I began our fourth form year as roommates. Although we were very different in a host of ways, I think we went ahead and roomed together because it seemed a forgone conclusion. We liked one another, but we really did not have much in common. Mike had much more in common with many of the white boys with whom he associated than with me. I understood why that was and I swear I was ok with it. I was popular in the circles in which I moved.

We had a double room in a dormitory called Corner, one of the newer dormitories. Our room was actually two separate rooms that shared a common door inside. We used one room for sleep and the other to study.

Living with Mike demonstrated for me just why he excelled. He was very good about putting in the time hitting the books. I was lazier and much more interested in simply getting some extra sleep, so there were very few late night extra grinding (studying) sessions for me unless I was in a panic and hopelessly behind on some overdue schoolwork.

Mike and I were veterans of the SPS game and for about a minute that gave the two of us great power among the new black students, but very soon after we began meeting with the new guys and spending time with them, Mike and I began drifting apart. This was despite the fact that we remained roommates for the first semester of our fourth form year.

At the start of the semester, Mike Shivers, Mike Nelson, Mike Russell and me had gathered in the double room that Mike and I shared in a dormitory called Corner, surrounded by several of the new black boys. We were explaining the particulars of life at St. Paul's School to several of the new guys, except that now, only a year later, you had a situation where all of the nearly fifteen guys in the room were black or Hispanic. Like me, they were anxious to know what to expect. I loved the feeling of power and confidence that my knowledge of the school experience gave to me.

I felt an immediate connection with a few of the more outspoken of the new boys. I believed that this was in some way disloyal to Mike, but there was no denying that I had a lot more in common with at least a few of the new black boys. With the memories of the relative isolation that I had endured last year fresh in my mind, I desperately wanted something different this year.

With what I knew about Mr. Grant, I had no doubts that these new guys would be a new source of irritation to him, and of course, that made them all my new best friends. I no longer felt alone.

These guys were loud; they joked and cursed, did outrageously funny things and showed unabashed irreverence for much of the staid, stiff behavior that was the norm at this boarding school.

Mike, however, soon chose to maintain a guarded and discreet distance from most of the older of them. I could clearly see that he had decided to continue along the lines of the homogeneous existence we had known as third-formers, when most of us simply blended into the SPS background. That suited Mike, and why shouldn't it? It worked very well for him. It would not do for me.

More of the new boys were like me, just barely tamed and unpredictable. Mr. Grant was going to have his hands full with there being so many new black and Hispanic guys at once. I'm not sure if anyone had considered what would happen if so many black and Hispanic students were introduced into the SPS environment all at once; and even though the system did not break down, it did shudder a good deal.

By this time, I was beginning to stabilize academically and Mr. Grant spent less time hassling me, giving me a little breathing room. Yet, there continued to be the same baffling antipathy between us.

Much of my free time during my next three years at SPS, with the exception of classes and athletics, was spent almost exclusively with the other black guys. To be frank, quite often I did not even want to be around the black guys either.

Often I took long walks in the woods, or sat around in one of the many comfortable and isolated nooks around campus, often the Sheldon Library. I was discovering that I was somewhat of a loner, but it was still good having more black guys around. There were more of us now and in the spirit of the times, we had not only found a voice, but a very loud voice!

Some of the black guys with me at SPS believed that our being there was one other great social experiment of the 60's, born out of the nation's guilt over slavery and Jim Crow.

Someone had decided that it would very likely be of great benefit for these young white men at SPS to receive some exposure to young black men from the tough streets of this diverse nation, a benefit that is quite likely arguable. For many of them, this might be their only chance for such exposure. We thought it was our duty to show them what real black folk were like.

*****

CHAPTER 44 - COOK, HIPP, PRENTICE

John Cook and Robert Hipp had come from the housing projects of White Plains, NYC. The three of us roomed together for two semesters after Mike and I parted ways, and our room quickly became the central gathering place for many of the black guys at SPS. We became the core of our black student group, and were hell bent on making some sort of mark on SPS. We must have been obnoxious.

Cook had an exceptional knack for getting people to laugh, often by doing this thing called muggin' where he would twist and contort his body and face into the ugliest position possible and get the person to look at him, which would inevitably crack the guy up.

Cook used this device to great effect, particularly when he thought someone might be upset with him or needed a good laugh. Other guys also began doing this in the ensuing years. It was never something that I felt comfortable doing and I wouldn't, even if Cook were right up in my face. I thought Cook was very clever.

He was not unlike some of the toughest guys that I knew back in Harlem Park, but of course, he was much smarter. He was about 6'3" and lean, with very dark skin and a smooth complexion. He wore glasses. Cook's physical appearance belied how strong he was. He had speed as well as strength and eventually set a school record for the hundred-yard dash, as well as being a co-captain of the basketball and track teams.

Academically, Cook had rough moments like everyone else, but essentially, he did well in most of his classes. Cook had a strong interest in history and he was very interested in learning Spanish. He would later share a room with Jose Maldonado who is Hispanic. That association helped to improve Cook's Spanish.

He very quickly assumed a position of leadership among us because he was very outspoken and that was something we had been lacking, even though we did not know it. There was no doubt in anyone's mind that he would become president of our black student union. He won that position and held it the three years he was a student at SPS.

Cook's ascendancy in the pecking order may not have gone over well with the former heads of our Black student organization, but the vote for the lead position was not even close. It was Cook by a landslide.

Cook was very unpredictable. On more than one occasion he punched someone out for some slight or insult. He could be charming, but he did have an explosive temper if you fucked with him, yet we co-existed well. I gave him the space he needed.

I was probably better prepared to deal with Cook than most of the other boys. We had both spent substantial time with outlaws in our hometowns, not enough to have criminal records, but enough to know how to manage around volatile people.

Robert Hipp was from the same projects as Cook in White Plains, N.Y. and that initially placed Hipp closer to Cook than any of us.

Hipp was a much more reserved person, much closer to my own temperament.

Hipp and Cook were perfect for me. They understood the streets and they came in with this New York attitude, an aggressiveness that appealed to me. Their musical tastes were much more expansive than mine were, although my taste had changed a bit because of the constant drum of rock 'n roll I had listened to the previous year at SPS.

The two of them were listening to black rock 'n rollers like Jimi Hendrix, Buddy Miles, Sly and the Family Stone and the Chambers Brothers. In Harlem Park you were considered a freak if you were listening to rock 'n roll, although even in Harlem Park the sounds of rock 'n roll were creeping in. Michael Baskerville told me that his favorite song was Layla by Eric Clapton. It's a fantastic song, but I was still surprised to hear Michael say that. With these new guys at SPS, I felt free to explore everything.

Mr. Grant and Cook could manage to be civil to one another, certainly much more so than Mr. Grant and I could, which was further evidence that Cook was a very clever boy. However, Cook would certainly not have been Mr. Grant's first choice for leadership among the black students.

Mike Russell was closer to what Mr. Grant wanted to see, but most of the guys, while they found Mike an affable person, were drawn to Cook. He had loads of charisma, he was tough, he was cool and Cook knew how to make the guys laugh. Among a group of teenagers, that can give a person great power.

I was later elected the vice president of our group. Mr. Grant was not happy about that either. It must have horrified him to see someone like me assume a position of leadership ahead of someone like Mike Russell. I remember the look on his face when they elected me. He seemed so dejected. I could feel it. He must have felt that he was losing complete control of things.

The guys had a choice between Hipp and me for vice president and I barely won. There were no hard feelings between Hipp and me, it wasn't that important. Hipp was fast becoming my best friend. I was sure that Mr. Grant would have even preferred Hipp to me, although I knew Hipp did not like, or trust, Mr. Grant, any more than I did.

The previous year, when we first formed the black student group, the officers were Mike Russell and Charlie Nelson. Now, the two of them were out, reduced to marginal participation. Mike took it well. Charlie Nelson never seemed to get over it, and there was always simmering bad blood between him and Cook. The bad guys had taken over. Laissez les bon temps roulant!

I spent a lot of time with Cook and I know that everyone thought that there couldn't possibly be any tensions between us. That was true to a point, but the truth is, I was often on edge around Cook. He was very temperamental.

I wasn't afraid of him, but I was always worried about someone or something setting him off and thereby drawing me into something... unpleasant. Sometimes I could see a bad situation developing between Cook and someone else, and I would cringe in anticipation of the fallout.

One evening after a seated dinner, this white kid named Mike Prentice, a third-former, made the mistake of saying something, allegedly in jest, which seemed racially insensitive to Cook. According to some of the other guys, he said something like, "What do you mean boy?" in response to something that Cook had said to him.

I was there and I wasn't sure what he said, but I can tell you that I did not think of Prentice as especially racist, only a little silly at times, like everyone. I had seen him run off at the mouth a little. The previous year, Prentice was one of the white boys I had gotten to know reasonably well.

In a flash, Cook was in his face, and a verbal back and forth ensued.

Several others present noticed it. Prentice could see that Cook had become dangerously angry and tried to ease his way out of the situation by adopting a contrite, submissive tone, but it was too late. Something had started, but the attention the event had garnered helped to defuse it, for the time being.

Soon after, Cook, a few of the other brothers, and I left the dining hall and drifted onto the muddy path that ran behind the Library Pond. I had a bad feeling, because there was no good reason for us to be heading in that direction unless we were third-formers, which we were not.

As we approached Simpson House, Mike Prentice came along behind us and more words were exchanged between him and Cook. Prentice should have kept his mouth shut. Cook pounced on him.

He body slammed Prentice to the ground, and when Prentice got to his knees in an effort to stand, Cook sat on his back as if riding a horse and pounded him ferociously about the head and shoulders. Prentice could only try to cover up, and kept yelling for Cook to stop. Mercifully, Maldonado and Mike Shivers, both big guys, pulled Cook off him.

I did nothing. I knew that minding one's business was important to getting along with someone like Cook, and besides, it was just a good old-fashioned beat-down. Nobody was in any danger of being killed. What was happening between Cook and Prentice was their affair. Prentice had made a serious error in judgment; he did not know Cook well enough to take any kind of liberties with him, so he got what he got.

I stood by watching rather dispassionately (much like Kenard had back in Harlem Park as Bozy beat his girlfriend), and I could think of absolutely nothing to say. That may seem cold, but that is how it was.

I knew that Mike Prentice would not make that mistake again - whatever it was, and now, neither would anyone else. I'm sure that

Cook gave some thought to that. Word of this would go forth and conclusions drawn.

I imagine word of the incident got back to Mr. Grant, and looking at it from a purely selfish point of view, if Mr. Grant is disappointed with Cook, then he is disappointed in me as well. Cook and I were already becoming close friends. I'm guilty by association, another strike against me.

The entire incident seemed rather pointless to me, but you see, in my life I have always done everything I could to avoid a fight. When I was a third-former, there was one instance when I punched a tall guy named Chip Lamason in the face for piling on me (twice) in a football game after the ball had been whistled dead. I only hit him with one punch and I think he knew he deserved it.

My back was injured badly, yet after the game I waited until the moment when he had taken off his helmet and, in great pain, I popped him in the face good. As with Cook, I imagine that the word about me punching Lamason enhanced my reputation to some degree among all the guys, white and black.

Interestingly, in my fifth form year I was involved in one fight at SPS with, of course, another black guy. It was one of only a couple of fights that I have had my entire life. At the time, SPS was involved in a one-semester student exchange with an all-girls boarding school as SPS studied the feasibility of going co-ed, so of course the fight was over a girl.

It started in the dining hall at the 'black table'. You see, for all the notions about integrating St. Paul's School, we did a good job of segregating ourselves from the general population in the dining halls. Usually, the way the 'black table' developed was rather impromptu. One of the brothers would lay claim to a table at lunch and that would attract some of the other black guys, and quickly a 'black table' is born.

The white guys were not prohibited from sitting with us. Yet, it was the rare white boy who was brave enough to subject himself to the ribbing and abuse that we would dish out. Still, there were those who were unafraid. Clint Van Dusen was one of them. He seemed hell bent on being accepted by the brothers no matter what he had to endure. I was impressed by his persistence.

Of the girls who came to SPS for that semester, only two of them were black. Cook and Maldonado immediately began to woo the two new female black students. Charlie Nelson and Mike Jones were interested in them as well. At that time, Cook and Maldonado were roommates, and Nelson and Jones were both sixth-formers. There was no real love lost between the two pairs of boys.

This black kid named Newman told me about a conversation he had overheard between Charlie Nelson and Mike Jones, about what would happen if the two camps came to blows. Mike Jones said that he would have no problem kicking my "little skinny ass." I didn't appreciate that, especially since I wasn't even in the running for either of the two black female exchange students, but since I was close to Cook and Maldonado, somehow I was part of the whole thing.

The next day at lunch, when there were several black students gathered at one table (though it had not become a black table), I confronted Jones.

"Hey Jones, I hear you've been talking about kicking my ass."

He answered in his thick Boston accent, "That's right. I said that."

"So why do you want to drag me into your business? I'm not involved with either one of those girls."

"It's because you got too much mouth," he answered.

"Oh... ok... I see. So why haven't you kicked my ass Jones?"

269

"That's because I like to give everybody three chances." he snapped back.

Now all the guys at the table are locked onto this. They could smell a fight. My head was spinning from the adrenalin rush. This was so out of character for me, but I felt I had to respond to Jones. Guys were sitting there waiting to see if I was as tough as my reputation.

To be honest, I was not that anxious to fight Mike Jones. He was on the wrestling team and a sixth-former. He wasn't especially menacing, but I wasn't sure if I could take him.

"Tell me Jones, how many chances have I used up already?" I asked.

"Only one so far."

"Oh, I see. Well fuck you Mike Jones, and fuck you again. Now I've used up all my chances,"

I stood up, Jones stood up, and then my boy big Mike Shivers stood up and Charlie Nelson stood up. The surrounding crowd was expectant. Newman, an obnoxious but harmless kid from Washington, D.C., said, "Ya'll need to take this to the hall."

Jones and I headed out to the area just above the Lower School lounge followed by 10-15 guys; some of them white guys. They probably couldn't believe their good luck; they were about to see two black guys beat the hell out of each other.

Once we were in the hall, Jones and I were standing a few feet apart, when he very suddenly ducked his head and charged me, just what I had feared. I wasn't sure how strong he might be.

He knocked the wind out of me as he drove me into a wall, but my arms were free and I began landing solid punches to his head and body. He rammed me into the wall a couple of times before I was able to shove him away. When I did, he went side-ways and hit the wall hard, at which time I was able to get in one very good punch to his face, which I knew stung him. Again, I heard that familiar 'Oooooh' sound come from the onlookers. I thought I had left this shit behind in Harlem Park.

We were about to square off to continue, when there was a sudden rush of nervous guys past us, running ahead of an approaching faculty member, and we all began moving along as though nothing had happened.

The fight was over and I left the Upper to get to my next class, accompanied by some of the guys who had witnessed the whole thing. When that kid Newman spotted Cook and Hipp walking on another pathway, he yelled to them.

"Yo Cook; Jones and Wid had a fight. And Wid won!"

When Jones graduated later that year, he wrote in my copy of the yearbook that on that day in the dining hall I had taught him not to bullshit. That episode didn't hurt my reputation among the fellas either. I suspect that word of it did nothing for my less than stellar reputation with Mr. Grant.

*****

CHAPTER 45 – IT'S SATURDAY NIGHT!

Cook and Hipp brought in with them some unexpectedly galvanizing force that propelled us all to bolder and more constructively political behavior. Unfortunately, there was some anti-social behavior as well. None of it was egregiously bad. None of it was unusual for a bunch of teenagers. Everybody was trying to have some fun. Yet, sometimes we did take things too far.

We were isolated in the countryside on the SPS campus, and getting to town meant hitching a ride with a faculty member or spending money for a cab. No students were allowed to drive and only sixth-formers were allowed to have bicycles. There were almost no black people in town and very little to do if you were broke, so most of the black guys simply remained on campus much of the time.

On Saturday nights there would usually be a movie shown at Memorial (Mem) Hall. Sometimes that might be the only thing to do, unless you were out in the woods getting high or at the Library or something, so lots of guys would go, depending on the film.

I saw the film The Lion in Winter at Memorial (Mem) Hall. It was the kind of film that I don't think that I would have seen at the Harlem Park Movie Theater. All of my SPS boys hated it and they left me alone sitting there, but I was hypnotized.

I did not understand it, but I was fascinated by the story and completely in awe of the acting of Peter O'Toole, Katherine Hepburn and the rest of that talented cast. I thought the film was extraordinary. I could not understand why I felt compelled to stay and watch it, but looking back, I do understand it now. I was simply more sensitive than I would have liked to admit! I was watching something great and I knew it. I had never considered being an actor, but that film made me want to try it.

Memorial Hall had a balcony. On Saturday nights, sometime after the start of the movie, Cook and a couple of the brothers might come in at the balcony entrance and begin loudly calling out something like,

"Yo' Hipp, Shockley, Kenny, Wid! Where y'all at man?"" he yells.

"Over here man!"

"Up here man."

"Stop playin' man, where y'all at?"

"Down here man."

"This movie any good?" Cook asks.

"Out here man."

"Under here man."

From somewhere in the safety of the darkened theater an anonymous white boy yells. "The movie stinks OK…now for God's sake would you please be quiet and leave!"

"Shut the fuck up!" Cook yells back.

There will then be a cacophony of voices as everyone reacts to what could very easily turn into an ugly situation. The voice of a faculty member will usually be enough to quell the noise.

Some nights, when we were bored, we did stuff like that. It was stupid and we would laugh like crazy. It was the sort of thing that drove Mr. Grant to distraction – always the black guys cutting up.

*****

CHAPTER 46 - FAUX THUGS

One of the big fears for almost all of the black guys was that we would come out of SPS as carbon copies of these seemingly pampered and very proper white boys. Like me, many of the black guys hated the flack we would take from the folks in our hometown communities when we came back – 'changed'. Some of us were determined that we would change very little.

The fear of someone suggesting that you were 'acting white' is something with which many intelligent black children must contend. I hated hearing anyone imply such a thing about me back in Harlem Park, but it seemed to be an inevitable part of the price for high academic achievement in the black community, and indeed, I did hear it. It's backwards thinking and everyone knows that, but it continues to this day. In the Black community we should be encouraging every black child to do their best, and yet our friends often ostracize us and say we're trying to 'act white' if we do too well, or speak too well. The best way to get around it is to ignore it, and continue to do well.

That's what Mike Russell tried to do. He performed well. The 'ignoring' part was more vexing for him. I think he would have liked a bit more acceptance from the more hardcore of us. I was a part of that hardcore group and I knew there was no chance for him. No one trusted him.

I wanted it all; complete acceptance from the boys on the streets, and I still wanted to do well in the academic world. I was fighting like hell to hold onto a part of me that most reasonable people would insist that I must renounce in order to get ahead. I refused to do it. I think I was right to do so, even today.

I believed that the two parts could co-exist. Intuitively I reasoned that if I were to go back to the community from whence I came with this SPS education, and try to make a difference, I would need to retain some of that rough-edged piece to get the job done effectively for those needy black folk. It is a very fine line to negotiate.

Malcolm X is someone whom I admire a great deal, and his early life was not a pretty picture. Yet, I believe all that street hustling, and the hard knocks he endured, helped to prepare him for the great service he later rendered to black folk (indeed all folk); serving in the profound way that only Malcolm X could. At least, I wasn't committing any felonies.

Someone like Mr. Grant, who appeared to loath and disavow all of the supposedly unsavory manifestations of that 'street mindset', must have hated what he saw me hanging onto, and he may have been right. Who knows?

Guys like me, Cook and Hipp tried to walk that line. Consequently, we were slightly more thuggish at SPS than we were anyplace else. I think at SPS, a lot of us were trying-on-for-size that street persona that was denied us back home, where we were the 'good kids.'

I know that I was going for a Tony Stewart meets Joel Finney kind of combination; a sort of tough, yet quiet cool, tempered by athletic skills and a good grade or two. Obviously, such behavior did not go over well with Mr. Grant. I'm sure he felt responsible and it embarrassed him greatly.

Some of us did a fair amount of stealing. Now I know that is not a nice thing to admit but we did, and believe me, it was way too easy given the expressed and implied honor code in operation at the school. There were no locks on the doors at SPS and most of the guys were in the comfortable habit of leaving their money, watches, etc. in plain sight in their rooms.

At the gym, these guys did not even lock their lockers and for me it proved to be simply irresistible. It was at the gym that I committed my first theft of cash. I was late getting to football practice and I mistakenly opened the wrong locker. When I saw some guy's wallet sitting there, cash plainly visible, looking around I thought,

"Oooooh! This is way too easy!"

I helped myself to some of it, but I never took it all. If the guy had $60, I might take $25. That way, he might think that he had misplaced some of his money or he might not remember how much he had, but he wouldn't be flat broke and steaming mad. I considered that very thoughtful of me, and it became my pattern. I would hit a few lockers whenever I needed some extra cash for the expensive books, laundry or snacks at the Tuck shop. The expression 'hitting lockers' became part of the lexicon among some of the boys.

I always worked alone and almost never told anyone exactly what I was doing or how much I had taken. My conscience suffered very little because, after all, these guys were wealthy. I imagined my thievery as a perversion of the tale of Robin Hood, where I was 'the poor.'

It's despicable I know. At that age, while I knew it was wrong and felt bad about it, the remorse was fleeting. As an adult, I can't imagine how I could cross the line like that. I know I was thinking, "But these guys have so much," which will never do as an excuse. There is no good excuse.

I preferred to steal cash, but I would occasionally take a watch or a gold ring, stuff that was easy to hide. One thing I would not do is to wear certain stolen items while on the SPS campus. I would stash it away until I was home in Harlem Park, where I would make gifts to friends of some of the items. My first year, my third form year, I did much less stealing and then I was more likely to only take a pair of gloves or a scarf.

Sometimes I would lift a few sodas or snacks from the Tuck Shop in the old Lower School. That store was run by an eccentric old white-haired guy named Art who wore thick half-glasses, a ratty old sweater buttoned over his considerable belly and had a habit of touching everyone familiarly and calling them 'dear', which of course to our adolescent minds gave rise to speculation that he was homosexual.

Art was probably just a friendly, sweet old guy. However, he was not in any way equipped with the kind of vigilance necessary to foil the brazen and unheard of thievery we brought to SPS. I would go in the store when it was crowded and wait for Art to become engaged in a conversation. I would then simply stuff several cans of soda under my armpits, beneath my coat, and casually saunter out of the small crowded room.

Now, there were more guys around who, like me, were a little crooked and that emboldened me. Many of the guys began calling me Big Al because I used to sit in the Sheldon Library and read about gangsters, and Al Capone was a gangster that everyone knew, even though as bad guys go, I thought Capone was a stupid bad guy.

Other guys were also stealing things, and I know that because they would brag about it to me or ask me to give them advice on the best way to take things, especially the younger guys. Guys knew that I could keep my mouth shut. When I saw too many guys using my methods, I would move on to something else.

"So tell me man, what do you think is the best way to get some beer out of one of those places in town?" this young black kid Wilford from NYC asks me.

"First of all man, you need to stop thinking about stealing anything from any store in town. You're under-aged and black. If you get caught they will call the cops on you and maybe even lock your ass up to scare you." I tell him.

"But, what if I put it down the back of my pants and walk out?" Wilford says.

"Did you hear what I just said to you? You're not hearing me man. You steal here on campus and they catch you at it, at first, you get a lecture and they might let you go, but not in town. Don't do it!"

Wilford did it anyway. He was found out and later ended up being sent home, expelled. There were probably other issues involved. I liked Wilford. He could talk about anything non-stop, especially sports.

It must have been rough for him in the third form Quad. Wilford was so strident, so severe. The other kids probably saw him as scary. He was always stopping by our room. Wilford was fighting to survive, and I could see him struggling. I talked to him whenever I could, but he was not yet ready to do much listening. SPS is not for everybody.

I was sorry to see him go even though he had once managed to get me into a good deal of trouble. Wilford used my B.B. rifle to shoot one of the faculty members, Mr. Morgan, from a window in my room. Mr. Morgan figured out where the shot had come from and crept up to the window where he spotted Wilford and a few others laughing hysterically. They almost crapped in their pants when Mr. Morgan's face, flushed red and puffed up, suddenly appeared at the window from nowhere.

As I expected, Mr. Grant heard about it, and promptly came to see me, resulting in the confiscation of my rifle – forever. Incredibly, and to my great surprise, that was the end of it. For some reason Mr. Grant let me off easy.

Possession of the B.B. gun on school grounds was against about a thousand school rules. He could have nailed me good and I fully expected him to do so. I figured he had waited a long time for this opportunity and he showed up at my dorm room looking like the angel of death.

"You know why I'm here. Hand it over," he demanded.

Something in his smarmy tone suggested that he knew I had the gun all along. I knew I was losing it because I had been careless in allowing Wilford to shoot someone with it. After all, Mr. Morgan was not a stray bird or a squirrel. Mr. Grant and I understood one another. It was an issue of personal accountability. He simply could not look the other way on this now, and I understood that.

Sometimes I think that he let me go because it would not have been worth the trouble that would have ensued if St. Paul's kicked me out. I feel confident in saying that a good number of the brothers would have made a lot of noise about it; we were a loyal bunch. I had a lot of friends among all of the boys, black and white. Maybe someone put in a good word for me.

That B.B. rifle was a popular item with many of the boys because it was against the rules. For many of them it made them cool to be in on the secret. Cook had a B.B. pistol that we would often keep in our dormitory room as well. At that time, Hipp and I were roommates living in this cavernous corner room in Nash, one of the nicest dorms. There was carpeting in the hallways. I loved that.

We would fire both guns out the window, being careful not to be too conspicuous. Taking a position far back in the room, away from the open window, kept us hidden and muted the sound of the air gun.

Dinnertime was a favored time for shooting at people, as they passed by on the way to the Upper.

We had no concerns about anyone getting hurt. Neither of the guns was very powerful, unless you were right up on a person. There was an unwritten rule that you only shot at people wearing a heavy coat. Most passersby did not even realize anything had happened. It would just bounce off the back of their coat. I'm guessing Mr. Grant did not know the full extent of our mischief, or he might have come down harder on me.

One day, inside our room, I shot this kid named Porter in the leg with the rifle. Porter could be annoying, and you always wanted to take him down a notch. He made a big fuss about me shooting him and actually cried. I apologized, but he continued fussing.

In order to shut him up, I offered to shoot myself with the rifle so that he could see that it did not hurt that badly. There were several guys in the room and they did not believe that I would do it. They all crowded around.

I put on my coat, placed the B.B. rifle flush against my chest, and pulled the trigger. The impact knocked me down, but I went down more out of reflex, than in reaction to the blinding pain of the impact. It hurt like hell, but I bounced right back up smiling.

"Damn, that stung a little bit," I joked.

I then removed my coat and shirt and showed all of them my bare chest. There was a big round dark bruise. It was impressive.

Not that it excuses our behavior, but you should know that some of the white boys also did some stealing. It would often be one of the white boys who was hanging out with a black guy and trying to show how cool he was. Of course, there were those white guys who would take/borrow things from someone without their knowledge, but that isn't really stealing is it?

We were petty crooks, but decidedly the minority. I believe most guys at SPS were honest to a fault. For my part, I would almost never work with anyone and no one ever caught me. However, there was one instance when I had taken some money from a guy's desk and he walked into his room before I could leave. He came in to find me standing next to his desk and I had no good reason to be there.

"Hey Lloyd, do you have any extra ping-pong balls?" I ask him quickly.

"Yeah sure, look in my desk." he says.

I had remembered seeing some ping-pong balls in his desk as I was rummaging through the top drawer and stealing his money; he loved the game of table tennis and played constantly.

I enlisted the aide of my boy Hipp to help me make this situation right. I trusted Hipp as I trusted no one else at SPS and I knew he would help me. Hipp challenged Lloyd to a table tennis match in the basement, while I returned to his room and put his money back. There was no sense in being greedy.

*****

CHAPTER 47 – SUMMER LUST

In the summer of 1970, my boys and I had come a mighty long way from our days of softball, in the back alleys of Harlem Park. Allen was going out with Cheryl, who was as cool as could be and athletic as well. She would eventually become his wife. Bruce was in love with Roxanne, who also would become his wife. They were falling in love, and I knew that a natural consequence of that was that we would be spending a lot less time with one another.

As for me, I was paying the price for my life of mobility. The fact that I always seemed to be leaving Baltimore on a jet bound for New Hampshire, or vice versa, made a permanent relationship somewhat difficult.

Then, there was also the fact that St. Paul's School was an all-male institution. They were experimenting with co-education, but had not yet made a full commitment to instituting it into the curriculum. Opportunities for love can be somewhat limited in an all-male boarding school, but I think that was part of the point of it all.

I don't believe I deserved any pity however, because there were always a few women around who relished the idea of a guy who lived something of an exciting jet-setting sort of life. As a matter of fact, there was already someone around who fit into this category - perfectly.

She had been living in Harlem Park only a couple of months, having recently moved to Baltimore from somewhere down south, and I had seen her a few times walking around the neighborhood with another girl named Colleen whom I had known from way back.

To my pleasant surprise and eternal gratitude, my old friend eventually stopped at my front steps to introduce me to this new girl, whose name was Teri. I had this feeling that it was actually Teri's idea that they stop.

She had captured my attention from the very first moment that I saw her. It was strange, but I remember that in some ways she reminded me of Allen's mother Ms. Alma, or the way I pictured Ms. Alma looking when she was a young girl – kinda' cute and sexy.

One afternoon, I saw Teri was walking down the alley near Club Astoria with Colleen. She was wearing these short pants that were this weird shimmering purple color. Even today, it amazes me that I can remember the color of her outfit because what really caught my eye were her legs.

She was short, but her legs were wonderfully smooth and shapely. The fact that she was wearing very short pants helped to accentuate her legs and gave them a graceful athletic aspect, not to mention that she had an ass that shivered and bounced ever so slightly with each step she took. I loved that.

Uncharacteristically for me, I had made up my mind that day to follow them so that I could put my case before this girl Teri. I was feeling emboldened, by lust no doubt. It made me get my ass up off of my steps and hurry past the Club to catch them. They were walking down the alley in order to go into the back entrances to their respective houses, something a lot of us kids did.

When I reached the corner, I sort of peeked around the building thinking that I would first get another good look at her ass as she walked away. Teri was standing there all alone waiting for me, with a kind of smirk on her face. I was totally busted.

"Caught me huh...you knew I was going to come and take a look... didn't you?"

"I've been feelin' you lookin' at me all week...I was thinkin' you were 'bout ready to do somethin' more," she answered, still smirking.

"Well...uh...nice outfit." a dumb thing to say. Damn, I was choking like some kinda' punk!

"Thank you."

I'm standing there thinking she was not going to make this easy.

"So ...let me ask you...you have a boyfriend?"

"Yes..."

"Does he live around here?"

"No, and you don't know him...he works at night and most of the time he comes to see me in the early evenin'."

All right, that was more information than the question merited, so now I'm thinking that I had somewhat of a chance for something here.

"So...what are you telling me?" I asked.

"Well...Why don't you meet me out here on the playground...at about eleven o'clock tonight and let's talk about it...OK?"

"Good...eleven o'clock...real good...now do you mind if I stand here and watch you walk the rest of the way home?"

She looked me directly in the eye as she answered, saying each word very distinctly.

"Whatever you want...you hear me?"

Oh, man! After she was gone, I went back to sitting on my front steps and tried to suppress a desire to jump around, because even to me her message was pretty clear, and I can be a naive idiot sometimes.

This girl Teri had not only caught my notice, but a lot of the older guys had been talking about her as well. I had listened to some of the guys as they were speculating about her just a couple of days before, when we were all sitting on the playground behind Allen's house. Tony, Sammy, Alfred and this big country boy PeeWee, had all been going on about how hot she looked, and all of them wanted to fuck her but she wouldn't talk to any of them.

Part of the reason that I approached her as I did was because I decided that if they all struck out, then I might have better luck. She was a couple of years older than I was, but I was thinking that it just might be possible that she liked younger guys. The idea that she might prefer younger guys wasn't such a stretch from my point of view. Already, I had seen that occasionally one or the other of the older girls around would take a light fancy to me.

A friend of my sister Plum, who lived across the back playground, once gave me this sort of booklet she had written on kissing, describing the proper way to kiss a girl. Her name was Julie and she was a beautiful girl, and I mean really - a stunning beauty. She came from a large family of similarly beautiful girls.

She instructed me to read her kissing manual over and over, and then sometime later, she and I would get together to practice what she had written. I was maybe only thirteen or fourteen then, and I could not believe my good luck.

Julie kept her word too. She came to the house one day and asked me if I had studied her book, then asked me if I was ready. Of course, I am looking at her like, "Are you kidding?"

She had me sit in my father's favorite armchair and she sat in my lap, and we kissed and kissed and kissed. No sex, no fondling, only wet sloppy kissing that went on for the longest time.

Looking back on it now, our practice sessions were as much for her benefit as for mine. She was using me for some purpose, which of course made no difference to me. I really missed it when it stopped.

One other crucial piece of information I picked up from Julie had to do with discretion. It proved to be an invaluable lesson. She asked me,

"Do you want to get the pussy; or do you want to be that guy who talks about getting the pussy?"

The obvious point being, that if a girl thinks you can keep your mouth shut, you stand a much better chance with her. Of course, such a thing could be a little self-serving for the girl if she is trying to run a game on someone, but even so, I found it to be a sound piece of advice. From then on, I made sure to let women know that I was not the type to go around running my mouth. Julie sensed that I understood that.

As she had promised, that night Teri came out to the playground behind our houses, where we sat on some monkey bars and talked for a good long time. She seemed to have checked me out pretty well, because she seemed to know a lot about me. I could see that she was intrigued by the fact that I was constantly going back and forth to boarding school, that made me seem very different from most of the other guys around.

Since she was relatively new to the neighborhood, I think she felt some sort of affinity with me. In some respects, to her I seemed new to the area as well, which I guess I could understand, although nothing could be further from the truth.

Her main topic of conversation was her relationship with this guy she was seeing. It was plain that she was not all that happy in the relationship. Apparently, he had a good job and was nice to her most of the time, but he was older and worked at night. That meant that he could only spend time with her on a limited basis, in the evening. She told me that she was all right with that part of everything.

What bothered her was that she thought he should be able to spend a little more time with her during the day, but he said that he slept during the day and had other business to take care of. He thought that she should understand that. Teri was convinced that the guy had another woman, and that was the real reason that he only came around irregularly, and then, only in the early evenings for a quick fuck before he went to work.

After that candid revelation, she became even more specific about the core reason for her dissatisfaction with him, above and beyond all that she had already revealed. By this point, I realized that I was dealing with a girl with a remarkable propensity for frank talk. I found it tremendously sexy.

She explained to me that while she enjoyed sex with her guy, she usually came away from the experience feeling unfulfilled, and she told me exactly why. She told me that all he wanted to do was eat her pussy. That further increased her suspicions that he must have another woman somewhere. It seems that this guy, in her mind, was far too fixated on pleasing her orally; but she conceded that she did really enjoy that. However, as she told it to me, "I wanna fuck!"

Given this, she felt that it would not be so horribly wrong if she found someone of her own. However, she made it crystal clear that what she really wanted was someone who wanted to fuck. She was equally plain about the fact that she had no intentions of breaking up with this other guy. She admits that he did sometimes do nice things for her and she really did care about him, somewhat.

I knew I was her man.

It appeared that my instincts were right in more ways than one. Teri was attracted to me because she felt that by my being younger and in the full bloom of youth; I would have the stamina and raw lust necessary to quench her desire for some good old-fashioned fucking.

Furthermore, my impending departure in a couple of months would guarantee that I would not eventually become a pest if I stupidly fell in love with her. As far as I could see, there were not many flaws in this thing, as long as everybody managed to stick to their assigned roles.

This was a situation that called for a guy who could keep his mouth shut, and I had already demonstrated that I could do that. I had my suspicions that someone else had already informed Teri of as much.

It was probably the very next night that we started what were to be almost nightly sessions of sweaty, bold bouts of frenzied fucking, first on the couch and then on the floor in the living room of my parent's house.

Ever since I had begun attending St. Paul's, my folks were giving me a wide berth. They allowed me to stay out as late as I wanted. They seemed to be sympathetic to the fact that I only had the summers to spend any real time with my friends.

Something else that facilitated our passion sessions was that my parents were notoriously predictable in their sleeping habits. They both worked during the day, so they were generally in bed and asleep by about eleven-thirty.

That hour coincided nicely with when Teri was available to come to the house. Her guy would have gone on to work and she had time for a nice freshening bath. She lived with an aunt and uncle and very likely they were also probably in bed by that time.

Our house on Edmondson Avenue was a big old house and the

living room had the French doors that we could shut to keep noise inside the room. If anyone did come down the stairs from the second floor, those old wood stairs made a god-awful racket. That gave us plenty of time to straighten our clothing.

My brothers and sisters had a good idea of what I was up to, so they all stayed away from the living room or used the back staircase to get to the kitchen, which is about the only place anyone would be going late at night anyway. It was perfect.

With the entire affair infused with an exhilarating sense of urgency, Teri and I did most of our screwing nearly fully clothed. It was hot and sweaty. It was a lot like what kids would resort to in the back seat of a car, but a lot more comfortable - thank you. All the intrigue surrounding what we were doing only served to make the whole thing more exciting for both of us.

Yet, apparently, it was not enough, because she decided that we needed to figure out a way to get her upstairs to the third floor where my bedroom was. I mean, why not go where we could stretch out more, at least once, especially since my room was on the third floor at the back of the house far from my parents' second floor front bedroom. No one would hear us.

I already knew that getting her upstairs was not an unsolvable problem, because the boys and I had devised a solution for it some time ago. We would have girls climb the fire escape at the back of the house. The fire escape back there served our house, Club Astoria, and one other nearly deserted building, so that in making this climb, the girls did not have to be concerned about anyone else seeing them because there were no apartments back there.

It was really dark and you had to negotiate this long space across a wide divide to get to get onto the fire escape, and the first step onto the fire escape was a crucial one. If you slip, you will fall about one story down into a sort of basement stairwell - in pitch-black darkness.

You did not want to miss that first step. There were rats and all kinds of filthy shit down there. That was one reason why it took more than one person to pull it off. We were really careful to take the girls by the hand and make the climb with them. We were a chivalrous bunch.

Figuring out these types of situations had long been one of my functions in our gang of three, and I felt strongly that the fire escape was not the way to go with this particular girl. I was sure that for this, I could use the help of my boys. Teri agreed, so I let my boys in on what I was up to with her.

Up to this point, they knew vaguely that I was talking to her, but they were not fully aware of exactly how far matters had progressed. Like I said, I knew how to keep my mouth shut, and both of them were far too preoccupied with their own budding romances to miss me much. Most of the time that I spent with Teri was in the wee hours of the morning, when they were up to the same thing as me.

My plan was simple.

The boys would wait with me at the house until Teri arrives. While we are waiting for her, we carry on in our usual way, in order to establish that the guys are in the house, and we are just messing around. Once Teri gets there, Bruce's job is to go up the stairs, behaving normally, maybe even go to the bathroom; anything to announce his customary presence in case my parents are still awake.

His main purpose is to stop at the top of the stairs on the second floor and listen for sounds of activity from my parent's room. They always keep their bedroom door open so he had to be careful. The staircase is just outside of their open bedroom door but they cannot see out into the hallway if they are in bed, which is almost always was the case. When Bruce is satisfied that they are asleep he will quietly signal Allen at the bottom of the staircase. Now comes the part of our escapade that calls for real nerve.

Allen will start up the stairs as naturally as possible, even speaking to Bruce as he goes up, which again is a natural thing to do even in the context of not wanting to make too much noise and awaken my sleeping parents. At the same time that Allen starts up the stairs Teri and I begin climbing, but I walk behind her, being careful to take a step at the precise instant that she does.

Although agonizing over each creak of the staircase, we easily reach the third floor in this way. From there, the boys will exit via the window of my room and go back out by the fire escape.

Quite likely, the whole thing was overdone but it worked like a charm, and once again, for my boys, when it came to getting pussy, "I was the man!"

After a couple of hours in my bedroom, Teri and I would walk quietly back down the stairs. I would lead the way to check things out and Teri would follow a few steps behind. It was two o'clock in the morning by this time and everyone was surely sound asleep. Even if someone did hear us, there was still the implied illusion at work that it was only Allen or Bruce leaving.

On subsequent visits, Teri and I worked the "step drill" on our own. We did not do it every night because it was risky and if only once you screw up – well it's over. Anyway, we still enjoyed the sweaty humping on the living room couch.

After several weeks of this, Teri and I had an interesting conversation one night while she was upstairs in my bedroom. There was no way to see it coming. We were hot, sweaty and completely nude, which was nice because she had a lovely body. As we lay there, she was looking off absent-mindedly.

"You know ...I really like what you do to me... the way you do it... you know what I mean?"

Right then, I did know something was coming.

"Good... that's...that's...good to hear." I said

"Can I ask you somethin'?"

"You can ask me anything... whatever..."

"Well... you know how in the beginnin' I told you I wanted somebody who really wanted to fuck...'cause my boyfriend only wanted to eat me...you remember?"

OK! I had a good idea where she was going now.

"Look," she said, "I'll suck your thing...if you'll eat my stuff."

My sweet lord! She had a way of getting right to the point.

"Hey Teri...I've never done that before... (PAUSE...PAUSE... PAUSE...) I mean...I've thought about it...but I just haven't done it." I told her.

"You can try it for the first time with me...I'll show you."

"OK.... OK...I'll think about it...just...just let me...think about it...all right."

She seemed reasonably satisfied with that answer, because she smiled broadly and was again as warm as always.

Therefore - here's the thing. In our neighborhood, and some would say in the Black community in general, there was a certain stigma attached to being perceived as someone who eats pussy. On this topic, many Black people will know what I'm talking about.

"Y'all know what I'm talkin' 'bout!"

Those of you, who are upstairs, rattle your jewelry.

Among the older guys, if someone makes such an accusation, it is the sort of thing that could set tempers flaring. Now, maybe I am wrong, but I had always felt that a lot of those guys were lying, but the general consensus was, "You don't eat pussy!"

There was a guy in the neighborhood that people whispered about. They said, "He liked to perform oral sex", but no one put it so delicately. The fact that he did this made him somehow nasty. There is nothing much worse in the Black community than for people to think you are nasty. You can be pretty much anything you want as long as you are not nasty.

Even the guy's own girlfriend, whom I knew very well, appeared to participate in deriding him. "But he's doing it to you. You're letting him eat you, and later you make fun of him for it?" I thought.

It did not make any sense to me. Nevertheless, the community prohibition was clear, and I was much too much of a punk to buck convention.

How sad: (When I told Teri that I could not do it and why, she seemed to understand.) Things between us went on as normal through the rest of the summer. She was a good girl - and I suppose she thought, "a deal was a deal." At the end of the summer, we parted amicably.

I ached for that woman for a long time after I had gone back to boarding school. It wasn't too long after that when I said to hell with convention and jumped into the pool of lascivious pleasures with both feet. The water was - exquisite.

*****

CHAPTER 48 – SUMMER FUN

Having beat out all of those older guys for Teri's attentions did a lot for my self-confidence, even if they had no idea, from me at least, that I had upstaged them. That was fine with me. As tough as these guys were, all of them could have some unpredictably fragile egos.

Lately, I found myself on the basketball court with those guys practically every day. They could be unbelievably petty and ready to fight about the stupidest things. I was only out there on the playground trying to improve my game, playing that tough street brand of inner city ball, which could translate to stardom with the white boys at St. Paul's in sedate New England.

I really loved being on the court with those guys. They were all so enormously competitive and it always seemed like it was no big thing for them. Unlike me, they did not seem to find it necessary to spend endless hours on the court practicing dribbling the ball or making left handed lay ups and that sort of thing.

A few of them were naturally gifted, with a sort of down in the gut kind of street toughness that gave them the stamina to play game after game, even as they were smoking cigarettes or taking a hit on a joint between games. Of all of us out there on the court on any given day, two guys in particular were almost always the focal point of the game, and they were a study in contrast.

One was Glascoe, who did not smoke, drink or do drugs, and as I said before he was legendary in Harlem Park for his skills on the basketball court. He could run all day, and had a presence on the court that made others around him play better. Glascoe was a natural leader on the court. He was tolerant of those who were less skilled than he, and generous as a teammate.

Quite often, after playing a few games, Glascoe and I would go back to his house for some water. We would have a snack consisting of something like cold applesauce and bread, a cool way to cool off after the games. That was one way.

Then, there was Tony who did everything wrong, smoking, drinking, weed and coke, and yet Tony could still run with Glascoe all afternoon. They seemed to give one another the appropriate respect; and everyone knew that it was going to be a good game to watch when they were both on the same team.

Tony was not all that tall either, but he could leap in a way that allowed him to get right in there with big muthafuckas. He had such a sweet, soft shot. I wanted a shot like his. Sometimes I was glad that I wasn't in a game, because I enjoyed watching him on the court.

The guy had such uncanny control over his body and played the game with an awe-inspiring gracefulness. There is this vivid picture in my mind of seeing Tony rise in the air, reaching over the backs of three other taller players and snatching a rebound from their midst. Smooooth!

Tony was playing a pick-up game with me once, and I noticed that he was carrying a thick and worn copy of Mario Puzo's The Godfather bulging in his back pocket. It was strange to see him carrying a book around, and this was before the movie had come out.

"Tony, what are you doing with that book in your pocket?"

"Kenard told me to read it."

"I don't mean any harm man, but it looks odd to see you carrying a book around. What's it called?"

"The Godfather. It's about these New York gangsters, but it's not like that show The Untouchables or those movies. This seems more real."

"Is there a lot of killing in it, like in The Untouchables?" I asked.

He replied, "You know man, people get killed and everything, but they do it only when it helps the business they have. Ain't nobody being shot over a nickel bag! You know what I mean. It's all like organized, like Bethlehem Steel or like the government. Reading this book is showing me how there ain't a whole lotta difference between them."

This book had him thinking. Tony liked the idea of learning. That's part of the reason he let me hang around. He wanted his good ideas to be understood by someone he considered intelligent.

"Yeah man, I go to school with those rich white boys at St. Paul's and you can believe that at least some of their families got their fortunes by doing something slightly crooked; now they're all respectable." I said.

"Kenard and me are puttin' our money together man. We need a real business, not running around here shootin' dudes and getting' shot at. Once we get a good bankroll together, we gonna have our own business, respectable family men, you know what I mean?"

'That sounds about right man. I might read that book." I replied. That pleased him.

Today, The Godfather is still one of my favorite books and movie.

Thinking back on a few of the conversations I had with Tony, I begin to see that he seriously, and I thought soberly, looked at selling drugs as mostly just a way of putting together the capital he needed for starting some kind of business. The moral questions aside, Tony and Kenard were doing what a lot of guys on the streets resorted to. For them, drugs were the best and fastest way to get you in a position to be legitimate.

Of course, the whole idea is flawed. For one thing, it is predicated on the assumption that no one innocent is harmed and it's only another business, but I don't think many of them think about it that deeply. They thought of themselves as simply fulfilling a need – plain old capitalism.

I had looked into his eyes and I could see that he was deadly earnest, and I did not doubt him. He and his partner Kenard really had some sort of a plan, and they had really been working on it for some time now. They were scratching and clawing their way towards some dream they shared; and I could only hope that they would live to see it.

By this time, I was at the point where I was smoking herb fairly regularly, and I bought it from Tony much of the time because I knew I could trust him. He had moved from his Mom's house and gotten an apartment with his girlfriend, so I assume business was good. I would often go by his apartment to pick up a bag of weed from him.

One time I walked into his place and there was a whole crowd of guys there. They were a lot of the older boys from the neighborhood, Michael, Cardy, Wine, Alfred, Kenard and a few others. Everybody greeted me like one of the boys and told me to come on in and have a seat. They were getting fucked up, big time.

As I sat there in the room feeling young and awkward, I was strangely conscious of a realization that a day would come when I would surely look back fondly on days such as this, when I was in a room with all these good neighborhood boys. Some of them are outlaws, some of them nine-to-five Joe's, most of them teetering between both worlds.

I was aware that I was flirting with my own two very incongruent worlds. Me - a student at one of the most exclusive boarding schools in the country, down here, down the way in Harlem Park - gettin' high.

Much of the time, I felt like an outsider looking in on my own life. I knew that it was largely because I was constantly coming into town, doing whatever and then jetting back to SPS, where I would repeatedly process all that had gone on. There was a lot of time for reflection.

For all their foibles, idiosyncrasies, mistakes, these boys were my very good friends. I knew that they would not allow anything to happen to me, and my enemies were their enemies. All of them were interested in seeing me succeed in what they saw as that school hustle that I did. I had come a long way with them. I was comfortable with them and I loved them, some more than others, but they were all an indelible part of who I was.

Tony sat down with us and started rolling a big joint; it was going to be special he said. I watched him as he put some marijuana in the papers, then he ground up and added some hash to it as well as a sprinkling of cocaine, and started rolling it up.

Now, I am thinking that there is no way that I am going to smoke any of that. It looked to be way out of my league, but damn, I didn't want to look like a punk. Especially since, this was the first time I had sat in with so many of these boys all together like this. Hell, even Kenard was there!

I was hoping someone else would balk at it first, so I wouldn't have to be the first to punk out, but as they started passing it around, I could see that I wasn't going to have any such luck. Michael Baskerville almost gave me a delicate way out, by jokingly suggesting that I was too young to try it, but I let that opportunity get past me. I decided that today I was going to see what these boys were into.

"I am here watching all the other children jump off a cliff, and I am not going to go home this time – not today. Today, I plan to jump off the cliff just like them," I thought.

So, when my turn came to hit it - what could I do? I took a tentative hit, but I hit it. Of course, then I coughed for about a half-hour, but, "I'm cool – 'ma'an," I said choking and trying to hold it in.

Wine and Alfred let me have it.

"Told y'all that young boy couldn't smoke that!"

'Who let that young muthafucka up in here?"

"Y'all sure he ain't no cop man?"

Everybody in the room had a laugh.

It was the end of summer. My head cleared and I floated back to St Paul's in milky white Millville.

*****

CHAPTER 49 – THE BODY BLACK

We were the resident experts on all things Black or so we thought, and we relied on one another to remind us of who we were and from whence we had come.

Nearly all of the people of color were considered members of our black student organization, the Afro-American Society. Not everyone actively participated, but if you were black or Hispanic you were considered a member, whether you wanted to be or not. A few of the black guys and Hispanic guys did choose to have nothing to do with the whole Black student union thing. We gave then their space – but we counted them in our number!

There were a couple of Native-Americans students and they also found their way into our group. We welcomed them. The few Asian guys at SPS made it clear that they were not interested in being members of such an organization. Had they been inclined to hang out with the black guys in general, we certainly would have welcomed them, but they had other priorities.

Our political agenda was not very bold, but we were earnest about it. One of our priorities was to encourage more recruitment of minority students and faculty. Occasionally, carefully selected black guys were chosen from among us to attend recruitment events in other cities, guys who could be counted on to behave themselves, like Mike Russell. No one ever asked me to go along on one.

Mr. Grant would sometimes go on recruiting trips to other cities accompanied by Mike Russell. Mike was like a poster-child for what a boarding school education at a place like St. Paul's could do for your poor black or Hispanic child.

A couple of forums were held with the SPS faculty and administration to look at ways to increase the levels of cultural sensitivity on the part of the SPS community. A few of us spoke to the faculty about our life experiences. We tried to explain what it meant for us to be Black and a student at SPS, or some nonsense.

I remember speaking to the assembled faculty and administrators and going on this long-winded ramble about having rocks thrown at me by white boys back home and therefore I knew from personal experience what racism was etc. I'm not sure where I was going with all that, but I do recall that I had everyone's full attention for a minute. They were horrified.

One Weekend, Bishop John T. Walker, an important Black Bishop from Washington, D.C. visited the school. He had been the first Black teacher at SPS and the first Black Episcopal Bishop of Washington, D.C. I liked him immediately. I could feel that he was a genuinely decent man.

To my eyes, he was everything that Mr. Grant was not. We would have been fortunate to have such a man as an advocate. When I met him, he remarked that I reminded him of Africans he had met in East Africa, which made me feel important. He was a very warm man with a nice family, yet it was clear that he was no pushover. I respected that.

My boys Cook, Russell, Turville, Charlie Nelson and me wanted to do something in his honor. We decided to salute him by singing at a Sunday chapel service. It was somewhat bizarre to see the five of us working on a project together, but we could all sing and we had put off deciding how to honor Bishop Walker until the last minute, so it made sense. We all believed we could pull it off.

The five of us saw one another in close quarters practically every day, so all sorts of tense, juvenile melodrama was percolating among us, but we put it aside in a show of unanimity for the school. We did it gladly, and we received the award of SPS school blazer buttons in chapel for doing so. That was a big honor at SPS. I still have those buttons somewhere.

That day we performed in chapel went well, but what I found sweeter was something that happened a few days before, when we got together in Conover/Twenty dormitory to choose a song. We (more easily than I would have expected) decided on the song Let Us Break Bread Together after quickly rejecting some of the more revival meetin' sort of Black spirituals. We wanted to do something dignified.

The five of us sang it through one time, everyone finding their way in the harmonies. It wasn't bad, but it was sloppy. After some discussion, we tried it again - and something astounding occurred. We began singing, and while the harmonies flowing from the five of us in that dormitory room were still improvisational, this time they were perfect and achingly beautiful. The five of us had managed to put away our egos for the sake of that piece of music, and it was lovely.

When we stopped, there was a period of silence, during which I looked around at the other four boys assembled and wondered if they too had any idea of how good we sounded. They all knew. It was plain from the smiles on their faces. We were all equally impressed.

I think I have a decent feel for good music, partly born out of my experiences playing classical music in the school orchestra at Harlem Park, and having grown up in a house filled with music, mostly gospel and rhythm and blues. That day in Conover/Twenty, it was beyond thrilling for me to be personally involved in such a perfect musical moment. The five of us had our differences, but when we spoke as one voice, that voice was transcendent. That was a life's lesson about cooperation for each of us - me particularly.

We rehearsed the song a few more times but we never again performed Let Us Break Bread Together as well as we did on that second take, not even at the chapel tribute. It turned out to be another one of those fleeting, pure instances of perfection that don't repeat. The kind of thing you never forget.

*****

CHAPTER 50 – THE POLITICS, BABY

We lobbied for a room for the establishment of a Black Student Lounge. We were given a room in an isolated building called Scudder near the front of the campus. We regarded that as a huge coup.

When we would visit other boarding schools, or especially the various colleges in New England, some of them had rooms reserved for similar purposes. At the University of Massachusetts, the Black students had an entire building. We were pretty impressed by that. The phrase Black Power carried some weight back then.

We mostly used our lounge to conduct meetings and parties. Mr. Grant liked to point out that we were too concerned about having parties and not concerned enough about things that are more important. He wanted us to take our responsibilities as young black men and women more seriously. Our response to that was that we were slugging it out in boarding school, trying to get a first class education. That's pretty serious. Why can't we dance a little?

The lounge was decorated with posters of Black leaders and the like, with institutional-looking tables and armchairs strewn about. At that age and for those times, a lot of us leaned more towards Malcolm X and Huey Newton, rather than Martin Luther King in our political thinking, but we weren't holed up in the Black student lounge planning the overthrow of the school or anything. Mostly we had Sunday meetings and listened to music - not much different from Sunday church.

There was a stereo system in the lounge. That would draw some guys to hang out there, but the lounge was in an isolated corner of the campus so there were not a whole lot of reasons to hang out there, unless you wanted to be alone. Its isolation made the Black student lounge a good place to spend time with a girl. If you think about it, the vast majority of the school would not dare come there, and once the initial joyful buzz of having the room wore off, none of us wanted to walk way up there either.

When I arrived at SPS, it was an all-boy's school. Looking back on it, it wasn't that bad! Not everyone wanted the school to open its doors to girls. I'm sure it was disappointing and overwhelming for some people when girls were admitted, especially after having only recently witnessed an explosion of lively black male faces in their midst.

More girls were on the way; they could occasionally be spotted taking tours of the school, with the first 19 girls arriving in the winter of 1971 when I was a fifth-former. At the beginning of my sixth form year, the school moved closer to being fully co-ed by admitting 72 women.

I liked SPS just fine when it was all-boys and I liked things after the girls came. Other than the expected boy/girl flirtations, things didn't feel that much different. Undoubtedly, my personal viewpoint is the result of my being less consumed with the exclusive all-male tradition of the school, than those people who revered it.

A few of us quickly paired off with some of the black women who enrolled. Consequently, a sofa in the black student lounge became the setting for a lot of heated sexual activity. I must confess that I also spent some time there. The reputation of that particular sofa was so bad that some people refused to sit on it, leading to exchanges like,

"I don't know if you want to sit in that spot Loretta," Kenny will say.

"Why, why not? What's wrong with it?" Loretta replies.

"Just take our word for it...OK."

"Shoot, y'all just want this seat for yourself. I'm not sitting on the floor for this meeting."

"Don't say we didn't try to warn you...oh no ...she sat right in it."

"What? I don't see anything, just a white stain on the cushion." Loretta says, scraping at it with her finger.

"Damn... don't touch it! Ah man...she touched it."

"Y'all being silly. Somebody probably spilled some yogurt or...it looks like ice cream most likely," she says looking confused.

"When you ever see somebody eating yogurt up in here?" Kenny says.

"Yeah, they spilled some yogurt all right. He spilled his entire yogurt," another guy adds.

"I have no idea what y'all talking about." a bewildered Loretta replies.

After that, for a while, guys will be walking around cracking up whenever anyone says the word yogurt.

Some of those meetings were a hoot. There were some very witty black guys and gals in that room and they could make me laugh.

Things among our small Black student population at SPS were far from perfect. Just as back in all-black Harlem Park, where we had to contend with intra-racial prejudices, there was some similar nonsense at SPS.

It generally involved instances of pettiness and subtle cruelties to guys who were perceived as too accommodating or too friendly with the white boys, or the faculty. We sometimes had a mob mentality, that kind of thinking where you were either with us or against us. Several guys were not treated very nicely at times. Mike Russell was a frequent target and so was Turville, although Turville sidestepped the problem by avoiding everyone at all times.

Part of the problem that guys had with Mike, was that he sometimes seemed too eager to blend in with the white guys; he roomed with a white kid. He seemed not as eager to blend in with the black guys and I suppose some of the boys found that offensive.

I had known Mike for at least a year and I was already used to Mike going his own way and doing just as he pleased. We were friends, but we never spent very much time hangin' out, and it didn't bother me. Mike was on his own mission.

What was more significant was the perception that Mike also got along too well with Mr. Grant, who now had several guys who required his stern supervision. We were afraid that Mr. Grant would use Mike to find out what trouble the rest of us had in mind, so guys were suspicious of him.

Mr. Grant was particularly kind to Mike, giving him gifts, even lending him some of his personal albums and often taking Mike on recruiting trips. Most of the rest of us fell far short of Mike's example and received no such goodwill.

Mike did make an effort to come around the rest of us occasionally, but he never seemed very comfortable and never stayed very long. The fact that he was on the basketball team, and a co-captain no less, kept him in closer contact with the rest of us, during basketball season alone. Beyond that he was largely absent from us.

In the fall, Mike played varsity football and in the spring, he played varsity baseball. Not very many black guys participated in football at the varsity level and still fewer played varsity baseball, so we didn't see Mike very much during those seasons.

I think Mike wanted greater acceptance from the rest of us, but he wasn't willing to compromise himself, and you can't blame him for that. He wanted no part of the noise, the stealing, or any other questionable behavior. It embarrassed him, and I understood that, because sometimes it also embarrassed me.

As much as he may have wanted to, like the besieged and virtuous Sir Thomas Moore in A Man for all Seasons, Mike couldn't find the 'other way'. I believe that there was 'another way' that would have allowed Mike to fit in and still be the outstanding and conscientious fellow he wanted to be.

For some reason, Mike couldn't find it. It could be that he just didn't care to and that, rightly or wrongly, was construed by some of the boys to mean that he thought himself better than the rest of us. It was on that score that several guys objected to Mike, although some of the younger boys and the girls (when they arrived) still looked up to him. The whole thing was stupid teenaged boy bullshit.

Everyone was reasonably civil to one another but that undercurrent of suspicion and frostiness with Mike persisted. Slowly, he stopped coming around and no one was going to invite him.

I'm sure Mike had demons of his own with which he had to contend. He and I still talked frequently, and things between us were friendly, but on a much more superficial level now. He didn't seem comfortable around me anymore either.

Many, many years later, I felt compelled to apologize to Mike for my tacit participation in that whole business. For my part in it, it was one of those situations where the problem wasn't only what the outlaws were doing; the problem was what the good people had not done. In other words, there were times when I might have spoken up for him, or at least explicitly expressed some disapproval when guys appeared to be treating him coldly.

Yet, at that time, the way I looked at it, Mike and I had both made choices, deciding what track we wanted to take. The price I paid for the choices I made was to live with the constant ire of Mr. Grant because he thought I was behaving like a street punk and not living up to my potential, and other more obscure costs.

I'm not completely sure what price Mike paid for his choices, but I know that what he was experiencing, the good and the bad, was perhaps an inevitable part of it. We were supposed to be big boys – right.

One day, we cornered Mike in our room and began asking him to honestly, no holds barred; tell us what Mr. Grant really thought of each of us. I believe it was Cook, Hipp, Shivers, Nelson and maybe Kenny and Ed and a couple of others present, and me. We always acted as though we couldn't possibly care what Mr. Grant's opinion of us was, but deep down we wondered. I know I thought about it.

Although grilling Mike like this was not my idea, when I heard what they were asking, I really wanted to hear what he would say. Even though doing so was like picking at a scab over a sore, where you know you should leave it alone but you just can't help yourself, and you end up bloodied.

After some vigorously spirited resistance, Mike surprised me by finally relenting. He then immediately looked into my eyes and said slowly and distinctly,

"He just absolutely hates you!"

And it was like – Daaaammmmn! That was cold-blooded! I'm telling you, that statement, and the look of contempt on Mike's face when he uttered it, landed so heavily among us that there was now little reason to talk about anyone else.

Immediately, all the boys present protested strongly in my defense, but I did not hear them. I put on a brave smile after Mike had spoken because I knew all eyes were on me, but inside I was numb, wounded, and yet surprisingly calm as I absorbed what he had said. I got up from where I was sitting on my bed and without a word left the room. I took a walk.

It is one thing to suspect such contempt, and obviously I wanted to believe that it might not be true because I felt, "Why would he hate me... how is it possible that he could not like me that much?" I mean - I did everything I could to stay out of Mr. Grant's way. To my knowledge, I had never knowingly done anything to him. I certainly had no power to hurt him. What was his fucking problem with me? I didn't understand it then, and I don't think I shall ever know what the truth is, and ...well, none of it matters now.

Of course, there is the question of how much of Mike was in the statement. Mikes revelation aside, I already knew that I could handle Mr. Grant. I had learned to do that. Mr. Grant was aware that I had absolutely no use for him, and I was aware that such a thing was probably insulting to him and to his position as our adviser.

I thought all we needed to do was to stay out of one another's way. As far as I was concerned, that was still the best likely course. I could succeed without him, I thought. The thing with Mike was more complicated. I had been careful to avoid ever ganging-up on Mike, but like me (dealing with Mr. Grant) - he was on his own after that.

I know Mike felt betrayed by me.

*****

313

CHAPTER 51 – FACULTY, ENGLISH

I was able to get along with nearly everyone, students and faculty. I did have more than one verbal altercation with a couple of the faculty during my career at SPS. No real harm ensued. One of them never spoke to me again, but I convinced myself that I didn't care.

The rector during my first two years was a man named Matthew Warren. Mr. Warren sometimes wore a clerical collar but it did little to soften his rigid visage. He always struck me as a pretty tough guy and for me he was an unlikely choice to spearhead this stepped up opening of the pearly white gates of SPS to minority students. I figured that there had to be something reasonably decent about him to take on such a challenge. I also suspect it turned out to be an unexpectedly difficult task for him. I liked him.

It was Mr. Warren who spoke with me on the phone when I missed the SPS bus upon my arrival in Boston. He left after my second year and was succeeded by William Oates, who was flashier and wore brighter suits (grey instead of black), but was not much less old school from my vantage point. Mr. Oates was stern, but his short stature made him appear accessible. He supervised the enrollment of the first girls, who probably thought he was cute.

Mr. Warren and later Mr. Oates were both charged with navigating the St. Paul's School ship. I had very little contact with either of them, although I know that they both kept a wary eye on my boys and me. I'm glad we never tangled because they were both tough men.

I never formed any especially close relationships with any of the faculty in particular, although there were several members of the faculty of whom I was fond. These were most often the guys that most of the black guys liked and who were generally well liked by the SPS student body in general. Three that come to mind are Jim Buxton, Richard Lederer and George Carlisle. Each of them was able to relate to our youth without condescension. They all taught English. Lederer and Buxton were especially cool.

Also well-liked were Cliff Gillespie (the Rock) and Bill Matthews for their firm but honest bearing, you could trust them to be straight with you. There were other good men at SPS, but these are some that stood out for me personally. I cannot imagine that any one of them would remember me now – well maybe a couple of them might.

Anyone in the athletic department was a friend to us all. We had tremendous respect for Maurice Blake who coached a few varsity sports and Mr. Barker, with his gravely voice and endless stories of the old days at SPS.

Hipp and I especially liked an athletic trainer named Mr. Harris. He was a funny guy, with a pleasant face and a great bedside manner. He was good at his job. Mr. Harris had a good sense of humor.

"What did Mr. Harris say about your sore knee, Hipp?"

"I don't know man, seems to me like every time I tell him something is wrong he tells me that it is the pre-patella, whatever that is. I could be talking about my ass and he would say, 'I think it's the pre-patella, Hipp."

I thought all of the other boys had a better knack for developing close ties and genuine friendships with various faculty members than I did. Usually, it was only through hanging with the other boys that I ever came into close proximity with any of the faculty, other than in classes and sports. I avoided them.

It was always difficult for me to relax in their presence. Talking with them felt too much like being on stage for me, particularly when there were other guys around, because then it seemed that everyone was fighting to be noticed or to impress. That's how it often was at seated meals.

Most of the black guys had close ties to Mr. Lederer. He had done a year's Sabbatical at Simon Gratz, a tough inner-city public high school in Philadelphia, and all of us had tremendous respect for his commitment to education, and his bravery in working at that particular school.

Guys would often stop in to see him at his dormitory apartment and he would invite them in to hang out with his family and give them things to eat. I believe I stopped by his place once.

Mr. Lederer taught English, and he offered a course that explored literature and popular culture. Several of us signed on for it. It was one of the few classes that Cook, Hipp and I had together other than a creative writing class with Mr. Carlisle where we primarily wrote poetry or short stories.

At each session of the writing class, someone had to read a short story he had written. The three of us were constantly trying to shock and amuse the class with our often provocative stories of Black life. Writing short stories was fun for me and I was usually anxious to read mine. The boys knew I was good for a few laughs.

Mr. Lederer assigned a class project to us and for my project; I decided to explore the history and progression of jazz music. What was great about Mr. Lederer was that he was willing to allow a student to experiment with form and content as much as he wanted - within reason.

I decided to do a very low key, quiet exploration of various styles of jazz by turning the classroom into a sort of speakeasy joint, with closed blinds, lowered lights. The class members were allowed to get comfortable, lying on the floor, propped between chairs, whatever.

I ran into one problem with the music. None of the black guys on campus had many jazz albums. I knew that Mr. Grant had some, but he did not like to loan out his albums and I would not have taken on that perilous responsibility if he had.

I asked around, found that a formmate, Doug Chan, was a jazz buff, and had an extensive collection of jazz albums. He was kind enough to give me complete access to them.

Over a few days, I listened to tons of jazz music, and then assembled a tape that included long and sometimes complete samples of music by artists such as Herbie Hancock, Miles Davis, Billie Holiday, Count Basie, etc. Between songs, in a quiet FM radio-like voiceover, I gave the history of the artists, music styles, the chronology of jazz history, with anecdotal facts sprinkled in,

"Next we will be hearing from Billie Holiday aka Lady Day, born Eleanora Fagan. Her turbulent personal life is a well known fact and indeed her personal troubles were as haunting as the songs she sang. We'll be listening to a song entitled Strange Fruit, a song based on a poem about lynching..."

My boy Hipp told me how much he enjoyed my presentation. He said he learned some things, and he also thought I had some potential as a radio DJ. Occasionally Hipp would imitate my narrative by coming up to me and saying,

"Relax, and dig the sides."

Mr. Lederer gave me high marks for that project and the guys loved it because they were able to spend the entire classroom period in a way that didn't feel like class at all. They also loved the jazz music. Mr. Lederer shared my tape and narrative with one of his other classes.

There was something imminently likable about Mr. Lederer. He had a way of making you feel that he took you seriously, that you were significant, that you had possibilities. I think I needed some of that kind of affirmation. I think Mr. Lederer realized I was somewhat of a loner, but he was never pushy. My first year, he used his own time to help me become a better basketball player. Some of my best work came out of his class. I liked him a lot.

I imagine some of the lessons Mr. Lederer learned during his sabbatical at Simon Gratz, that inner city school in Philadelphia, helped him to extend to me the sort of compassion and empathy that a man like Mr. Grant could never muster. I couldn't imagine Mr. Grant ever reaching out to help needy kids by spending a year where they live.

How ironic!

*****

CHAPTER 52 – HIPP, AN INVISIBLE FORTRESS

My closest personal connection with anyone at SPS turned out to be with Robert Hipp. Hipp and I roomed together for two years. We were proud of that fact. Not many of the black guys lasted that long together, often they only lasted a semester or two. When we first met, I told him I was from Baltimore. Hipp said he didn't know anything about Baltimore and I was the first person he had met from there.

He said, "The only thing I know about Baltimore, was that during the riots the newsman came on TV and said, 'And Baltimore is in flames!'

At some point, Hipp acquired the nickname Invisible. A photograph in our senior yearbook shows Hipp in cross-country gear running down a country lane, with the caption 'Invisible takes up the rear.' This was because he was often overlooked when people gave out the accolades for athletic achievement or other types of accomplishments.

One day in chapel, the Rector announced that Cook had made All New England in basketball, and Russell and I had received honorable mention, but there was no special recognition for Hipp. Hipp was too good-natured to complain, but privately he told me that he hated the way he was often over-looked. I didn't like it either.

It was Hipp who was the soul of the b-ball team. When Hipp was not in the game, I always felt that we stood far less a chance of winning, even though he wasn't the star of the team. He just knew how to keep it together. He had a strong drive to win and his presence on the basketball court comforted me.

Often and quite unexpectedly, I learned something from him. There were nights when I would be in our room studying late, which was called grinding at SPS, and Hipp would walk in,

"Burning the midnight oil man?" he asked once.

"I don't know...What? What do you mean by that?" I asked.

"You know, studying late and all. C'mon man, you never heard anybody say that before?"

"No, I have never heard that before," I answer, which makes him laugh and shake his head.

I once complained to him that I had a zipper that wouldn't stay up.

"Well, did you try locking it?" Hipp says.

"What do you mean by that?" I say, looking confused.

"Don't tell me you don't know that you can lock a zipper by pushing that little piece down?" He says giggling.

"Really man? No one ever showed me that," I tell him.

Hipp would tell me stories about this robot toy he had when he was a small kid. It was called The Great Garloo. I had never heard of it and he was amazed at my ignorance. He showed me a photo of him as a young child in his pajamas sitting next to The Great Garloo. When we graduated, Hipp wrote in my yearbook, "Will we ever forget the Great Garloo?"

I never will.

Hipp never made me feel stupid and Hipp was never invisible to me - quite the opposite actually, even now. Hipp was one of the best people I have ever met.

He was exceedingly practical. At basketball practice, he once told us that he had a bank account with a few thousand dollars in it. We were amazed. Unlike many of us, Hipp did not spend every penny he had, and cared little for running out to get the latest fashions. I admired that about him, and given my background, I knew that I felt similarly.

I just wasn't as courageous about bucking the prevailing adolescent conventions as Hipp. I wanted to look sharp. When all the guys on the b-ball team bought expensive leather sneakers, Hipp was the last to give in. I was one of the first. Hipp hated spending all that money for sneakers.

Our room in Nash, a newer dormitory, was one of the biggest double rooms on campus and was highly sought after. We couldn't believe our good luck in getting it. There were always a lot of guys hanging out in our room because it was so spacious; often Hipp and I were not present.

At night, Hipp and I would talk. He would be lying on his stomach on his bed and I would be doing the same across the wide room. Hipp liked to listen to music before he went to sleep and he would have it turned low. I would sing along sometimes and Hipp discovered that I could sing. I confided to him that I would like to sing in a group like the Temptations one day. He thought I could do it.

Hipp talked about his girlfriend Alma most of the time. They were a cute couple. It was impossible for me to understand how he could spend every spare minute with her, but I think it came easily for him. Hipp wasn't the type to pursue women indiscriminately. He seemed more suited to something more settled. His infatuation with Alma, and hers with him, was a heartwarming picture of mad young love.

She was one of the few people in our crowd to call Hipp by his first name (Robert). I always thought she seemed to be pronouncing it – Wobert. Hipp probably fell in love with her based on the 'cute factor' of her southern voice alone. Alma was funny and smart, but Hipp said that he was always explaining a lot of common-sense things to Alma. He liked to say that she was smart, but with no common sense. She was adorable.

We would also discuss some of the dynamics of life for the black guys at SPS. We both had few complaints with anyone and tried to stay clear of much of the inevitable jealousy, pettiness and animosity that afflict teenaged boys. When we were together, there did not have to be a lot of phoniness or small talk. We were good friends.

I was going out with someone myself, she was my new girl at SPS actually, and her name was Addie. She was younger, only in the third form, and I often felt slightly guilty about going out with a girl so young. There were not a lot of girls enrolled at SPS and the competition among us teenaged boys to win their favor was fierce. My politics strictly forbade me from even thinking about going out with a white girl.

I had the edge with Addie because I was her old boy and had written to her the previous summer. Once she arrived at SPS and met me, I'm sure she was caught up in the usual starry–eyed wonder that many young girls exhibit for an older teenaged boy, "Oooh, a sixth-former."

Our relationship was off and on. Addie was confined by the school rules for third-formers that did not allow her the freedom of movement that a sixth-former had. In addition, I had become such a relative loner by then that I wasn't interested in hanging out with the other third, forth and fifth-formers that essentially comprised her circle of friends.

The entire affair was difficult on her I think. She was not totally naïve, but she was in no ways prepared to deal with someone of my dubious experience and aloofness, and I say that with all the humility and regret that I can muster. Addie was a sweet, caring and bright girl and I liked her a lot. Even now, I'm sorry I did not behave as maturely as she did.

Although Hipp was a pretty gentle guy, old fashioned and almost frumpy in his style of dress, he did have a vicious streak, that killer instinct.

He was sitting on the bleachers once (nursing a badly injured hand), watching some of us play a 3-on-3 pick-up b-ball game. This guy named Rodney Williams (Oobs) was guarding me. Cook had given Rodney the nickname of Oobs, which was a reference to his fat butt that Cook said was as big as an ooba-tuba. Cook had a penchant for making up nicknames for people.

Oobs was Black, but his family was comfortably stable, financially, according to him, especially when compared to those of us from the projects and slums. For that reason and some others, Oobs was perceived as soft among the black guys, a fact that caused Rodney to try too hard to fit in.

It meant that you couldn't allow him to beat you at anything, because you knew that if he did, he wouldn't ever shut up about winning against us ghetto niggers. Yet Oobs desperately wanted to spend as much time as he could with those of us he considered to be the toughest and most popular, particularly Cook.

Oobs once had the misfortune of jokingly referring to us as ghetto niggers when Cook was not in the mood for it and Cook kicked his ass pretty bad. I did not try to stop Cook that day either. That time,

I simply found the whole thing to be funny, the price Oobs had to pay for his 'hero worship' of Cook.

Oobs thought that since he was Black he could get away with that remark. Any other time he might have gotten away with it, but that day his timing was bad and he got beat down. Timing can be everything with that stuff.

I can still see Cook punching Oobs, who was on his knees curled up in a ball on the floor, with the quiet and reserved housemaster, Mr. Ball, running in a circle around them.

Mr. Ball kept repeating in his soft monotone voice, "John...John... stop it John. I think he's had enough John." It was a riot.

So, I am out on the basketball court and Oobs is guarding me one-on-one, and Hipp is yelling at me from the bleachers, seemingly right in my ear,

"Dick that muthafucka man. Dick that muthafucka, Wid! Don't let him get shit."

Hipp played on the varsity baseball team in the spring, as did Mike Russell and Wiltshire. I participated in track and field in the spring and that meant that I did not see Hipp as often because we operated on different schedules.

One day near the end of winter, at about the time when baseball practices begin, Hipp and I started playing this game where I would rush at him with a knife and he would defend himself. I had this Swiss army knife that I liked. It sounds stupid, but sometimes we were as silly as little boys were. I would make these wide sweeping stab motions, being careful to turn the blade away from him, and Hipp would grab my arm and wrestle me to the ground.

We did this many times, but on one turn, Hipp made a grab for my wrist and I accidentally sliced his hand open pretty badly. He bled a good deal. It was completely my fault because I neglected to turn the blade. We took him to the infirmary and from there he was taken to a hospital in town, where Hipp received several stitches to close a deep and ugly wound near his thumb.

I felt terrible. To make matters worse, Hipp had to miss playing baseball while he healed. When I would be on the track participating in a track meet, I would see him sitting alone at the end of the baseball team's bench, watching the team compete. Hipp never blamed me - not a word.

Sometimes in the mornings, after chapel, Hipp would race from the chapel in order to get to our first class that morning before anyone else arrived. He would then write the title of that morning's hymn on the chalkboard, but he would insert his name into the title somehow, so it would be something like, A Mighty Fortress Is Our Hipp. The morning after a special performance in Memorial Hall by the great French mime Marcel Marceau, Hipp wrote on the board, Marcel MarHipp. That stuff always cracked me up.

*****

CHAPTER 53 – BASKETBALL, TRACK, VALIDATION

All of us loved playing on the varsity basketball team; and as I said, the team was nearly all Black, Hispanic and Native-American. During our sixth form year especially, we generated some real excitement at SPS for basketball. SPS was a hockey school, but for the first time in probably many years – maybe ever, there were busloads of students coming to our away basketball games. My senior year, we came close to winning a championship, but we finished a heartbreaking game or two short.

On Sunday mornings, a lot of the black guys would meet in the gym for pick-up games. This was when we had the most fun playing ball. It was that street, playground, run-and-gun kind of game, the brand of ball that we could never practice on the SPS varsity team run by Coach Blake.

Coach Blake was a no nonsense guy who insisted on disciplined team play. All the guys respected him. Proof of that, was when he insisted that we all shave our tentative adolescent mustaches and goatees to be on his team. That was a hard thing to do for a bunch of guys trying to look as manly as possible, but everyone did it.

I loved those Sunday games. I played better basketball then. It was like being on the playgrounds of Harlem Park. I was a starter for the SPS varsity, but I was not a very complete player. My strengths were rebounding and defensive hustle and I staked out that particular niche for myself on the team. On Sundays, I could be a scorer. I had a fairly decent shot. Had I a little more weight on me, I might have faired better over-all, but I was painfully thin.

Size was not as important in track and field as it was in basketball, and it is there I found my personal sports kingdom at SPS. I never trained very hard for track, but I found that I had some natural skills, especially in the long jump.

As a fifth-former, at the annual New England Interscholastic Track Meet, I was hoping for at least a fair showing against some of the best track and field talent in New England. I had long jumped for the first time that day, when this kid from another private school came up to me. He was tall, had crazy wild hair and he was wearing glasses.

"Look, you don't know me and we're competing against one another and everything, but I've been watching you warm up and I watched that first jump you took, which was not bad, if I might add. Anyway, you're much better than you think. I know that I have no ways near your talent, but I noticed that, with your speed, if you would hold your legs up for a split second longer, you would go at least a foot farther."

"Yeah, I've tried that man, but it always feel as though I'll pull something." I told him.

"Just try it one time. I think you'll be surprised, that's all I'm telling you, one time."

Another guy walked over as he was saying this. It was this black guy from Chicago named McPherson, whom I had met during the six weeks at Dartmouth. We had developed something of a rivalry in the long jump over the past two years.

"Why you trying to help him dummy, he's on the other team." McPherson says.

My next jump, I take that kid's advice, straining to keep my legs extended, and the jump is explosive. I don't remember any sound, just the thud of landing. Someone told me later the crowd gasped because I flew so far and it was so completely unexpected.

"Then I heard an official say "22 feet and eight inches."

"Whoa…you sure you're not mistaken?" I said to him as I struggled to contain myself.

"No mistake son, congratulations. I shouldn't say it, but I don't think anyone here will beat that today."

"You haven't won yet man, still a lot of jumping gonna happen here." It was McPherson whispering in my ear.

I was jumping around like an idiot, still in disbelief. McPherson's words gave me cause to settle down, but the day ended with me winning the long jump at the New England Inter-scholastics. I set a new SPS school record for the long jump, smashing the old record by nearly two feet, which is not a bad day.

It gave me a certain stature at that track meet for the rest of the day and then on the SPS campus when we returned to the school. It was my grand moment, the sort of validation of my athletic abilities that I had been craving.

What made it even better was that I had injured my leg running in a relay, so I returned to school with my leg heavily bandaged, and walking with the aid of a cane. I looked like I had been in a train wreck. That only helped to bolster my heroic image.

That was a very good day. I felt that I had attained a substantial place in the collective SPS school consciousness that day, my own distinguished place in the history of the school. Someday, my own long jump record will be broken, but for now, I am the king.

Coach Blake's wife prepared a celebratory spaghetti dinner for me at their private campus residence. It was my first time inside one of those lovely, typically white and shuttered New England homes that dotted the SPS campus here and there. Some of the staff members lived in those homes with their families.

Originally, Coach Blake had promised a special dinner if I broke the high jump record, but Coach decided the long jump record would do. Hipp came along, at my invitation, to help me out with the small talk. He kept them laughing. I'm not sure if I would have gone if Hipp couldn't attend.

I never again long jumped as well as I did that day. At a subsequent track meet on our home track, there were great expectations that I would break the SPS track record for the long jump. A huge crowd had assembled to witness my effort. All of St. Paul's was pulling for me.

To my amazement, Mr. Grant was there with his expensive camera and tri-pod. He set up at the back of the long jump pit to get a photo of me making the jump. Many times, I had seen him with his camera taking photos of campus life and the inhabitants, but this was the first time I remember him being focused on me.

As it turned out, there was to be no new track record in the long jump that day, although I did record some very good jumps and Mr. Grant was able to get a nice photo of me gliding through the air, slicing the crowd. In the photograph, the support of the SPS community for my effort is evident on the many faces of the people surrounding the long jump pit.

Maybe for just a moment, Mr. Grant had to hate me a little less.

*****

CHAPTER 54 – WANTED, AN SPS REVOLUTION

I have always thought that the white boys in my form at SPS all wanted to be John Lennon, whom we could all agree was one of the coolest white boys ever. I greatly admire John Lennon. He managed to combine his working class cool with a brilliant mind to create some groundbreaking music.

He had the sort of edgy persona I was shooting for, and from what I have read, he could be a bit caustic too. He had just the right something. I think they call it genius. The Beatles, The Stones and Hendrix ruled the day at SPS and you would hear some incarnation of their music, or an assortment of other rock n' roll music coming from every room.

The release of the Beatle's Sgt. Pepper's Lonely Hearts Club Band and later the 'White Album' were transcendent moments of musical history on the SPS campus. I would hear the Beatles song The Continuing Story of Bungalow Bill echoing down the dormitory halls countless times. I loved that song. There was so much good music everywhere, so many smart and courageous people speaking out, trying to make sense of the world.

Many of the white boys were buttoned down and conservative. However, there were a good number of guys in my graduating class who flirted with existence on the edge. These were the guys who were writing songs and playing jazz or the blues, creating art projects, doing some photography and maybe a little marijuana or acid, the drugs in relatively strict moderation because one's grades were still critical to remaining at SPS.

There was more drug use at SPS than many might have imagined. It was an underground thing that only certain guys knew about. We were not even allowed to smoke cigarettes on campus, until a rule change during my fifth form year.

In order to get high, it was necessary to spend time at night in the woods surrounding St. Paul's School. That made it prohibitive for me because I was unwilling to go into the woods at night. The mosquitoes in those woods were numerous and hungry. Some guys would cover themselves in this smelly tar-like woodsman's insect repellant, so that they could go out and smoke.

Guys were also getting high inside the dormitories, but that was very risky. Getting high was not a big priority for me. It didn't make sense to get high just to study. In addition, there was no place to buy it, and I had no money to spend on such a thing if there was. Much of my free time, I was only interested in getting some extra sleep.

I did smoke with some of the black guys from SPS, but we were in Boston, away from campus. I wasn't much of a drinker either and I don't believe that I ever had any alcohol while on SPS grounds. Compared to some of the other guys, I was an angel. How could Mr. Grant not like me?

I was considered cool enough that I was privy to some of what was going on in the school underground. Besides, I had spent a lot of time around guys who were getting high in Harlem Park. Just as I could spot the junkies at home, I could spot many of the guys who were getting high. It was a simple matter of knowing who a particular guy hung out with, and when.

Many of the white boys looked liked the stereotypical drug user anyway, with their long hair, scraggly stubble on their faces and torn jeans. Such lapses in personal hygiene were more prolific once the dress code became more relaxed.

They were learning how to be cool with black guys. I suspect many of them had never had an opportunity to measure themselves against black guys from the inner cities. We were amused by the whole 'torn jean' thing'. None of us would willingly wear torn jeans.

There was a coffee house for students near the Lower School Pond. It was a place to stand around a roaring fire, talk some trash and have something hot to drink. Often a few guys would come in with instruments and try to play a little jazz or blues.

I didn't go there much, but when I did the white guys always wanted me to sit in and play or sing with them despite the fact that my only real musical expertise was on the trumpet, and no one ever brought one of those.

I would sit at the piano and play a few chords I had picked-up fooling around on a toy organ back on Edmondson Avenue, and the white guys would try to follow me. It wasn't very inspired music, but I could sense that they felt themselves to be enormously cool, jammin' with a black guy. That amused me, because I stunk!

There were some interesting people among them. At times, we would sit around in the coffee house and have these spirited, weighty discussions on issues of the day. We all brought wildly different perspectives to the table, making for conversation that was passionate, witty and sometimes brilliant – even I had my moments.

When we were senior classmen, there was a lot of fearful talk about the Vietnam War. There was a military draft lottery then. Everyone was afraid of getting drafted, even at St. Paul's School.

John F. Kerry, an SPS alumnus and president of Vietnam Veterans Against War, visited the school and spoke about his personal experiences in the war. That got a lot of guys thinking. I personally knew several boys back in Harlem Park who had been drafted and at least one who had been killed in Vietnam.

One of the boys in our SPS class was drafted before he could graduate from St. Paul's – from high school! The war in Vietnam had fallen apart, and by then the United States was aware that we were losing, but this kid had already been drafted and had to report. His graduation portrait was a photo of dense forest undergrowth since he had to leave before his senior portrait was taken. Luckily, he never had to do any fighting.

One night, a meeting of the entire student body was held in Memorial Hall at which no faculty members were to be present. Today, I do not remember what it was that brought us there in the first place. What I do remember is that the meeting began to degenerate into a boring gripe session about unpopular school policies. However, things took a sudden turn when a new flash point was found.

Someone yelled, "We should ask them to change the school dress code. What's the point of us sitting in class all day in a jacket and tie; it doesn't help us learn any better."

How lame! However, the issue of abandoning jackets and ties for classes was a topic that would always rear its head when there was talk about school policies and it had lately acquired a new urgency for those of us who wanted a revolution – well you know?

"They're not going to change the dress code in a million years asshole!" someone else offers.

"It's what makes SPS," someone else throws in.

"I know for myself, I can't afford all those clothes," one of the brothers says.

"Me either, I have one sport coat that I wear all the time." another black guy pipes in - and a way forward was revealed.

In my opinion, this seemed to bring a slightly different complexion to the issue for everyone. It was almost as though everyone suddenly saw that this was an issue of social injustice. A change in the dress code was needed, if only just out of fairness to the kids who were less fortunate, like the black guys. Yeah! Yeah!

"Let's see by a show of hands, how many people here want an end to coats and ties."

Hands shot up all over the room. A lot of those guys were cheering and hooting, totally caught up in this moment of revolution. Most of them had no clue as to why they wanted to go along with this, but they became swept up in a wave of cool disobedience. They had no idea how much they were kidding themselves.

"OK! Tomorrow - anyone that no longer wants to wear a coat and tie - don't wear it!"

A loud roar of approval welled up from the assembly.

"Won't we get kicked out of class?" some of the younger guys ask.

"Of course we will, but we will be there to help you. Just find one of us older guys."

I bet nobody figured on this kind of thing when the brothers were let the in.

The next day, at least 70 to 80% of the boys, punked out and wore their ties. However, there were a good number of guys, black and white, who did go to classes without their ties and we were thrown out of our classrooms.

When I was asked to leave my classroom, I spent a long time talking to the teacher about why he felt it necessary to expel me from his room. Apparently, it wasn't personal because he had served in a unit with Black men in Korea, and there was the usual talk about his many Black friends, etc.

This failed demonstration did precipitate a more aggressive school dialogue on the dress code. To the school's credit, after some studies, meetings and experiments, at the start of the next year, the dress code was relaxed substantially. Ties were no longer required for classes and we could wear jeans that were 'clean neat and in good repair'. It was a good practical lesson in civil disobedience, very minor league John Lennon!

After our protest, I felt a sense of power, because many of the black guys were at the center of the strike and I believe that gave courage to the white guys. We came to St. Paul's, and irrevocably insinuated ourselves into the fabric of the place. Louie Grant was not impressed.

Our attempts at social protest aside, life at SPS was still rich and predictable - safe - yet I complained every day. I swore that I would never send a child of mine to such a place. I don't feel that way anymore.

St. Paul's School did evolve. Girls were admitted and the first class of graduating girls was in my class. There were only three or four girls graduating, but things had come a long way from my days as a freshman at SPS when the only girls we saw on a daily basis were the children of faculty. We no longer had to settle for the one or two black girls who might attend the Tea Dances.

Starting with my fourth form year, when more black guys were enrolled at SPS, we began to organize our own parties. That required contacting maybe ten private girl's schools to cull a group of perhaps twenty black girls for a party. It was all pretty desperate.

On one occasion, we threw an impromptu party in the black student lounge when some kids from the ABC program in town came on campus. Initially they had come to attend a Tea Dance that was scheduled that night in the Gates Room.

However, some of our boys decided that the Tea Dance was boring and that we could have a much better party in our own black student lounge, with some R&B music and some seriously dimmed lights if no adults were present.

A plan was hatched; some of the boys went to their rooms to gather the necessary music, with perhaps a quick change into more casual and provocative clothing, and a party was born. We did all of this without Mr. Grant's permission or knowledge.

At first, there were not a lot of people privy to the party. Initially, the idea was to have a more adult-like house party for those of us who were older, fifth and sixth-formers mainly. We planned to go back to the Tea Dance in the Gates Room before it ended, and nobody would get hurt.

That scenario went bust the minute that word of the thing started getting around. If too many people showed up we were sure to get caught, and soon everyone knew about it.

The confounding thing is that we attempted to pull off such a thing in the first place. We were bright kids, yet we decided to dismiss the obvious. We knew we were headed for trouble with Mr. Grant, but that night we just didn't care.

A part of it was, unfortunately, we fell into a trap. We didn't want the ABC program kids to think that we were afraid to break rules. There was a guy named Julius in the ABC program and he would often goad us by suggesting that the black boys at St. Paul's were a little soft and pampered.

"Ya'll know ya'll scared to do anything. You got the perfect room where we can go listen to some slow jams. I ain't scared of no muthafuckin' Mr. Grant. Ya'll a bunch of punks."

No way could we let him get away with saying that. We were sunk by our own raging egos.

I have no idea how Mr. Grant found out about the party, but after we partied for about a half hour, he came storming into that room in a rage. There was no warning. When I looked up, he was already in the room.

At first, he said nothing. He stood there looking around the room, fuming. Then he recited the usual talking points,

"...who gave permission? ... Does the ABC chaperone know? ... Irresponsible ... displaced values ... no hard work...,"

Not to mention the issues of safety and liability and all that other perfectly reasonable shit. After exhausting all that, he really lost his temper.

He went on a rampage, a real honest-to-god raging tear, and began ripping posters off the wall, turning tables over, slamming books and things and eventually smashing the stereo system. He completely razed the temple. Those of us who did not flee stood by in stunned silence, and we had no defense.

My one thought as I stood there watching him was, "Boy I'm glad that I am not him."

No rational person could argue that we weren't wrong, we were way out of line, but I thought Mr. Grant's reaction was just plain loco. It was more like watching a toddler's temper tantrum than looking in on the actions of a mature professional educator, and he should not have let that happen under any circumstances.

In that instant, any respect I may have had for him evaporated into thin air. I now think that Mr. Grant's shocking display of blind rage that night may have been the single event that completed my liberation from his oppressive influence. I can't speak for anyone else.

Whatever was troubling Mr. Grant was clearly a deeper and much darker issue than any of us could comprehend? He had every right to be angry. After all, he was the adviser to our Black Student Union. Still, he is an adult and a teacher of history at the prestigious St. Paul's School. In that context, his behavior was entirely, to use his word, inappropriate. He and I were finished.

Therefore, by the time I had neared completion of sixth form in June 1972, Mr. Grant did not worry me any longer. I had found my way. I was an accomplished and confident young man now. My report cards now actually contained a few High Honors and the finish line (graduation) was in sight. It had been a tough four years, but tough in a good way.

I found myself thinking back to the Annual Turkey Crawl cross-country race that I had run when I was a new third-former, and how I had arrogantly assumed that I could win that race easily. Well, it wasn't an easy race, and as I staggered across that frozen country landscape, I suffered through painful cramps and blinding fatigue, before finally up-chucking all over the nice white snow. I learned some things about myself that day. I didn't finish first, but I finished respectably distanced from last.

Now, I felt a sense of pride that for four years at St. Paul's I had navigated an academic course that was decidedly more difficult than I could possibly have imagined. I learned some things about myself along the way. I didn't finish first, but I believe I finished respectably distanced from last.

The important thing is I finished what I had begun and gained a lifetime's worth of knowledge along the way. I was filled with the realization that (like at the end of that Turkey Crawl race) it was all downhill on a bed of snow and pine needles from here.

*****

CHAPTER 55 – GETTING IT

There were moments during which I knew I was as capable as any other student at St. Paul's School. Actually, there had been many small occasions leading up to this realization, specific instances when I performed well academically.

One such occurred while I was in the third form, in an Ancient Religions class. I had written a paper examining Jesus as an historical figure, which was singled-out as an outstanding essay by our instructor, Mr. Howard White (Howdy). He said that it was the only paper from the class that was any good and he thought it was very good. He read it to the class.

The strange thing was that even though he had lauded my paper, as he read it, I remember thinking that the language I used sounded infantile and simplistic, not what one would expect from the best paper in the class. I think that was what Mr. White liked about it.

Everyone in the class was astonished, because I rarely spoke in that class. There were some really smart guys in there and they loved to debate; Mike Russell was in that class. You knew not to open your mouth in there if you were not prepared, and I never felt fully prepared to debate them effectively.

When I was a fifth-former, I was taking a required course called Ancient Civilizations. A team of instructors taught it. They grouped a couple of classes together to form a large lecture class of maybe - twenty boys. We were focusing on ancient Greece and were looking at the city-state of Sparta.

For a couple of weeks our instructors, led by Mr. Kellogg and Mr. Knickerbocker labored to make some important point about the origins of Spartan law, a point that it seemed none of us could figure out. They lectured and prodded, and moderated intense classroom discussions, to no avail. There was another large lecture group taking the same Ancient History class and they couldn't figure it out either. Outside of the class, everyone was trying to figure out what they were getting at.

The frustration on the faces of the faculty was very apparent. They wanted us to figure-out something very specific. After a few days of this, as I sat listening to all these really bright guys mouthing off, I had a thought; and very tentatively asked to speak.

"I was thinking that it was possible that the Spartans may have been influenced by the culture of Crete, because they had similar Gods, half-man and half-animal. That had to be more than a mere coincidence. There must have been some exchange of ideas between them." I said.

Mr. Kellogg stopped everything, silenced everyone. He walked up to me and looked in my face.

"Did you think of that all on your own?" he asked.

"Yes." I replied.

"No one told you that?" He asked again.

"No sir. It was just a thought."

"That was very good," he said.

I am certain that I remember the whole thing imperfectly, but the feeling of it I do not forget to this day. On that day, my mind had worked beautifully. That day, I knew that on any given day, I could be as brilliant as anyone in the room could - critical thinking.

Shortly thereafter, Mr. Kellogg called me into his office and told me that I was being assigned to a History tutorial class. It was a real surprise because, quite frankly, Mr. Kellogg and I did not get along that well.

He had been my Housemaster when I lived in Simpson in the third form, but in the intervening years we had some disagreement and he soured on me and me on him. To his credit, he did not let that stop him from doing something special now, for what he saw as a promising student.

I was told that I would be studying ancient civilizations privately with Mr. McDonald, who was this very grave, serious history scholar. That meant that I would only have class once a week, a time when we would sit in his apartment for 90 minutes and discuss my history assignments.

So now, I had no choice but to read the materials and come prepared and it was excruciatingly painful for me. You could not bullshit with Mr. McDonald. He was brilliant and a little scary.

I knew that they were thinking this individual attention might spur me to more serious work, but that wasn't going to happen. I found history interesting, but much less so than - say – English and Literature. The attention I received was flattering, and I do concede that the experience of the tutorial with Mr. McDonald was not all that bad. He would get me talking and there were times when he did get me excited about the subject matter.

In another history class, the instructors conducted an exercise that taught me one of the most valuable lessons that I took away from SPS.

They showed the entire class a very short film of a riot in progress. We had no idea why we were being shown the film and none of us knew what we were supposed to be looking for. At the end of the film, we were all given questionnaires with questions about the purpose of the riot, about how many people were there, who started it, etc.

I was astounded as I listened to everyone take turns describing what they had seen. There were so many different interpretations of what had taken place in the film. Guys had wildly varying estimates on the numbers of people present, what the riot was about, and everything else. I found it hard to believe that we had watched the same film.

I loved that lesson and I paid acute attention to the classroom discussion of it. The range of the discrepancies reported fascinated me. Since that day, I have made a careful effort to see things as they are and not as I want them to be; to pay close attention to what is going on around me; to strive to look for the truth. The message of that lesson was beautiful and it has served me well since.

After all that tutorial business, my confidence in my own abilities was cemented for me. I knew that I could compete with these guys and I still felt that I was tougher than most of them. I imagine that all the other black guys, and the white guys as well, had analogous moments of enlightenment. It is difficult to imagine that anyone could go through St. Paul's and not come away vastly improved.

I was aware that even my musical taste had matured. That may not seem very important, but it is indicative of my enhanced capacity to open myself to new things, a new level of maturity. I was now more interested in what I liked, and much less influenced by peer pressure or the social music taboos I had observed in Harlem Park. It was liberating.

Besides listening to Motown and R&B, I was listening to the Beatles, The Byrds, Pink Floyd and Yes. Bruce and Allen thought I was crazy at first, before their tastes also began to change as a wave of radical changes of all kinds swept the world during those years.

At the end of my four years at SPS, I was polished and open to everything, certain that I could handle it. I was aware that I had learned a great deal at St. Paul's in spite of myself. I was growing up.

*****

CHAPTER 56 – COLLEGE

When selecting a college, I made visits to the Ivy League schools and schools like Brandeis University, the University of Massachusetts and Tufts University. Harvard made an impression on me, but only because we got excited when we saw that they had soda fountains in the dining halls, where you could drink all the soda you wanted. We did not have that at SPS, so for a moment Harvard was my first choice.

Mr. Grant had consented to taking us on this college tour trip. I thought it was daring of him to accept the responsibility of supervising me, Cook, Hipp, Shivers, Nelson, Turville and Mike Russell, but other than being loud, we didn't make any real trouble for him.

Mr. Grant took us all to see the original Night of the Living Dead in Cambridge, Massachusetts and we all got a kick out of that. That gesture on his part generated a fair amount of goodwill among us. We were all feeling positive. Graduation was just around the corner.

I decided to apply to Brandies and Tufts, but Brandeis put me on their waiting list (which I viewed as an insult) and I don't believe that

I ever completed all the necessary paperwork for admittance to Tufts. As a safety school, I chose Temple University in Philadelphia, even though I had never visited Temple University. I had never even been to Philadelphia - in my life!

I had reservations about spending four more years in the northeast. It seemed to me that going to the Ivy League schools would be like going to four more years of boarding school. All the same, boys would be there, and I wasn't sure if I wanted that. I'd had enough.

Unlike the other guys, I was thinking (and I actually believed this) that the time was right for me to return to the 'people.' I also liked that Philadelphia was half way between Baltimore and New York. I could visit my NYC boys when they were in New York and I could run down to Baltimore on a moments notice. It was all very unscientific and incredibly bone-headed, but that is how I made my selection. I have lived with it since. It was a choice that ultimately allowed me to remain grounded, connected to ordinary folk, and I think that is important.

Mr. Quirk, my college placement adviser was furious with me for what he saw as my cavalier attitude towards selecting an institution of higher education. In retrospect, I see that he had a valid point. His good counsel was all but wasted on me, because I stubbornly chose to go to Temple University anyway. I knew that I could run track at Temple and maybe play basketball for them. Temple snapped me up right away, offering me what was nearly a full scholarship.

The other guys all opted for the Ivy League. I will never know if I had the grades to get into an Ivy League school, but with the reputation of SPS behind me, and having some other unique qualities to offer, I know I stood a chance.

I will say this in my defense. I came away from St. Paul's School feeling so thoroughly prepared, academically and intellectually, that I thought my choice of a college was not as important as it might otherwise have been.

One of the very important things I had learned while I was at St. Paul's was that the process of learning was something that one did for one's self. I felt that I had learned the means by which to educate myself for anything. Thus, my choice of a school was not so big a deal.

*****

CHAPTER 57 - GRADUATION

My parents and I had talked about the possibility of their attending the graduation ceremonies, which is called Anniversary Weekend at SPS. They had not been able to afford to visit the school during my four years there. My mother desperately wanted to come and see me graduate.

Anniversary Weekend is an entire weekend steeped in tradition, with SPS alumni coming from all over the world. That weekend there are dinners, brunches and athletic events including boat races, award ceremonies, class reunions and a parade, then finally the formal graduation ceremony, all of this culminating Sunday in the departure of the graduating sixth-formers.

My parents had become slightly better off financially in the four years since I had come to SPS, and they decided to scrape together the money to fly to New Hampshire, even though I had tried to talk them out of it. I have no doubt that my mother applied considerable pressure on Reverend Johnnie Watkins to make the trip happen. She did not do it often, but occasionally she would insist that Johnnie Watkins do a particular thing for me.

Secretly, I was happy that they were coming, but I was also apprehensive. Regrettably, I know that I was afraid that they would embarrass me around all those upper crust folk. I even considered not attending the ceremony, but then I learned that attendance at graduation was required if one wanted to graduate.

When they arrived in New Hampshire, it was weird relating to them in an environment so far removed from the concrete and asphalt of Harlem Park. I went to visit them in a hotel room and we all went to dinner at the hotel restaurant.

We all behaved as though it was all completely normal, and you know, it almost was normal. My folks acquitted themselves very well I thought. I realized they were no more embarrassing for me than any parents are to their teen-aged children

Reverend Watkins handled it all pretty well. All of his 'people skills,' his schmoozy preacher skills, came in handy as he charmed the faculty and the parents of my buddies. Johnnie Watkins was reasonably articulate; he read the bible a lot. When I was a kid, he used to conduct spelling bees at our house for us kids, which I always won, of course. Hipp told me he noticed that my father had the 'gift for gab.'

My Mom did not say much, as was her custom. I showed them around the school grounds and they seemed very proud of what I had accomplished. I sensed that my mother, Mary Jane, was filled to overflowing with joy for me. She had hoped and dreamed, and now she could relax a bit about my future.

At the big athletic medals ceremony, the high point for my family was when I received my medal for outstanding achievement in track and field, a medal I had also received the prior year. I had set the school record in the high jump and the long jump, and I was a member of the Athletic Association.

There was none of the towering academic achievement that had set me slightly apart from the crowd at Harlem Park, but that was all right, since I had managed to learn one or two things in my four years. Here at SPS, I was decidedly just one of the crowd, but at SPS, that is not such bad company actually, and I still felt that I had held onto my essential self.

Mike Russell received a lot of accolades for his academic achievements, as did Cook who was treasurer of our class, but it was Mike's name that we heard over and over that weekend.

Mike Russell: president of the Athletic Association, vice president of our class, School Medal winner for excellence in the performance of school duties; the Gordon Medal (one of the schools most prestigious honors) awarded to the best all-around athlete and sportsman.

Cook and I decided that as a final act of defiance we would wear our leather jackets to the graduation ceremony, his was black and mine was burgundy. My jacket wasn't even genuine leather. We really stood out among our class of about one hundred and twenty boys, almost all of them clad in a blue blazer.

Seeing us, I wondered what the families of the white boys thought of their alma mater now. The other graduating black guys, Shivers, Russell, Nelson, Turville and Hipp dressed appropriately.

We had learned our lessons, had our fun and we were now making our exit, managing not to lose a single man. Our graduating class had the highest number of black guys graduating from St. Paul's in the history of the school, as well as being the first class with graduating women.

We were at St. Paul's during an important juncture in the school's history; a time filled with change. Many more black students were admitted, 72 girls were admitted, more female faculty were hired including the first black female faculty member, the dress code was substantially relaxed, the Lower School was being phased out and smoking cigarettes was allowed on a limited basis. There were other changes that were subtler, but looking back, I can now see that it was a very special moment in time for the school.

The formation of a receiving line, comprised of the entire faculty from SPS, was a tradition at graduation. Each sixth-former was to walk down the line and shake hands with each of the Masters.

Doing so elicited more emotions for me than I expected. This outcome was never a foregone conclusion for me. It could have been derailed a number of times. I now felt that I had done something substantial. I was grateful to many of the men and women standing in that line.

When I reached George Carlisle who taught English, he shook my hand and proclaimed me the student who had taken more English courses than anyone else in my class had. I did that to avoid some of those science and math classes. I enjoyed English and I liked Mr. Carlisle. I wrote several short stories while in one of his classes and one of my stories was published in a school magazine called the Horae Scholasticae. I was surprised my short story was selected, and a little proud.

There were many men on the faculty for whom I had great regard. They poured themselves into us and I was aware, even then, that I had received the extraordinary gift of a truly first class education from them.

Before I finally left St. Paul's I tried to start a tradition. There was this wood sculpture that resembled an African Pygmy's head, which I had made in an art class; it was a mainstay of the décor in the room that Hipp and I shared. I gave it to Maldonado and asked him to try to pass it down to whoever the leadership was among the minority students. Maldonado was the next likely leader. I don't think that tradition held up.

My career in boarding school had ended well. I graduated

respectably distanced from the bottom of my class, and my final year saw me getting grades reminiscent of my high marks at Harlem Park Junior High School.

My most notable accomplishment, I thought, had been in how much more comfortable I felt inside of my skin, and how supremely confident I had become in my abilities to make my way in any place, at any time.

This sort of polished civility was what the boarding school experience was supposed to do for all the young white men and women who managed to get through the program successfully. I admit that even I came away from four years at St. Paul's School a believer. They gave me the gift of knowledge, and now I would see how far it could take me.

However, in all other respects, not much was different for me. I had no trust fund, no powerful friends, and no clear plan for the future, but I was strong inside and I knew that was worth a great deal.

I thought about how, about halfway through my four years at St. Paul's, a meeting had been organized so that the current black students could talk with a Black student alumnus. There were only a few of those in existence.

We were given a chance to ask him what it was like for him as a student here, and about his life after graduating SPS. It was helpful for many of us, because it helped us to put our daily lives at the school into a larger, future context; and as a consequence, perhaps more bearable for us in the short term.

He told us that he was somewhat ambivalent about his years spent at St. Paul's, and he was not sure if he ever really enjoyed being there, being one of only two black students. When he used the word "ambivalent" all of us sort of looked around at one another.

It is not even a 'big' word, but none of us knew what it meant. We sat there smiling uncomfortably, looking at one another with puzzled expressions, until Jose Wiltshire had the guts to tell the guy that we were laughing because no one in the room knew what the word ambivalent meant. Therefore, the guy explained it to us.

I knew then that I wanted to get to a place in my life where I could use words like that in front of a group of people and know what I was saying; or at least have the ability to understand the babblings of any other intellectual show-off.

I think what I wanted was an ease of movement between the two worlds in which I lived, something that was akin to what an undercover cop might aspire to. I have always deluded myself that I would make a good undercover cop.

I tried to be with the bad guys without stepping over a certain line, at which point I felt that I would have become one of them. I thought that if I could walk this tightrope well enough, I could ensure that I would always be able to go back home, be one of the homeboys in Harlem Park.

I desperately wanted to secure that alternative for myself. My thinking exhibited all the classic signs of the shortsightedness of youth. The Harlem Park I loved will never last – but, of course, what does?

Perhaps as a final dig at Mr. Grant, I submitted a blurb to go beneath my photo in our senior yearbook, which raised some eyebrows. It was out of character for me, but I wanted to say something provocative when I wrote, "One black day, the nigga' in me will set us free."

Writing such a thing was my way of embracing that part of me that Mr. Grant found so objectionable. Mr. Grant undoubtedly saw what I wrote as proof of every objection he had to me.

Today, I am a little bit embarrassed for having written such a thing. I was trying to express my conviction. I felt it would be the toughness I had gained in Harlem Park I would draw on most as I moved forward; the rough canvass upon which I would paint the knowledge and skills I had acquired at St. Paul's School.

My Mom, Dad and I flew on a jet back to Baltimore together, something that I could not possibly have imagined at one point. It was an evening flight and we flew in a rainstorm. I sat there alone in my seat, in a contemplative mood, fascinated by the sight of raindrops running up the window of the jet.

The sound of those bells never leaves you.

*****

CHAPTER 58 – PHILADELPHIA TO HARLEM PARK

Throughout my four years at Temple University, I continued the same kind of back and forth pattern between cities that I had adhered to in boarding school. I would return to Baltimore for most of my vacation breaks and always spent the entire summer in Baltimore, usually working a summer job to make money to defray the cost of the next semester at school. As a result, I was spending less time on the streets.

Now that we were moving into young adulthood, people were starting to scatter. Sometimes Edmondson Avenue felt like a ghost town. My presence on those streets was eerie in itself. I had graduated from one of the finest boarding schools in the country. How does one go back to living in the badlands again?

My own family moved away from Edmondson Avenue around this time. There had been some row houses renovated a few blocks away on Carey Street, and my parents seized the opportunity to own their own home. We were still in the neighborhood, but officially, we now lived in Franklin Square.

I still spent most of my free time on Edmondson Avenue, although now there was almost no one to hang out with anymore. Of course, that was not truly the case. It's just that everyone had more complicated lives and more responsibilities. Unless you were unemployed, dealing drugs or on a school break like me, you probably had a real life to manage.

Many of the girls from Edmondson Avenue, whom we used to refer to as our girls, had babies to take care of now. One day I was sitting with a girl from the neighborhood named Sherry, on her grandmother's steps. She was telling me about the many problems she was having with her boyfriend, Chuckie, who lived up on Carrolton Ave. I was familiar with the guy and I knew him to be pretty damn tough, a little mean, and frighteningly unpredictable. He was from a large family that was very tightly knit. No one wanted to get on the wrong side of Chuckie's family.

One of the older boys from up on Stricker Street once said of Chuckie's family, "I'm sure glad they love me 'cause if you cross them - watch your back!"

I had spent a little time around them myself and I too tried never to give them any reason to think badly of me.

Sherry was saying that she had gotten to the point where she had finally begun to be afraid of Chuckie. She now worried that he might hurt her bad. They were the parents of a beautiful little girl, and I thought that it was exactly because of that little girl that Chuckie was so threatening. He really appeared to love that little baby girl and would be extremely reluctant to risk losing his daughter or Sherry for that matter.

"I've always been calling Chuckie crazy, but now I'm beginning to believe that he is really mentally disturbed," Sherry complains.

"You really think that? I know that he's a little crossed-eyed, but he's probably no crazier than these other crazy people around here." I say.

"You don't know him like I do. He don't want me to do anything," she moaned.

"Your little girl looks just like him," I remark.

"Yep, he loves her to death. She's like a piece of property to him. He might kill her and me if I tried to take her anywhere," she says tragically.

"Where would you be taking her Sherry?" I ask.

'I don't know…anywhere else but here!" she sighs.

"Well…you're right. Anyone can see that he does love that baby," I admit.

Sherry told me that she had made an important decision about what she was going to do, and she wanted my help. She had made up her mind that it was absolutely necessary that she obtain a permit to buy a gun for herself, as protection against the violence directed at her by her boyfriend Chuckie.

Sherry wanted me to go with her to the Western District Police Station so that she could look into the matter. I believe that she thought that I would be useful in helping her to navigate the legal requirements of such an undertaking, and to help her hold onto her resolve.

I sympathized with Sherry's plight. There were many times when I would walk by her house and she would be out there with her child, and I would stop to talk and play with her baby. Sherry was a good Mom and doing such a good job of raising a bright, happy child. I was fond of Sherry, in a way that is somewhat inevitable when you have spent a large part of your childhood together.

When I was away at St. Paul's, Sherry wrote me a couple of letters.

She gave those letters to Allen and Bruce to mail to me, but they assumed that I would not want them and never sent them to me. In a way, they were right, because I was too young and goofy to consider any sort of relationship between Sherry and myself.

I do remember thinking at the time that I actually wished that I had seen the letters, because being so far from home; I valued mail from the home front. I kind of regretted never knowing just what it was that Sherry was feeling about me.

I thought Sherry's plan to secure a gun was something that she had not thought out enough. Going out and getting a gun was the kind of thing which would only anger Chuckie and make things worse - maybe even get her killed?

I was sure that I did not want to be a part of such a thing. I worried that Chuckie would think that I had put her up to it. That might seem cowardly on my part, but I had seen Chuckie's family in action and it was not a pretty picture. These were people who could be extremely dangerous.

Try as I might, it was very hard for me to understand how Sherry had managed to get involved with Chuckie and his family in the first place. However, she did have a child with the guy and in some respects; she was stuck with him, for the time being at least.

Chuckie and his family were all enormously popular with almost everyone, because they were a lively bunch. Their house on Carrolton Avenue had become a popular hangout in the neighborhood. They had given a few parties at their house that had been pretty nice. It was a good place to get high, and of course, a few of the girls around were interested in Chuckie's crazy-assed brothers. There was always something going on with them.

One night I was hanging out in front of Allen's house on Edmondson Avenue with Allen and Bruce, when we saw this girl named Pat rushing our way. As she passed by, she yelled back at us that she was going down to Club Astoria because there was going to be a fight. She said that Chuckie and his brothers were going to kick someone's ass. So, of course the boys and I headed on down there to see what it was that Pat was talking about. This had to be good!

Once we got down to my block, we sat down and waited on my steps for whatever was going to happen. While we were waiting, some of the other people who were known to spend time around Chuckie's house filtered onto the block. They were fired up to lend support to whatever it was that Chuckie's family was going to do.

They were saying that Chuckie's father had gotten into some kind of argument with another man inside Club Astoria; both men had been drinking and things had gotten out of control. At some point, using some brass knuckles, the other man sucker-punched Chuckie's father injuring him badly.

This is what had Chuckie's entire family worked up to fever pitch, not to mention all of their fringe friends, who suddenly had become very loyal to the family. They all began to group together on the block, waiting for this guy to come out of Club Astoria.

Whoever this guy was, he did not know what he had gotten himself into, because a veritable mob was assembling. Even some of the women from Chuckie's family were there, and one of them was carrying a big stick. Chuckie was carrying a baseball bat.

After a short wait outside the Club, they found out that the guy they wanted had already left the Club, but he had only gone across the street to the Yat-Gaw-Mein Joint for some Chinese food.

We watched as they all stealthily gathered around the Yat-Gaw-Mein Joint entrance and waited for him to come out. Chuckie and one of his brothers stood on one side of the door with the baseball bat, and their sister was on the other side with her big stick. That guy inside did not know it, but everyone watching could see that he had stepped into some deep shit.

Completely unaware of what was awaiting him just outside the door, we watched as the guy nonchalantly stumbled out of the Yat-Gaw-Mein Joint door. He was a fairly big guy and it was obvious that he was a little drunk. They let him stagger out the door, and he was even allowed to take a couple of steps across the sidewalk towards the street before Chuckie and his sister simultaneously swung that bat and that big stick at the guy's head.

Chuckie's sister had the better aim. She broke her stick in half over the top of his head, while Chuckie's bat glanced off the guy's back and shoulder. I had a sense that the guy immediately knew what was happening, because without looking back at all, he blindly darted across the street in what was to be a futile attempt to get away.

All hell broke loose as Chuckie and his family stormed after the guy whose escape was deliberately slowed by friends of the family who stepped into his path. He was stumbling and pushing forward through the crowd in a drunken panic as they jumped on his back, forcing him to the ground.

Then they all piled on top of him and he disappeared beneath a barrage of fist and flailing arms. He was down on the ground beside a car, but still partially out in the street. It did not matter anyway, because traffic was forced to a halt.

The guy had already been beaten up badly, when I saw one of Chuckie's brothers climb up on the roof of the car and attempt to leap down onto the guy's head - but he missed and simply stomped on the guy's chest instead. By this time, we are all right on top of the whole scene, and I marveled at the dude as he managed to push to his feet. He was a big strong looking boy, although by this time he was very bloody and disoriented.

Again he tried to run, but he tripped over a trashcan, disturbing a couple of big nasty looking rats, that sent everyone scurrying back. The guy then lunged forward and blindly crashed into my boy Allen, getting blood all over Allen's clothing. That, and the diversion of the rats, afforded the beating victim a chance to make another break for it.

He made a frantic dash up Edmondson Avenue towards Carey Street, where they caught up to him again. Once again he was beaten to the ground next to a car, and once again Chuckie's brother tried to stomp on the guys head by jumping off the roof of a car, except this time he did manage to deliver a glancing blow to the guys head.

Amazingly, the guy was able to struggle to his feet again. This time he ran back in the direction from which he had started and this time he was allowed to escape up an alley where he disappeared.

By the time the police showed up just about everyone had left. The cops went up the alley in search of the guy who had been beaten up. I don't know if they ever found him.

The next day, I checked the newspapers to see if there was any mention of what had happened. I thought it was entirely possible that the guy who was beaten might have died from his injuries, but I guess he did not. There was nothing in the papers.

In the aftermath of this gory assault, Chuckie's family and their many friends were in a celebratory mood, because just about everyone was feeling that the guy had gotten what he deserved. Something inside my gut suggested to me that the whole thing was not all that clear-cut. I could not help thinking that the beating he received was disproportionate to the report of one sucker punch between two men drinking in a bar.

Hell, everyone in the neighborhood knew that what happened was mostly a case of Chuckie and his brothers showing off. Having observed Chuckie's family over a stretch of time, I knew that they had a propensity for violent behavior.

Yet, despite my misgivings about them, like everyone else, I was drawn to them by the promise of the unexpected. So that, when

Chuckie and his brothers suddenly decided to give a party, just about everybody from around Edmondson Avenue stopped in for it.

They chose to throw the party in the basement of their house. It was really hot down there, so at intervals people would head outside for fresh air. I found myself standing outside with a group of people, most of whom I did not know that well.

There was this young kid out there named Jeffrey who was sort of loud and boisterous. He was going on about how much of a gangster he was, and how much ass he was going to kick and that kind of shit. The boy was determined to make a fool of himself!

At the same time, I was pretty sure that he was not the type of person you wanted to cross. He was obviously immature, insecure, and therefore dangerously unpredictable. He soon did something that night to confirm all of my suspicions about him.

He was dancing around on the sidewalk giving a real show, and he had a rapt audience of people out there that appeared to know him well. Although I had seen him around a few times, he was essentially a stranger to me, so other than an uneasy feeling I had, I wasn't sure just exactly what to expect from him.

As he continued to act the fool, he also began walking away. At the same time, he was fishing around in his pocket. Then, quite suddenly, he spun around to face us; and at the same time, the very distinctive sound of an automatic weapon being cocked could be heard. He was now standing before all of us waving and pointing this nickel-plated pistol in our faces, laughing hysterically.

Naturally, everyone started taking cover by ducking behind cars and steps, shoving each other trying to get out of the way. He just kept laughing and lunging at folk, pointing that cocked gun at them. Some of his friends did try to tell him to cut it out before he accidentally shot someone, but he just kept laughing and ignored them.

Right after that, I decided to go back into Chuckie's house and tell

Allen and Bruce what had happened and that I was going on home. That kid Jeffrey had ruined the evening for me by acting stupid. Even as I said that, it occurred to me that I was thinking and even acting like Tony, except Tony would have told him he was stupid.

Tony told me that some nervous guy with a gun had once tried to rob him and Kenard. "He was real nervous man and he kept waving that gun around." Tony said.

"Damn Tony, what did you do?" I asked.

"Both of us told that nigga to stop waving that gun around in our faces before he shot somebody. That muthafucka ran."

My impressions of the way Tony handled himself while on the streets was often a model for my own behavior. The thing to do was to be calm, to be confident and most of the time, be quiet.

****

CHAPTER 59 – CROSSFIRE

Several months after the party at Chuckie's house, I was with Glascoe down on my block while he waited for an order of food from the Yat-Gaw-Mein Joint. As we stood there waiting, Tony Stewart walked up and decided to hang around and wait with us. It was another one of those steamy Baltimore nights. It seemed as though everyone was outside in an effort to cool off.

As if on cue, every single person on the streets turned to look up the street towards Carrolton Avenue near the top of the hill, at precisely the same instant. It was like every single person's head was wired together and we all turned with a snap.

We heard gunshots, lots of them. Even in a neighborhood where people were relatively accustomed to hearing the occasional stray burst of gunfire, this was extraordinary. This had to be a gun battle of mammoth proportions that we were hearing. The gunfire was so sustained that Tony had time to leisurely walk out into the middle of the street, listen for a moment and conclude that it was coming from somewhere up near his mother's house. He turned to look at Glascoe and me. That's coming from up my way...come on man!"

Tony then started running the two blocks up the street. All the while, the shooting was still going on, with a few shorter burst of gunfire being heard, a brief pause, and then more shots. Then there were two loud booming explosions, as if a shotgun was being fired - and finally silence.

It took every bit of courage I possessed to start running toward a place where I knew, for certain, a gun battle was going on, but I began running up Edmondson Avenue with Glascoe. We both followed Tony up the hill.

We heard the last two shotgun blasts when we were about a block from Carrolton Avenue. Tony was at the corner of his block when the shotgun went off, and we saw him quickly disappear around the corner in the direction of his mother's house.

Glascoe and I were practically the first people on the scene, other than the people who lived up there. Most of them were still inside or hunkered down behind something until they were sure the shooting had stopped. The immediate area was absolutely deserted, except for someone who we noticed laying on the curb near a tree on Edmondson Avenue. Glascoe and I went over to see who it was.

He was positioned on the curb near this skinny little tree, with his legs still in the street, as though he had fallen while running to reach the only available cover. His right arm was outstretched and his head was resting on that arm, making it look as though he had casually laid down for a nap.

As Glascoe and I knelt down beside him, we could hear his labored breathing, which seemed to me to be coming from under water. He was trying to breathe through the blood spewing from a wound to either his right cheek, or his right shoulder. It was difficult to say which, because he had his face buried in his shoulder and there was so much blood and tissue surrounding the area of his wound.

I reached down to roll him over a little, to see if he wasn't perhaps blocking his airway by lying on his arm the way he was. Right away, I wished that I had not touched him. What I heard was a prolonged, wheezing exhalation of air from him and a gush of blood poured from his mouth. At that moment, even to my unpracticed eyes and ears, I knew that this man had just died.

I let him go and tried to move away from him, but I was unable to move because a sizeable crowd had gathered behind us. They were pressing forward to get a look at the man on the ground.

"Oh shit! That's Jeffrey."

Some guy behind me had recognized Jeffrey in that instant when I had rolled him over. Until I heard his name, I had no idea that the person on the ground was that kid from the party with the nickel-plated pistol.

Next, I heard a wailing sound that was the most pitiful sound that could possibly come from a human being. I at first thought that it was a woman's voice.

"That's my brother... that's Jeffrey...that's my brother...They shot my brother Jeffrey...Oh lord...they shot my brother Jeffrey."

I looked behind me and I saw a guy on the verge of hysteria, beginning to collapse. As people in the crowd moved to console him, a break opened up in the wall of people behind me and I was able to back on out of there. As Jeffrey's brother sobbed uncontrollably, Glascoe and I walked across the street to Tony's house where we found Tony standing outside with Eggy. Eggy had been sitting on Tony's steps and had witnessed the gunfight.

"Oh, man...you should have seen it...it was like the Wild-Wild West out this muthafucka'.... niggas was hiding behind steps and firing

...hiding behind trees and shit...Some of them niggas was shootin' while they was running down the street...That shit was wild, man. People were duckin' for cover and shit, all over the place...wasn't no time to get inside...I tell you man...cause they was blasting away."

No one from Tony's family had been hurt, and except for Jeffrey lying dead in the street, only one other person had been injured. A lady had been hit in the foot in the first moments of the gunfight. She was just sitting on her steps trying to beat the heat.

Tony thanked Glascoe and me for coming along with him and the two of us began heading back down Edmondson Avenue. Neither one of us said much of anything. Glascoe continued on up to his house and I walked the two blocks to our new home on Carey Street.

When I arrived home, I went directly up to my room, turned on the radio, and sat there in the dark for a while. The first song that I heard was Stevie Wonder's Blame It on the Sun, which was probably the very worst song I could hear at that moment. I soon found myself caught unawares by an incessant wave of melancholy that moved me to tears.

That kid Jeffrey meant nothing to me, and in truth, I did not even like him. Yet, Man! He was sixteen years old, and I had stood over him as he took his last breath.

As if that were not powerful enough, I kept hearing that wounded wail of his brother. The memory of that sound kept tearing at my heart.

It was all a little too close, I thought.

This time, there was something in the papers the next day, the inevitable news story about a sixteen years old teenager who had been tragically cut down in the prime of life on the mean streets of Baltimore. Same old - same old!

I heard later that there was some sort of dispute between two drug factions with whom Jeffrey was involved. There was a meeting being convened on the streets that night to resolve some issues, when the gun battle erupted.

Jeffrey was caught in the middle.

*****

CHAPTER 60 – HEROIN & DEATH

For a few days following the death of Jeffrey, I had a difficult time reconciling my fascination with street culture and the hard truths of the drug trade. The neighborhood was in a bad downward spiral. Everywhere I looked, there was another abandoned property and the streets were scarier than ever.

It was fairly plain that the businesses being burned out during the riot of 1968 had badly maimed the local economy of Harlem Park. That decline was now being accelerated by the exploding preponderance of crack and heroin, and also by what I thought was a noticeable breakdown in the level of civility on the streets. A lot of the older residents were leaving. They were scared.

Much of the violence was still primarily something which transpired between the guys who were directly involved in the drug trade. They would generally end up shooting each other, and usually only each other. However, that woman getting shot in the foot during that running gun battle near Carrolton Avenue was a harbinger of things to come. The streets of Harlem Park had always been dangerous, but not quite like this.

At that time, there was no such thing as "drive by" shootings where guys indiscriminately shot up a whole block, not caring if innocent bystanders were hit. The bad guys still seemed to prefer to find the guy they wanted to hit, walk up to him and shoot him in the face. Allen once told me about a shooting that he witnessed in my block that happened in exactly that manner, in broad daylight. I was sorry I missed that!

Sixteen-year-olds were routinely running around with pistols. Now, many of the guys selling drugs were much younger, and many of them were strangers to me. I finally had lost touch with the old neighborhood.

Many of the guys I had grown up with in Harlem Park were now involved with the drug trade in the area in a substantial way, either as users of hard drugs or dealing hard drugs. What they were engaged in now was no pastime anymore, but was becoming a way of life for them. I harbored no illusions about my old friends. Any idiot could figure out that if those boys were as mixed up in the drug trade as they were, they had to get a little dirty doing so.

I was sitting on Allen's steps one afternoon, when Eggy came up to me and asked me if I would do him a favor. He said he wanted to go down to Club Astoria, but he did not want to take the bundle of heroin packets he had in his possession with him. He was concerned about getting stuck up. Although the whole thing made me nervous, I agreed to help and he furtively handed me the heroin, which I put in my pocket, and he left.

I was now as nervous as he was; but he soon returned, retrieved his drugs and continued on his way. Stupid of me ...yes...but hey! Eggy was my boy! What Eggy did was his own business, and I would never come right out and ask him if he was dealing hard drugs, but I had suspected as much and now there was no doubt in my mind.

On another afternoon, I ran into Michael Baskerville who recounted for me something which had happened early in the day. He had to put Eggy and Alfred into a cold bath, in order to revive them after they had both overdosed on heroin. OK...so, now I definitely know that they are firing heroin.

I was hanging out with Tony Stewart one day, when he asked me to take a walk with him over to Kenard's apartment to pick up something. This was a first for me in a long while. Very seldom did I get that close to Kenard in any way, other than on the streets. That is probably how Kenard wanted it. Even though, by this time, even Kenard knew that I could be trusted to keep my mouth shut -- and besides, I was with his partner and brother-in -law Tony.

Entering Kenard's apartment, I saw a coffee table piled high with more packets of heroin than I had ever seen. There was also a huge mound of loose powder on the table. I was instantly struck with that familiar sick feeling of having crossed a line over which I should not cross. This was big time stuff!

I kept thinking that the police would surely burst through the door at any moment, and I would go to jail with Kenard and Tony. Why should they believe that I was only there with a friend to pick up his sneakers or some such dumb shit? At that time, we were not yet in the era of the open-air drug markets. If you wanted to buy weed, coke or heroin you went to the house of the guy who sold it and purchased it there, or maybe met somewhere and make the exchange that way.

If the cops had come in and found me there, I was facing some kind of serious drug charge for sure. Yet, I was really far more concerned about the possibility of a bunch of guys with guns storming in there. Something like that could be fatal. Those kinds of bad guys just might decide to take out everyone in the place. They aren't going to listen to me explain that I was there by accident.

Lately, Tony and I had been spending more time sitting around on the block, just talking. I was not in school at the time. I had taken a semester off to make some money to supplement my scholarship and make my last few semesters a bit easier.

When the time came for me to return to Temple University, I needed someone with a truck to help me move my belongings, which this time, included a bed and a couple of other large items. I was moving into an apartment rather than into the dormitories.

I knew Tony had a pick-up truck, so I tracked him down and asked him how much he would charge for such a job. He quickly said he would do it and he told me not to worry about the cost, because he would do it cheaply.

In the fall of 1974, on a warm and sunny fall day we loaded up his pick-up truck and set off for Philadelphia. It was a good day for a long drive, especially when there was no hurry to get where you were going.

We smoked some weed on the way up the road and snorted a little cocaine. One day not long ago, Tony had asked me if I wanted to try cocaine and we ended up snorting some in my house while sitting on the floor behind a sofa. It was a good buzz, but too expensive for me to want to do it very frequently. Today's treat was on Tony.

Today, we talked about anything and everything - feeling good, both of us looking to the future. Tony told me how he and Kenard planned to purchase some small trucks and start some kind of moving and hauling business. For the moment, the pick-up truck we were riding in was their first and only purchase. He said they would try to do it right and legal. They would form a corporation and get the required licenses, bonding, and whatever else was necessary.

He explained how he was looking to get out of the business of hustling drugs and do something legitimate for his family, Tony's Godfather dream. The only response I could think of was to say that; "it was good to hear him talking like that." I mean, if you were going to start a business it was important to go about it professionally, because then people would take you more seriously – right? It probably also wouldn't hurt matters that they were both married men, with families.

Not long before, Tony had gotten married and he had surprised me by inviting me to his wedding. I watched the ceremony and left right after. I waited outside in front of the church to congratulate him. I remember walking away from him that day, him standing there in his brilliantly white tuxedo, feeling that Tony was trying very hard to put his life on track.

As he sat there in the driver's seat of his truck studying the road ahead, Tony took a quick thoughtful glance at me. I could see there was something he wanted to say.

"You know, man...a lot of the time I talk to you, it's because you're not a dummy like so many of the guys I know...I'll tell them what I just told you, about starting a business and getting incorporated and all... and you know what they'll say? They'll just look at me with a stupid expression and say something like, 'No shit!' ...And that's all those dumb muthafuckas will say...I can tell you know what the fuck I'm talking about... because you go to school and everything."

I didn't know how to respond to that.

"Thanks for helping me get back to school man."

That was all I could think to say.

In Philadelphia, we unloaded the truck and I told Tony to name his price. Not only had he driven the entire way, but also he had paid for the gasoline, tolls, and helped with the loading and unloading. Tony walked to the door of the apartment, opened it, and nonchalantly said over his shoulder,

"Don't worry about it," and he left.

Tony could overwhelm me sometimes with his uncommon decency towards me. There was no way to know that the next time I was to see Tony, he would be lying in a hospital bed at Bon Secours hospital, recovering from gunshot wounds.

By then, I was back in Baltimore, at home in my apartment in Mount Vernon in downtown Baltimore where all the freaks lived, watching the eleven o'clock news. The news anchor was reporting a story about two men being shot on Edmondson Avenue. He said the name of one of the men, which struck me as familiar sounding. I heard the name Kenard, but he gave it as a surname and I did not recognize the first name he gave at all. Then he said the name of the other man who had been shot was Anthony S. That name I did recognize!

Immediately, I got on the phone and called my brother, who still lived with my parents on Carey Street. I knew that if it were Tony and Kenard, word would have spread fast to people living down around Harlem Park. He confirmed for me that Tony and Kenard had both gotten shot near the Yat-Gaw-Mein Joint, but he did not know much about it. He told me that he had heard that Kenard was dead on the street, but he wasn't sure about that. Unfortunately, he had it right.

Early the next morning I called Bon Secours Hospital, where the newsman said they had been taken, in order to confirm that Tony was there. I was his very first visitor that morning. Tony looked pretty banged up when I first spotted him in his bed. They had him drugged for his pain, so he was more subdued than I was used to seeing him, but not all that different from when we might be high. He was, I think, surprised and pleased to see me.

"Damn, Tony! You looked pretty fucked up, man."

"Yeah...I know man... them niggas got us pretty good...and Kenard got hit a lot worse than me... but at least he was breathing when I last saw him...He was always saying that if he ever got shot in the gut again, it would probably kill him."

Given what Tony was saying, I couldn't be sure whether or not Tony had been told that Kenard had died, so I decided that I would avoid mentioning it. I mean, he probably already knew, but I didn't want to say it to him. It was also news to me that Kenard had been shot before, but I guess that really should not have come as that much of a surprise.

"So...what happened down there Tony?"

"It was just a plain ol' stick-up...and we sure didn't see it coming, man...Like...me and Stevie was sitting on those tall steps by that little alley next to the Yat-Gaw-Mein Joint...and Kenard was standing at the bottom of the steps...so like...I'm sitting there like this...with my head down...because I was rolling a joint...so I wasn't paying attention... Then I heard this dude say, 'Get in the alley bitch!' That's when I looked up...and I heard Kenard say, 'Fuck you, muthafucka', then all of sudden I heard ...POP...and I saw this guy standing there with a pistol ...and Kenard broke across the street holding his stomach...Right then, Stevie broke too, over the side of the steps...

So I like jumped down on the guy so he couldn't shoot Kenard again...and I grabbed him around his two arms...so now we're wrestling for the pistol. Then the guy started screaming, 'Bust him...Bust him', so I looked over, and there was another dude standing there in that little tiny alley with a shotgun...So I tried to shove the dude I was wrestling with into the other one, and he backed up and fired his pistol right at my face...but the gun misfired...Right then I broke, man...but I only got a couple of steps when the dude with that shotgun opened up.... and it hit me in the back of my leg...and pushed me forward... then at the same time the dude with the pistol fired again and I got hit in my hand...

Then them pussies ran after that...So I got up and went over to where Kenard was laying in the street...and I put my arm around him... and laid on the ground with him...'til the ambulance came."

Tony showed me his bullet wounds.

So here it was, all the danger and drama that I secretly craved.

I mean, I am sitting there talking to one of my boys and he has just got shot up. I was proud of Tony, because he had lived up to my tough guy image of him. When the time came and he saw his boy in trouble, Tony didn't run. He fought hard to stay alive and keep his boy Kenard alive. Deep inside, I wanted to be that kind of tough! I doubted that I was.

Sitting there listening to him, I could very clearly visualize the 1300 block of Edmondson Avenue, Club Astoria, and two bleeding men laying on the ground comforting one another.

I could also clearly see the great ugliness of it all.

As I left the hospital that day, I was afraid for Tony. What was he going to do without his partner Kenard?

I had finally seen enough.

****

CHAPTER 61 – EXODUS, TONY STEWART

A long time went by before I saw Tony again. When I would ask people about him, I kept hearing he was OK, but some would add that he was never the same after Kenard had been killed.

"It's like he doesn't know what to do with himself." people said.

Given the circumstances, I thought that seemed about right.

However, after a while, there was no one that I could ask about Tony anymore. Nobody that I knew ever saw him, and I just didn't move in those circles anymore. I had been living in Philadelphia and New York City, doing some acting. When I did come to Baltimore, it was almost never for more than one day.

To finish, even before Tony and Kenard were shot, I had all but completely cut out the amount of time I spent on Edmondson Avenue. Think about it! If guys like Kenard and Tony can get wasted on their own turf like that, I surely had no business being down there.

There were too many unfamiliar faces around. The young boys that were coming up on the streets seemed meaner, and more capriciously violent than their older counterparts did. Of course, I know that quite likely, that is exactly what people thought when Tony, Kenard, and the rest of our generation started to take over the streets.

The families of all my closest friends were either leaving Harlem Park or making plans to leave. Bruce's family had been gone a couple of years. Allen's family would be leaving soon, and although my family had moved a couple of blocks to the south, we were now removed from the center of things. The new expressway that was Route 40 served as a buffer for us - for the time being.

One day I received an email from Allen. In it, he said that sometimes he dreams about the old gang from Harlem Park.

"It was amazing that we all made it out of Harlem Park alive and well given all that was going on around us," he said.

Allen is right. Most of us, who either managed to avoid involvement in the drug trade and/or any of a dozen other fatal pitfalls of the streets, did come away from Harlem Park to lead productive lives. Even some of the guys who were caught up in the madness were able to eventually shake it off and live.

Nevertheless, it really wasn't as bleak as all that, not if you actually lived there. If you grew up there, in what I heard one person describe as "the sewer," it's ultimately just your home...right?

Bruce eventually married his sweetheart Roxanne; he was divorced, and then remarried. He and Roxanne put their son through college. Bruce has been self-employed as a manicurist for much of his adult life. He has always been my primary source of information regarding our old friends because he stays in touch with everyone. He was the most caring, the most sentimental of all of us.

Allen married his girlfriend Cheryl, and they have put a son through college. I recently learned that Allen developed a portable armrest and cup holder for home or automobile that he is trying to market. Allen remains a clever dude.

All of Allen's brothers and sisters were married and made out OK, with exceptions made for the predictable stray divorce and the other normal vicissitudes of life. Their oldest brother, Hubert, died suddenly of natural causes at a relatively young age.

Before their mother Ms. Alma died, I saw her one last time at her new home, far across town from Harlem Park.

"Hey Ms. Alma, you lookin' good" I said.

"Look who's here? It's so good to see you. How long are you stayin' in town? She stood to give me hug.

'You know that I am never here very long Ms. Alma, but I did want to stop by and say hello to you."

"Well I am glad to see you," she said.

Then she held me by my shoulders, looked at me and said more softly,

"Although I do wish you would come by more often."

"Yes ma'am." I said

I knew just what she meant. Back in the day, Ms. Alma treated me like one of her own children, and caring parents like to see their children come visit sometimes. I don't believe that I saw her again before she died. I felt bad about that.

At her funeral, I saw Michael Baskerville and John (Eggy) Reese, both of them are men with families now. They both still live in Baltimore, but far away from Harlem Park.

My own brothers and sisters stayed in the area of Franklin Square, and they have done reasonably well also. My younger sister got her son through college. My sister has refused to leave Franklin Square and raised her son there. Her son is Bernard Williams, a world-class sprint champion. He won a gold medal in the 4 x 100 relay at the 2000 Summer Olympics and a silver medal as part of the 2004 Olympic team.

Not bad.

Other than my family, my most sustained and cherished friendship is the bond between Bruce Johnson and me. I am pleased that the person closest to me is someone from Harlem Park. Bruce has been indescribably loyal and steadfast through all of my/our adventures over many years. It is that quality about him that helps some of us to maintain a thin thread of connection to others who lived in Harlem Park.

Some years ago, Bruce and I went back to Harlem Park to find Tony. We went to the house where his mother lived, and encountered a group of young men sitting on the steps. It was getting dark, and we were a little nervous about approaching these guys. When we asked them if they knew Tony, we could see in their faces that they thought we were cops. Even to ourselves we looked like cops. They were not going to tell us anything!

I singled out one slightly sympathetic face and explained to him that I used to live on Edmondson Avenue back in the day, and I used to hang out with Tony and Kenard. At the mention of Kenard he looked up at me in surprise and said,

"Kenard? That was my father. You knew my father, then?"

I remembered that Kenard did have a small son who must have been about three years old when Kenard was killed.

"Yes I did. He was all right. A lot of people liked him," I told him.

The truth is I liked Kenard a lot. I often think back to a seemingly insignificant moment years ago when I saw him walking quickly down the street, his jacket tucked in under his armpit the way the tough guys strolled, and I called out to him, 'Hey Kenard.'

All he did was look over at me and said, "Hey now homes."

However, that brief exchange is illustrative of the subtle and complex influence that a bad guy can have on the young and impressionable. I felt enormously proud that Kenard had simply acknowledged my existence, and as a homeboy no less. It's too bad his son had to grow up without him. There was something very decent about Kenard, the drug dealing notwithstanding.

Just then, Tony turned the corner and came walking down the street. There was still some of the old bounce in his step, and other than the fact that he was very thin and looked tired, there was no mistaking him. We got out of the car for hugs and handshakes. Then, we sat in Bruce's car and talked for a while.

I sat there listening to Tony talk about what he was doing and what he wanted to do and it was painful to discover that there was a slightly sad familiarity to it. It was the same kind of talk I used to hear from him years ago, but it rang depressingly hollow now, even though he was nearly as charming as ever.

Tony told us that he was going out with this girl Diane who I knew from my days back at Harlem Park Elementary School and Junior High School. I thought it was kind of ironic how people find one another if given enough time. Diane was a bright girl who was in one of the top classes at Harlem Park Junior High back when I was there. Apparently, Tony still preferred to associate himself with people who were not dummies.

Our boy Tony had made up his mind to remain right where he was, to see his life through on familiar ground.

We left Tony that night, feeling a little sad, although - I don't know!

People say that as long as there is life, there is hope. Tony was still alive!

*****

CHAPTER 62 – END OF AN ERA

In an effort to show my son, Colin, how much he should appreciate what he has, I took him to Harlem Park one warm afternoon. It was something I thought he should see. It turned out to be something I'm not sure that I needed to see.

Nearly the entire stretch of Edmondson Avenue, that had once been so alive with businesses and homes, was almost completely boarded up. The house that I lived in was a boarded up shell, as was Ms. Alma's old house. More recently, I heard that our old house on Edmondson Avenue and Club Astoria had been bulldozed flat, that there was a vacant lot there now. I could not help wondering where all the mice and roaches had moved to – and of course the people.

Jesse's barbershop was still there. You still had to wait two hours for a haircut; but Jesse took appointments. On the streets, there was ample evidence of open-air drug corners everywhere. Heroin and crack had taken over. The neighborhood was so thoroughly devastated that

I thought there was really nothing my son could gain from what he saw.

I am very sorry that I will never be able to show him what a wonderfully vibrant and nurturing place Harlem Park was for me. Inevitably, that Harlem Park faded away a long time ago and that fact compels me to bow in deference to the fleeting nature of all things.

Since I worked so very hard at drinking up every last drop of that neighborhood, Harlem Park seeps out of my pores even today. People look at me now and often remark that I appear to be very clean cut. They just don't know! Well - maybe now, they do know.

*****

CHAPTER 63 – POST SPS

After graduating from SPS, the guys in my class scattered and I don't hear from any of them very much. The two guys that I see most often are Ed Shockley and Kenny Williams. They are both from Philadelphia, and both of them from the class that graduated from SPS two years after my class.

Ed Shockley went to Columbia University, and later received an M.F.A. from Temple University. He has since become a fine playwright and educator as well as one of my most treasured friends; Ed and I have collaborated on several theater projects. He's written some outstanding stage roles for me. My son and I lived in a house in Philadelphia with Ed, his wife Terri and his sons for many years. We would baby-sit for one another's kids, operating very much like family.

Ed, better than many others, seems able to objectively view our experience at SPS and understand that it was dangerous to expect too much from life post St. Paul's School. We are, after all, still in America.

Kenny graduated from Boston University, where there were a few other SPS brothers, and he stays in touch with several of the SPS crew regularly. He lives in Delaware and enjoys a productive professional life, with a lovely home and a beautiful family. I love talking to Kenny. He has such a sharp mind and a laser-like wit.

The three of us have often discussed the intrinsic worth of our time at SPS. I often mention to them how I notice the black guys who graduated after my graduating class seem to do a better job of keeping in touch with one another. For whatever reasons, the boys in my class have generally elected to keep to themselves.

It appears to me that there is deafening silence among all of the boys of my class of 1972. It's like we all went missing in action after St. Paul's and that includes the white boys. It may just be a matter of perception, and maybe the reason for the perceived silence is that they do talk to one another, but not to me. However, St. Paul's does have a relentless Alumnae Association, and the names of my classmates rarely appear in the SPS alumni magazine. I have very little idea what most of them do now.

In 1980, about eight years after our graduation from SPS, I was living with a woman in Philadelphia who was a student at my alma mater Temple University, when I received a telephone call.

"Hey man, this is your boy Cook. Long time man, what's goin' on?"

Both Cook and Hipp were from the projects of White Plains, N.Y. I immediately felt that this was not good news. I had been dreading this.

Not long before I had seen Hipp, after having not seen him for a few years. I knew that he had been hospitalized for surgery on his brain. We had somewhat lost touch, but that is probably because Hipp was busy fighting for his life, and tragically I did not fully understand how critical things had become for him.

Standing there holding the phone, with Cook on the other end of the line, I morbidly reflected upon how when we roomed together at SPS many years before, Hipp would sometimes have severe headaches.

When Hipp was getting married, I attended the wedding in Washington, D. C. He was standing in a group of people with a broad smile on his face, dressed like a typical groom, but I remember that he looked very stiff. When he turned to speak to someone, it was necessary for him to turn his entire body.

In that instant, I knew that Hipp might not be alive very long and there was nothing that anyone could do about it. Hipp, on the other hand, looked exceedingly happy to be alive, and told me so.

"Do you miss playing ball Hipp?" I asked him.

"Oh yeah, sure I do, but I gotta' tell you, I love basketball, but I love living more." he said.

Hearing Cook's voice on the phone could not be good.

"Did Hipp die?" I asked, already cringing.

"Yes, he did man. His people called me. The cancer was too much."

"Damn Hipp? I whispered to myself. "I had a feeling we'd lose him Cook…you know he was the best one of us, don't you?" I said.

"He sure was." Cook said. "I'll get back to you about the funeral."

There was more said, but that was the gist of it.

I cried hard for Hipp that day, and I cried today just writing about him. I loved Hipp. Even his name was cool.

Little has been heard of Michael Demosthenes Shivers, but from what I have heard, he has been living quietly back home in North Carolina and managed to pull together a productive life. Mike Shivers was always somewhat private. I have known him longest, because we had spent that summer at Dartmouth together.

While I was attending Temple University I saw Mike Shivers only once, when I visited him at the University of Pennsylvania where he was a student. Shivers was all right, but even at SPS we did not hang out that much, basketball was about the only thing we had in common. I tried to track him down recently, but had no luck.

Michael Jay Nelson arrived at SPS when I did. He was something of a loner like Shivers, except, he did hang out with me a lot that first year. He helped me to get my 'prep- school legs' and he was a smart guy as well. He was always saying something… enlightening.

Nelson attended Tufts University for a couple of years and then finished up at Duquesne with a degree in journalism. Nelson actually called me once several years ago. When we talked, he seemed to be amused at the idea of my being an actor.

I spoke with him recently and found out he was still living in Pittsburgh, working at an insurance company. At SPS we used to refer to Nelson as Dry Neels, because he was so reserved and droll, so I was surprised when he spoke of his feelings about some of the SPS boys who have died – Robert Aurelius Hipp, Oobs (Rodney Williams) and Michael Renard Russell. We both felt that Hipp was one of the more exceptional human beings we had known. Nelson said that all of them were often very present in his thoughts.

Nelson said to me that there wasn't anything very remarkable about his life post SPS, but in his voice I still heard echoes of the quietly remarkable young guy he used to be. As we chatted about the direction our respective lives had taken since being at SPS, we both expressed our astonishment that we lived in a country and a time when even a boarding school lightweight like George W. Bush could become president – twice! However, as I said, Nelson's a smart guy.

No one has any information on George Leroy Turville, Jr. We do know that he was slated to attend Yale University after St. Paul's, that he spent some time in the military and at some point had changed his name to Eric von Gobe, but even the alumni association at SPS lists him as "Lost."

The two brightest stars of the seven brothers in our class, Mike Russell and John Cook, have the most compelling stories. Mike graduated from Harvard and attained a master's degree. We crossed paths when he was working for a while in advertising in New York City, making big money. He helped me get some jobs as an actor doing voiceover work.

Something began to go wrong at some point and Mike ended up unemployed and practically living on the streets in Philadelphia, moving from place to place, getting high. I would run into him occasionally when I too was living in Philadelphia. It was extremely difficult for me to see him like that, but I would only see him by chance. He did not seem to have a permanent address that he would give to me, and no consistent telephone number.

My son adored him. Mike would sometimes stop by my apartment for a meal and sit on the front stoop with my toddler son Colin and me. Colin found Mike to be highly amusing. Once, when Colin and I brought home a pinecone from a walk in the park, Colin kept it on a windowsill and named it Mike Russell. I thought that was pretty goofy. Mike was always an extremely charming guy.

One day I received a call from Mike's Mom who lives in Easton, MD. She asked me had I seen Mike, and if I did see him, to give him a message, "Come home!"

With Colin ensconced in his stroller, we went out looking for Mike and managed to find him and deliver his Mom's message. Mike did return home, and sadly, Mike died back at home on the Eastern Shore of Maryland in 1997, of AIDS. That explained for me some of Mike's baffling behavior, and it broke my heart. Who knows what happened with him.

I have often worried lest there is the impression that I was jealous or angry with Mike in some way. Mike and I were always ok with one another. I think that is why he opened up to me (somewhat) near the end. Mike put on a dazzling air show at SPS, soaring incredibly high. Unfortunately, at the very end of his life, the landing was a bit rough.

I did not hold Mike's success against him, and the same is true about his fall. It was the life he chose. I hope, for his sake, it was all worth it.

John Isaac Cook graduated from Princeton and received a master's degree from Iona College in New Rochelle, New York. He managed to accomplish some good things; even returning to SPS to teach for a short time, but around that same time Cook was also struggling with some substance abuse issues. While he was teaching at SPS there was some sort of low grade scandal involving an alleged indiscretion with a student, as well as other unnamed concerns, all culminating in Cook being asked to leave the school on very short notice.

Later, he took a job teaching English in Cali, Columbia before returning to the United States and settling in Florida where his life began to unravel further.

At one point he was tried and acquitted for attempted murder with a handgun; he received probation for discharging a firearm in public in another case, and did eventually serve some time in the Broward County Jail; all of which is documented in a book he wrote about his life called, From the Projects to Princeton.

Cook and I have talked a few times and it is always painfully apparent that he is struggling with the direction that his life is taking; he understands that he has allowed himself to get unbelievably far off-track. Still, he has created a website, www.educationalexcellence.net on which he offers his services as an inspirational speaker and apparently,

Cook has managed to find some of the solace he needs in his spiritual faith.

Like Mike Russell, Cook also delighted my son Colin. On one visit Cook made to Philadelphia, the three of us had lunch at the Reading Terminal, where Cook shared some of his corned beef sandwich with Colin. That made the two of them fast friends.

Cook may yet pull things back together. He's tough and he should never be dismissed, but I do worry about him.

I think that I miss Hipp most. Hipp understood me better than the others did. I honestly feel that my own life would have been improved if Hipp had lived to help me to look at myself occasionally. I think that I would have made fewer mistakes because Hipp was an extraordinary friend and someone to whom I would listen, but then again - maybe not.

The outcome for our group was supposed to have been more spectacular than this. Most certainly, I think many of my boys expected SPS would open more doors for us than actually opened. I think there was considerable disappointment for some of the boys.

Maybe at SPS we took more blows to our respective psyches than we realized, the damage only surfacing later. If we really were part of some social experiment, I would have to say that the results were somewhat ambiguous, and while it would be difficult to prove, I think the black kids who followed in the wake of my group seemed to fare better, generally.

I suppose it might appear that Louie Grant was right about us. Perhaps none of us worked hard enough to attain the good life that an SPS education promised. It would be interesting to hear what he would have said about Mike Russell's fate.

I heard from someone that Louie Grant left SPS after teaching for some years there, and also taught at Columbia University for a while. I also found out that Mr. Grant was gay, and that curious bit of information had me re-examining my interactions with him and wondering if his sexual preference had any impact on the negative dynamic between him and me, or indeed his interactions with the many boys in his charge at St. Paul's School. It's an interesting thought.

Then I heard Mr. Grant died - from AIDS, apparently. Imagine that!

My expectations were more vague. I entertained some hope that life would genuflect at my feet because of my outstanding intellect and wit, my boarding school pedigree, but I never have that kind of luck. It has always been an excruciating grind for me. I have slowly learned patience and to pay close attention to the merits of my daily life, to find the good in that.

Repeatedly, I have tried mightily to discern just exactly what it is that I gained from having gone to St. Paul's, and I can only say that I now have a markedly improved capacity to examine things and see life with some clarity. This has helped to make life much less overwhelming, even as I acknowledge that life is an imperfect thing; so of course I still struggle daily like everyone else.

The core of my being is this delicious blend of Harlem Park and St. Paul's School. The SPS piece keeps the Harlem Park piece in check. The Harlem Park piece gives me the courage to confront the world that SPS opened up to me, and who knows what wondrous things may yet be out in front of me.

One other thing occurs to me. Had I never left Harlem Park, I wonder if I would have come away with the same thing? Ed Shockley tends to believe that most of us would have risen to the top of any academic environment in which we found ourselves. It's an interesting thought.

Mine was a life lived in black, and in white - if you will. The benefit of that, I think, has been an enlightened life filled with color; informed about the way the world is, the way it could be. I feel fortunate to have had the chance to experience some of the best, and worst, that this country has to offer. I will leave it to you to decide what was what.

*****

CHAPTER 64 – THE GIVEBACK

One of my first jobs after graduating from Temple University with a B.S. degree in Therapeutic Recreation (don't ask!) was as a substitute teacher. My very first assignment was at my old school Harlem Park Junior High, and in my former section, unit-D. How's that for irony?

By this time there were even some white kids enrolled at Harlem Park. One white kid tried to give me some trouble in homeroom class.

"Yo dude, you need to find a seat," I tell him.

"I don't have a seat," he replies with all kinds of attitude, trying to act Black.

"Well you need to find one, class is starting. If you have to, just sit on one of those empty desks at the back of the room."

"My teacher told me we're not allowed to sit on the desks," he says.

"Ooooh good answer," one of the black kids yells out.

At that moment, I immediately knew the stakes. Here I am again, starting out at Harlem Park Junior High and I run smack into a make it or break it situation. However, this time I don't hesitate and I have no fear. I know exactly what I have to do.

"I'm going to ask you one more time to sit down, and if you don't, I will make you sit down," I tell him. By this time, I am standing right in his face, and at 6'1", I am a good deal taller than he is.

"Ain't nobody gonna put their hands on me, so you need to back the fuck up off me. You put your hands on me you bet' not come outside after school," he fires back, but it's clear he's beginning to waver, looking for a way out. The general atmosphere in the room was working against him, with so many Black faces about.

"Let me show you something man," I say to him while walking over to a window and opening it. "You see those houses across the playground, over on Edmondson Avenue? I grew up right in that block. This is my neighborhood. Looks to me like you bet' think twice about coming outside after school if you keep fuckin' with me. Now sit down boy!"

He stands there deflated, looking around at everyone in silence and struggling to hold onto his pride, but he just cannot seem to make himself comply, when suddenly one of the black kids who was sitting slouched in his seat behind me pipes in,

"He ain't lyin' to you man. He used to live right over there next to Club Astoria. Everybody know him over there. I think you oughta' sit your ass down white boy!"

Crisis ended.

I look around to see who is speaking and smiling back at me is this young boy we called Shoe. He was a little kid when I left Harlem Park, but he used to hang around The Club. Shoe always used to make me laugh and we had engaged in body punching a few times. He could hit pretty hard. He was growing up to be a thug, but I always liked him and at least he was still going to school. The whole thing was one more instance where it's borne out that it never hurts to know people on the streets.

My career as a Substitute Teacher was short lived and I took a job with the Baltimore City Schools in something called the Migrant Education Project. Essentially, I was a non-classroom teacher delivering educational services to families involved in migrant labor.

It was the sort of job that satisfied the youthful idealism and activism I had cultivated at SPS and then in college, but I knew that I would not remain there very long. The bureaucracy of the Baltimore City School system was far too stifling for me.

In my last year at Temple, I had discovered theater, and after a few false starts, I headed for New York to pursue acting and songwriting. The arts appealed to me as a discipline where I could explore and perhaps express all the ideas, contradictions and passions that were percolating inside me. Being an actor made me feel that my destiny was somewhat under my control, giving me the illusion of independence.

I did some minor parts in a couple of films, also some modeling, Theater, voiceover work, wrote a few good songs, etc., and for many years I was happy. I was struggling, but happy. Being a performing artist is the closet thing to an all-consuming passion that I have attempted. There's a good chance that I will return to it someday.

Then, I had a son and my focus shifted again, dramatically. I continue to feel like an artiste inside, but the practical considerations of raising a child have forced me to suppress my artistic leanings for a while.

Therefore, I dusted off my idealism and I spent about five years working with impoverished children, particularly infant children. I began this career track by first working for a few years in a daycare center as the lead teacher in the infant room, where I gained considerable experience and invaluable insight into the care and nurturing of small children. Then I set my sights on one of the biggest and best pediatric care centers in the country, The Children's Hospital of Philadelphia (CHOP).

At first, for about a year, I worked at CHOP (they hate it when you call it CHOP) with a pediatric literacy Program called Reach Out and Read (ROR). Its purpose was to promote the idea of exposing children 0-5 years old to books. Children who visited the Primary Care Centers (Clinics) at Chop would receive a few free books whenever they came for a well visit with their pediatrician.

This enabled families who might not be able to afford books to build a small library for their children. My job was to screen the books (new and donated) for non-age-appropriate content for the kids, distribute the books to the pediatricians and find book donors. It was a noble cause, but I knew that I could do more.

CHOP had an Early Head Start program and that seemed interesting. At first they completely ignore my application, but after a chance face-to-face meeting with one of the management team, I am hired as an Infant Toddler Specialist/Home Visitor with the Early Head Start program at the hospital.

My job is to visit the homes of low income families with at risk children from the ages of 0-3 years old, and provide them with child development activities in an effort to demonstrate the importance of a child's first three years, and to help the parents see that they are their baby's first and best teacher.

Most of the parents are very young single black women barely out of their teens, with a few Dads scattered in. Many of them are not much different from the girls I grew up with in Harlem Park, so I have an easy time relating to them. I think back to the girls from 'round the way' back in Harlem Park, and how vulnerable they could be beneath an often coarse exterior.

These women live in some of the toughest neighborhoods in West Philadelphia. Very often, there is no stable father figure involved in the baby's lives. Most of them have gotten off to a bad start in life and are now struggling to find their way. I thankfully find myself helping women who are probably not very much different from the one I witnessed being beat on the street back in Harlem Park when I was a teenager.

I arrive at their homes looking and sounding about as preppy as can be, knowing that the hustlers and dealers on the street are eyeballing me, but I don't worry too much. I know how to behave, how to walk, how to talk, what sort of eye contact to make and I have never had any trouble. Even so, I am extremely careful. There is always the possibility that one of those young street thugs might try me. You can't be afraid, but you must be vigilant. Long ago, I learned that on the streets you could never let your guard down.

Inside their homes, I know it is crucial that I communicate that I am not there to judge them or to do them any harm. I must demonstrate an ease in their environment, with the soiled furniture, the stifling heat in the summer, and lack of heat in the winter and the roaches and mice.

I remember one home where the roaches were so bold that they even crawled on the sofa, chairs and sleeping babies, not just the walls and floors. The roaches didn't have the decency to run away when the lights were turned on, but continued with what they were doing. That family did their best to exterminate them but they were fighting a losing battle.

Most of the families endure their circumstances with a stoic dignity and I endeavor to show them the proper respect for their efforts. I know that they are embarrassed sometimes, but I make them understand that they need not be embarrassed in my presence and they quickly realize that it is so. It is truly nothing I hadn't already seen.

Often, I am simply a sounding board for them, a person to whom they can express their hopes and dreams for a better life. Primarily, what I do is provide them with information about community resources from which they can seek help, the sort of information that might elude them due to such factors as lack of literacy skills, ignorance, or just plain distrust of the authorities.

I use toys, music and talk to engage their babies and toddlers in play activity in an effort to determine what their developmental skills are, nurture those skills where I can, or perhaps direct the parents to some sort of Early Intervention program for their baby, if necessary.

I visit once a week for 90 minutes, but even that small amount of attention is of value to them. Since I have come from the same place as them, I am well equipped to evaluate their needs and commiserate with them. I think the families I serve are comforted by my seeming worldliness, the range of my knowledge, and that helps them to put their trust in me.

I accept that I can never solve all their problems, but I offer concrete help where I can, and working in partnership with them, I try to demonstrate how they themselves can scrutinize their children for anything that might interfere with optimal, normal childhood development.

All the mothers and fathers possess a burning desire to see their baby's have the best chance for success that they can provide. Our program is voluntary, but they have all signed on, showing a willingness to do something good for their children. Not all of them get as much out of our program as they could, but we do help a lot of families.

Considering the length and breadth of my life, I know that I have a lot to offer them, even if none of their babies will ever remember me. Babies are such fascinating and prolific learners. They learn an unbelievably wide array of skills in an unbelievably short time. It never stops - the learning - but the pace of it quickly fades after three years or so, and it generally takes us a lifetime to acquire any real wisdom. You've got to reach them as early as possible.

Working with those young mothers and their babies is some of the most important work I have ever done. Every skill that I have has come in handy with this job, particularly my ability to sing and play songs for the children on my guitar. The babies and toddlers respond very powerfully to the music. It is an ideal way to reach their little minds. The older one's look to me expectantly when they come, hoping for a song.

Not many men do this sort of work and that has an appeal for me. For five years, I am the only male working at The Children's Hospital of Philadelphia's Early Head Start program. It is a challenge on more than one level! I enjoy proving to everyone that men can be nurturing caregivers to children, much as I had been with my son during his first three years.

It can be emotionally draining sometimes, particularly when I encounter a young child growing up in absolutely desperate circumstances and I wonder if he/she will someday have the sort of luck that I had, and find the means to a better life. I find myself feeling so powerless at times in the face of abject poverty. Yet, at the same time, I know that there are some possibilities, however remote, that things might work out for them.

When I am sitting in the homes of the families I serve, I am astounded that so much of America labors under the delusion that we have adequately addressed our problems of poverty, racial discrimination and class. We have not.

What I find tragic is that these good people, struggling as they do, continue to be very nearly invisible in American society. For too many people they don't even exist. It's easy to forget that there is still a lot of work to be done by everybody, a lot of human suffering to alleviate.

Looking back on it now, I find myself able to take some small comfort in the recognition that I accomplished some good in the tiny corner of the planet that I inhabit, sharing some of the secrets of the greater world with people who might not ordinarily hear it. It is my hope that such action was a satisfactory usage of an exceptional education.

There was a time when I thought that I could be the next Malcolm X, Martin Luther King, Jimi Hendrix or even John Lennon, but I was just dreaming, I don't possess such courage or talent. Most assuredly, I did not envision becoming a man who nurtures the minds of small babies. Perhaps I was just too lazy for anything else or maybe this is what I am supposed to be doing, but I'll tell you this, it's hard, and it is a grave responsibility. I tried to do what I did with some modicum of dignity and grace. The young black children I served are all important because - they are me, and I am them, if you know what I mean? SPS did that for me; gave me the ability to look at a thing and discern what is - or is not - important. I have learned that our children are damned important.

Currently, I am working with a program called Focus on Fathers. In many ways, it is like my job with Early Head Start, but now I am primarily concerned with helping men navigate the social service systems in Philadelphia as it pertains to child custody, child support, employment and housing. Not surprisingly, I believe that I have gained an even greater sense of satisfaction from this career.

So many of these men (mostly poor uneducated black men) have no clue as to what opportunities and assistance are available to them. My approach is to get them to first hone in on establishing a sound and substantial relationship with their children, and my belief is that everything else for them will flow from the nurturance of that important connection.

It appears to be working and I find these men willing to fight harder for a place in their children's lives. It may not seem much of an accomplishment, but I know it is huge. It is the kind of 'giving back' that I came to believe was required of me. Unfortunately, it is not the kind of work that American society values.

*****

CHAPTER 65 - FINALE

Looking back on everything, it has been pretty sweet actually. I would not have hesitated to send my son to St. Paul's School if I were able to afford it. We tried to get him in but he did not have the necessary grades, and I learned, in our case at least, me being an SPS alumnus was no advantage for him. It is a shame because I think Colin is more the kind of kid that St. Paul's would like to have. He is the sort of kid that they thought they were getting in me. He is a world ahead of where I was at his age, and unlike me, he knows exactly who his Dad is. I wish my mother could have known him. They would probably have gotten on well.

The death of my mother was as devastating a loss in my life as it is for most people I suppose. It was completely unexpected. She appeared to be a relatively healthy woman until a routine Pap smear revealed she had cervical cancer. She told me that she was going into the hospital to have a hysterectomy. Her manner, when she revealed this to me, was so matter of fact that I failed to grasp, in full measure, the seriousness of the thing. Of course, now I could kick myself for my cavalier attitude.

On the day that she was to have her operation, I went to see her and spoke with her briefly as she lay in her hospital bed. It was moments before she was going in for surgery.

"How are you Mom?"

"I'm all right. I am just trusting in the lord right now."

That was a strange comment coming from her. She never used such language with me, although she was deeply religious.

"It will be all right Mom."

"I know," she said.

At that point, I made a comment that was unusual for me.

"I gotta tell you Mom, you look prettier today than I have ever seen you look. You don't look so tired. I guess it's the good night's rest you got here last night – huh?"

She smiled. I was glad she smiled.

She went into surgery and the operation was purportedly a success. However, when I returned the next day there were a number of doctors and nurses in her room. Something had gone wrong and they told me I could not see her just then, but looking past them, I could see her face and she was in extreme distress. She appeared to be looking directly at me but her eyes were glassy, and when I called to her, she did not seem to hear me. I soon learned that she had suffered a massive stroke, one of the inherent dangers in undergoing a hysterectomy. After lingering for many hours my Mom died the next day.

I would have liked to have more time with her - in my adult incarnation. That was one of my more salient thoughts as I stood in the cool and dimly lit ICU staring down at my mother's cold lifeless body. Had she survived, we might have become even closer, more like friends and that would have been nice. I continue to miss Mary Jane Woody more than I can express. I imagine she would have been pleased with how things have turned out for her eldest son.

Years after my mother died and I finally went to meet my biological father's wife, about a year after he had died, his wife told me that he had inquired about me. My aunt Vinnie told him not to worry, that I was all right, that I had a scholarship to a New England boarding school, so he didn't press to see me.

So ironically, this remarkable thing that happened to me, this best thing that could ever happen to an at risk kid, probably kept me from meeting my father. I wish I had met him, but I can understand why he thought I was all right because I was, more or less.

Now, I think myself lucky. It could be that I am even luckier than those born to the inner-circle, because I have had the opportunity to know what they know, and that is terribly significant. I have concluded that it is always better to know things than not to know them. At the same time, I know some things about 'regular folk' that they will never know. All that knowledge has kept me centered in life, if not spectacularly successful.

Things could have turned out a lot worse, and I won't complain, but I am holding out hope that things might still get just a little bit better for me, and for all my friends and family as well. You see - I have this idea for a book....

My primary job now is to see that my son Colin gets some of the feeling of all of this. Perhaps he will learn something useful, and (in his time and in his way) make things a little better, which I trust he will understand is the responsibility of us all.

That's all I'm trying to say.

END